THE DICTIONARY OF
CONSERVATIVE
QUOTATIONS

THE DICTIONARY OF
CONSERVATIVE
QUOTATIONS

Iain Dale

Biteback Publishing

First published in Great Britain in 2013 by
Biteback Publishing Ltd
Westminster Tower
3 Albert Embankment
London SE1 7SP

ISBN 978-1-84954-539-6

10 9 8 7 6 5 4 3 2 1

A CIP catalogue record for this book is available from the British Library.

Set in Perpetua by Duncan Brack

Printed and bound in Great Britain by
CPI Group (UK) Ltd, Croydon CR0 4YY

Foreword

by the Rt Hon. William Hague

When Conservative Prime Minister Benjamin Disraeli commented that, 'The wisdom of the wise and the experience of the ages are perpetuated by quotations,' he was, more than likely, envisaging a collection selected from his own prodigious output. It is true, however, that dictionaries of historical quotations are an ideal way to discover the personalities which have dominated our political landscape, both past and present. To know that Burke is an important conservative thinker is not the same as understanding what he meant by saying: 'Liberty must be limited in order to be possessed.'

Quotations allow those of us who do not have time to pore over multiple learned tomes to access the thoughts of many brilliant, important, observant or just plain eccentric minds and to learn how the world looked through their eyes.

In the often frenzied environment that the modern politician inhabits, crammed with back-to-back appointments and three-minute interviews, it is hard to remember that words are never entirely spontaneous or disposable. Like particles of pure energy, words assume many different forms and can be turned to suit any purpose the moment demands, yet, as a consequence of being drawn on time and again, they accumulate their own histories and a wide range of meanings.

A word like 'conservative' has been around long enough for people to understand very different things by it – just ask Edward Heath or Margaret Thatcher! Occasionally, famous quotations will be rewarded by inclusion in popular idiom. Harold Macmillan's comment about the 'wind of change' in South Africa is an obvious example. Most political words will, it is true, be quickly forgotten but all remain available to be excavated and rediscovered by future generations. Dictionaries of quotations are, in many respects, exercises in political archaeology.

What is particularly pleasing to me about a specialist

Conservative dictionary of quotations is how it illustrates the breadth and depth of conservatism as a political tradition. Indeed, it has a proud pedigree, counting among its numbers thinkers of the calibre of John Locke, Edmund Burke and Michael Oakeshott; great wartime leaders, including Pitt the Younger and Winston Churchill; radical economic reformers like Robert Peel and Margaret Thatcher, and oratorical geniuses such as the Elder Pitt and Ronald Reagan. Less eminent, although no less conservative, are colourful characters like Edwina Currie, the might-have-beens like Barry Goldwater, or the forgotten – who can recall the key events of Henry Addington's premiership? Finally, there are those, like Alan Clark, whose wit can be savage but who can make us laugh.

What, if anything, do these conservative figures have in common? In consulting quotations from Aristotle (we claim him!) to Margaret Thatcher, from Abraham Lincoln to Karl Popper, certain themes recur: a suspicion of state intervention; an admiration for the traditional institutions of social and political life and a belief in the virtue of individual liberty – so far as it does not undermine these institutions. The pleasure of a book such as this lies in exploring the diversity of ways in which Conservatives have thought about these and a vast array of other questions. I certainly do not agree with all of the quotations in this book. Some, such as Abraham Lincoln's views on race before he became President, make for quite difficult reading. Conservatives, unfortunately, are no different from other kinds of people in falling prey to the prejudices of the day. They are perhaps a little better than some at maintaining a healthy scepticism towards passing political fads.

Any political organisation as old as the Conservative Party inevitably has its historical fault lines. The modern party which, to use John Major's words, believes in a 'classless society', was once led by Lord Salisbury, to whom democracy meant 'simple despotism'. Neither have Tories always been advocates of free trade, as Robert Peel learned to his cost.

Whatever the particular view expressed, I like to think that, on the whole, the quotations in this book show that conservatism is a political tradition alive with ideas and enriched by many thoughtful, intelligent and funny people. I can't deny that sometimes they have got it wrong, but I still have no doubt in saying that were Disraeli alive today, he would amend one of his quotations to read: 'The wisdom of the wise and the experience of the ages are perpetuated by Conservative quotations!'

William Hague
Leader of the Conservative Party 1997–2001, Foreign Secretary 2010–

Introduction

by Iain Dale

This book has been an absolute pleasure to compile. One cannot fail to learn from the words of wisdom or fail to be amused, entertained or informed. But the trouble with compiling a book of quotations is that one inevitably leaves out some obvious favourites. I am sure I have been guilty of that in this volume. Quotations have fascinated me all my adult life. Whether writing articles or making speeches they are invaluable for politicians of every hue.

I have purposely omitted quotes by non-conservative politicians on their criticism or definition of Conservatism. If you have enjoyed this volume but know of quotations you think should have been included, please feel free to get in touch by email – iain@iaindale.com – as we intend to publish new editions of this book in the future.

The quotes have been selected according to a number of criteria but, as with all books of quotations, the selection is somewhat coloured by my own choices. Where possible I have included the subject's biographical details. Please forgive any omissions or feel free to send me corrections. It has not been possible to source every quote, but in my view it is better to include a good quote than exclude it purely on the basis of lack of provenance. No doubt some quotations may have been attributed wrongly or have been printed in a slightly different form to the original. No doubt readers may puzzle over the exclusion of a particular favourite quotation. Please feel free to write to me with any corrections or suggestions for a new edition.

I would like to acknowledge other volumes of quotations which have been especially helpful in compiling this book. They include the *Oxford Dictionary of Political Quotations*, *Right Thinking* by Edward Leigh, Andrew Roth's *Parliamentary Profiles*, *Scorn* and *Read My Lips* by Matthew Parris among others.

The eagle-eyed reader might spot that I have drawn heavily

from my previous book, *The Margaret Thatcher Book of Quotations*, published by Biteback in 2012. I make no apology for the fact that there are a large number of quotes from Margaret Thatcher and Ronald Reagan. These two politicians shaped the world we live in today, no matter how much others might decry the fact. The world is a safer place and a more prosperous place thanks to them and let us never forget it.

Lastly, I would like to thank Grant Tucker, my executive assistant, for his assistance and enthusiasm in tracking down some elusive quotes. Grant is a mere twenty years old and was born two years after Margaret Thatcher fell from power, yet he seems to know more about her life and achievements than I do. Grant is living proof that Margaret Thatcher's legacy will be handed down through the generations.

Iain Dale
August 2013

A

Earl of Aberdeen

1784–1860; Prime Minister 1852–55

I consider war to be the greatest folly, if not the greatest crime, of which a country could be guilty, if lightly entered into. If a proof were wanted of the deep and thorough corruption of human nature, we should find it in the fact that war itself was sometimes justifiable.

Speech in the House of Lords, 4 April 1845

I think it clear that all government in these times must be a government of progress, Conservative progress, if you please; but we can no more be stationary, than reactionary.

Letter to Henry Goulburn, 2 September 1852

As we are drifting fast towards war, I should think the Cabinet ought to see where they are going.

Letter to the Earl of Clarendon on the Crimean War, 7 June 1853

Lord Acton

1834–1902; historian

Liberty alone demands for its realisation the limitation of the public authority, for liberty is the only object which benefits all alike, and provokes no sincere opposition.

The Home and Foreign Review, 1862

The man who prefers his country before any other duty shows the same spirit as the man who surrenders right to the state. They both deny that right is superior to authority.

Ibid.

Patriotism is in political life what faith is in religion.
Nationality (1862)

The danger is not that a particular class is unfit to govern.
Every class is unfit to govern.
Letter to Mary Gladstone, 1881

The law of liberty tends to abolish the reign of race over race, of faith over faith, of class over class. It is not the realisation of a political ideal: it is the discharge of a moral obligation.
Ibid.

Power, like a desolating pestilence
Pollutes whate'er it touches; and obedience,
Bane of all genius, virtue, freedom, truth,
Makes slaves of men and of the human frame
A mechanised automation,
Power tends to corrupt and absolute power absolutely.
1887

Great men are almost always bad men even when they exercise influence and not authority.
Ibid.

The one pervading evil of democracy is the tyranny of the majority, or rather of that party, not always the majority that succeeds, by force or fraud, in carrying elections.
History of Freedom & Other Essays (1907)

Liberty is not the means to a higher political end. It is itself the highest political end.
Ibid.

The great question is to discover, not what governments prescribe, but what they ought to prescribe; for no prescription is valid against the conscience of mankind. Before God, there is neither Greek nor Barbarian, neither rich nor poor, and the

slave is as good as his master, for by birth all men are free; they
are citizens of that universal commonwealth which embraces
all the world, brethren of one family, and children of God. The
true guide of our conduct is no outward authority, but the voice
of God, who comes to dwell in our souls, who knows all our
thoughts, to who we are owing all the truth we know, and
all the good we do; for vice is voluntary, and virtue comes
from the grace of the heavenly spirit within.

 Ibid.

John Adams
1735–1826; US President 1796–1800

Liberty cannot be preserved without a general knowledge
among the people, who have a right and a desire to know; but
besides this, they have a right, an indisputable, unalienable,
indefeasible, divine right to that most dreaded and envied kind
of knowledge, I mean of the characters and conduct of their
rulers.

 An Essay on the Canon and the Feudal Law (1765)

The jaws of power are always opened to devour, and her arm
is always stretched out, if possible, to destroy the freedom of
thinking, speaking and writing.

 Ibid.

I agree with you that in politics the middle way is none at all.

 1776

The judicial power ought to be distinct from both the legislative
and executive, and independent upon both, so that it may be a
check against both, so that it may be a check upon both.

 Thoughts On Government (1776)

Fear is the foundation of most governments.

 1776

The happiness of society is the end of government.
    Ibid.

Democracy never lasts long. It soon wastes, exhausts, and murders itself. There never was a democracy that did not commit suicide.
    1814

Phelps Adams

1903–91; American journalist

Capitalism and Communism stand at opposite poles. Their essential difference is this: The Communist, seeing the rich man and his fine home, says: No man should have so much. The Capitalist, seeing the same thing, says: All men should have as much.
    On capitalism

Samuel Adams

1722–1803; leader in the American Revolution

If ye love wealth greater than liberty, the tranquillity of servitude greater than the animating contest for freedom, go home from us in peace. We seek not your counsel, nor your arms. Crouch down and lick the hand that feeds you; May your chains set lightly upon you, and may posterity forget that ye were our countrymen.
    Attributed

Let us contemplate our forefathers, and posterity, and resolve to maintain the rights bequeathed to us by the former, for the sake of the latter.
    1771

We cannot make events. Our business is wisely to improve them. Mankind are governed more by their feelings than by reason. Events which excite those feelings will produce wonderful effects.

Letter to Samuel Cooper, April 1776

Lord Addington

1757–1844; Prime Minister 1801–04

In youth the absence of pleasure is pain. In old age the absence of pain is pleasure.

On growing old

The burden [of income tax] should not be left to rest on the shoulders of the public in time of peace because it should be reserved for the important occasions which, I trust, will not soon recur.

Address to House of Commons, on abolition of income tax

Konrad Adenauer

1876–1967; German Chancellor 1949–63

A thick skin is a gift from God.

New York Times, 1959

Aeschylus

c.525–c.455 BC; playwright

Every ruler is harsh whose rule is new.

Prometheus Bound

Aesop
c.6th–5th century BC; fabulist

United we stand, divided we fall.
The Four Oxen and the Lion

Little by little does the trick.
The Crow and the Pitcher

It is easy to despise what you cannot get.
The Fox and the Grapes

Be content with your lot, one cannot be first in everything.
The Peacock and Juno

Spiro Agnew
1918–96; US Vice-President 1969–73

If you've seen one city slum, you've seen 'em all.
Detroit, 1968

A spirit of national masochism prevails, encouraged by the effete corps of impudent snobs, who characterise themselves as intellectuals.
New Orleans, 1969

Yippies, hippies, yahoos, Black Panthers, lions and tigers alike – I'd swap the whole damn zoo for the kind of young Americans I saw in Vietnam.
On patriotism

Jonathan Aitken

b. 1942; Conservative MP 1974–97

I wouldn't say she was open-minded on the Middle East so much as empty-headed. For instance, she probably thinks that Sinai is the plural of sinus.

On Margaret Thatcher's views on the Middle East

Hervey Allen

1889–1949; American author

Every new generation is a fresh invasion of savages.

On civilisation

William Barclay Allen

b. 1944; Afro-American political scientist

This is a way of proceeding our country which leads to disaster ... People are in the habit of thinking in terms of race, or gender – anything except of being an American. Until we learn once again to use the language of American freedom in an appropriate way that embraces all of us, we're going to continue to harm this country.

Attributed

It is misleading to call affirmative action reverse discrimination, as we often do. There is no such thing, any more than the opposite of injustice, for example is reverse injustice.

American Enterprise Institute, 1985

James Madison thought that the most important test of American freedom would be the ability of our political system to guarantee the rights of minorities without exceptional provisions for their protection. Affirmative action is incompatible with that constitutional design. Whoever calls for affirmative action declares at the same time that constitutional design has failed and that we can no longer live with our constitution.

Ibid.

Leo Amery

1873–1955; Conservative MP 1911–45

For twenty years he has held a season ticket on the line of least resistance, and has gone wherever the train of events has carried him, lucidly justifying his position at whatever point he has happened to find himself.

On H. H. Asquith, speech in the House of Commons, 1916

Speak for England, Arthur!

To Arthur Greenwood in the House of Commons, 2 September 1939

You have sat here too long for any good you have been doing. In the name of God, go!

To Neville Chamberlain, quoting Cromwell, 7 May 1940

Conservatism recognises that individual effort, the individual desire to excel, the will for individual achievement and recognition will always remain the indispensable vitamins of human society. But the individuals it has in mind are also citizens. The qualities of cooperation, of public duty, of willingness to sacrifice personal interest and even life itself for the common cause are essential elements in the individuality we would strive to foster.

The Ashridge Journal, 1943

David Amess

b. 1952; Conservative MP 1983–

I am interested in everything and expert in nothing.
  Attributed

I do not believe in the equality of men and women ... If I were
pressed I would say that women are superior to men.
  Attributed

I would pull the lever.
  On hanging

Michael Ancram

b. 1945; Conservative MP 1974, 1979–87, 1992–2010

You can vote for Blair or you can vote for Britain. You can't do
both.
  June 2001

Thomas Aquinas

1227–74; theologian

Because the aim of a good life on this earth is blessedness in
heaven, it is the king's duty to promote the welfare of the
community.
  De Regno (c.1267)

Reason in man is rather like God in the world.
  Opuscule II, De Regno (c.1267)

Jeffrey Archer
b. 1940; Conservative MP 1970–74

She'll be Prime Minister until the middle of next century.
> On Margaret Thatcher, 1989

Hannah Arendt
1906–75; American philosopher

The most radical revolutionary will become a Conservative on the day after the revolution.
> *On Revolution* (1963)

The Third World is not a reality, but an ideology.
> On the developing world

Aristophanes
c.450–385 BC; Greek dramatist

A horrible voice, bad breath and a vulgar manner – the characteristics of a popular politician.
> On politics

Aristotle
384–322 BC; Greek philosopher

Democracy arose from men's thinking that if they are equal in any respect they are equal absolutely.
> *Politics* (c.335–323 BC)

Good laws, if they are not obeyed, do not constitute good government.
> Ibid.

Those who think that all virtue is to be found in their own party principles push matters to extremes; they do not consider that disproportion destroys a state.

Ibid.

Sometimes the demagogues, in order to curry favour with the people, wrong the notables.

Ibid.

Even when laws have been written down they ought not always to remain unaltered. But the law has no power to command obedience except that of habit which can only be given by time, so that a readiness to change from the old to new laws enfeebles the power of the law.

Ibid.

The most perfect political community is one in which the middle class is in control and outnumbers both of the other classes.

Ibid.

Poverty is the parent of revolution and crime.

Ibid.

... he who is unable to live in society, or has no need because he is sufficient for himself, must either be a beast or a god.

Ibid.

The male is by nature superior and the female inferior; one rules and the other is ruled.

Ibid.

Democracy [as literal majority rule] ... arises out of the notion that those who are equal in any respect are equal in all respects; because men are equally free, they claim to be absolutely equal.

Ibid.

We make war that we may live in peace.
  Nicomachean Ethics (c.350 BC)

Virtue, like art, constantly deals with what is hard to do, and the harder the task the better the success.
  Ibid.

No tyrant need fear 'til men begin to feel confident in each other.
  Ibid.

The generality of men are naturally apt to be swayed by fear rather than by reverence, and to refrain from evil, rather because of the punishment that it brings, than because of its own foulness.
  Ibid.

It is best that laws should be so constructed as to leave as little as possible to the decision of those who judge.
  Rhetoric (c.350 BC)

Dick Armey
b. 1940; US Congressman 1985–2003, House majority leader 1999–2003

Governments punish success and reward failure.
Know that euphemisms for restricting trade are created by those who benefit from restrictions.
  February 1993

Be sceptical of gloomy prognostications from people who are in the business of peddling more government.
  Ibid.

Mathew Arnold

1822–88; poet and educationalist

The world is forwarded by having its attention fixed on the best things
Fullness of life and power of feeling, ye
Are for the happy, for the soul at ease,
Who dwell on a firm basis of content!
But he, who has outlived his prosperous days –
But he, whose youth fell on a different world
From that on which his exiled age is thrown –
Whose mind was fed on other food, was train'd
By other rules than are in vogue today –
Whose habit of thought is fixed, who will not change,
But, in a world he loves not, must subsist
In ceaseless opposition, be the guard
Of his own breast, fettered to what he guards,
That the world win no mastery over him –

From Empedocles on Etna (1852)

… what a man seeks through his education is to get to know himself and the world.

A speech at Eton

Raymond Claude Ferdinand Aron

1905–83; French philosopher

The intellectual who no longer feels attached to anything is not satisfied with opinions merely; he wants certainty, he wants a system. The Revolution provides him with his opium.

The Opium of the Intellectuals (1995)

Communist faith justifies the means. Communist faith forbids the fact that there are many roads towards the Kingdom of God.

Ibid.

Far from being the ... philosophy of the Proletariat, Communism merely makes use of ... pseudo-science in order to attain its own end, the seizure of power.

> Ibid.

Nancy Astor

1879–1964; Conservative MP 1919–45

Astor: Winston, if I were your wife I would put poison in your coffee.
Churchill: Nancy, if I were your husband I would drink it.

> At Blenheim Palace, 1912

Nobody wants me as a Cabinet minister and they are perfectly right. I am an agitator, not an administrator.

> Attributed

Sir Humphrey Atkins

1922–96; Conservative MP 1955–87

Jim Prior is his own man. We all are.

> On Prior's resignation as Secretary of State for Northern Ireland, 1984

B

Sir Francis Bacon
1561–1626; lawyer and essayist

Alonso of Aragon was wont to say in commendation of age, that age appears to be best in four things – old wood best to burn, old wine to drink, old friends to trust and old authors to read.
Apothegus (1624)

In government, change is suspected through to the better.
The best governments are always subject to be like the fairest crystals, where every icicle and grain is seen, which in a fouler stone is never perceived.
To worship the people is to be worshipped.
Nay, the number of armies importeth not much, where the people is of weak courage; for as Virgil saith, It never troubles the wolf how many the sheep be.
Essays (1625)

There be three things which make a nation great and prosperous, a fertile soil, busy workshops, easy conveyance for men and goods from place to place.
Attributed

New nobility is but the act of power, but ancient nobility is the act of time.
Of Nobility (1625)

It is a strange desire to seek power and to lose liberty.
Of Great Place (1625)

Walter Bagehot

1826–77; essayist

In such constitutions [as England's] there are two parts. First, those which excite and preserve the reverence of the population – the dignified parts. And next, the efficient parts – those by which it, in fact, works and rules.

The English Constitution (1867)

It has been said that England invented the phrase 'Her Majesty's Opposition'; that it was the first government which made a criticism of administration as much a part of the polity as administration itself. This critical opposition is the consequence of Cabinet government.

Ibid.

The natural impulse of the English people is to resist authority.

Ibid.

An opposition, on coming to power, is often like a speculate merchant whose bills become due. Ministers have to make good their promises, and they find difficulty in doing so.

Ibid.

It is often said that men are ruled by their imaginations; but it would be truer to say that they are governed by the weaknesses of their imaginations.

Ibid.

The finest brute votes in Europe.

Ibid.

A constitutional statesman is in general a man of common opinion and uncommon abilities.

National Review, 1856

The most influential of constitutional statesmen is the one who most felicitously expresses the creed of the moment, who administers it, who embodies it in laws and institutions, who gives it the highest life it is capable of, who induces the average man to think: I could not have done it any better if I had had time myself.

    Ibid.

The cure for admiring the Lords is to go and look at it.

    Attributed

No real English gentleman, in his secret soul, was ever sorry for the death of a political economist.

    'The First Edinburgh Reviewers' (1855)

One of the greatest pains to human nature is the pain of a new idea.

    Physics & Politics (1869)

The electorate is the jury writ large.

    Parliamentary Reform (1883)

Dullness in matters of government is a good sign, and not a bad one. In particular, dullness in parliamentary government is a test of its excellence, and indication of its success.

    1856

There is no method by which men can be both free and equal.

    The Economist, 1863

The best reason why monarchy is a strong government is that it is an intelligible government. The mass of mankind understands it, and they hardly anywhere in the world understand any other.

    The English Constitution (1872)

In happy states, the Conservative Party must rule upon the whole a much longer time than their adversaries. In well-framed politics, innovation – great innovation that is – can only be occasional. If you are always altering your house, it is a sign either that you have a bad house, or that you have an excessively restless disposition – there is something wrong somewhere.

1874

Kenneth Baker

b. 1934; Conservative MP 1968–97, Cabinet minister 1985–92

Crime is always on the news. Crime prevention doesn't feature so often in the headlines but in the last ten years, and in the last five particularly, we have put crime prevention on the agenda for every police force, every local authority, every housing association, every car manufacturer and insurer, and on the personal agenda of many millions of ordinary people.

As Home Secretary, 1991

No Conservative government has ever accepted that parts of our inner cities might become no-go areas for the rule of law.

Ibid.

It's no use peddling the idea that unemployment and crime are the government's fault and opportunities are restricted by, for instance, lack of child care or racism. I see the growth of a so-called underclass as the most formidable challenge to a secure and civilised way of life throughout the developed world.

As Home Secretary, 1992

Socialists make the mistake of confusing individual worth with success. They believe you cannot allow people to succeed in case those who fail feel worthless.

Cited in *The Observer*, 13 July 1986

We have so reduced the power of the courts to lock up children – for basically good reasons – we now have a handful of young people we cannot really cope with.

As Home Secretary, 1993

Mrs Thatcher categorised her ministers into those she could put down, those she could break down and those she could wear down.

The Independent, 11 September 1993

Was I ever one of us?

To Charles Powell, BBC TV, September 1993

Stanley Baldwin

1867–1947; Prime Minister 1923, 1924–29, 1935–37

A lot of hard-faced men who look as if they had done very well out of the war.

Referring to the first House of Commons elected after the First World War

Four words, of one syllable each, are words which contain salvation for this country, and for the whole world. They are 'faith', 'hope', 'love' and 'work'.

Speech in the House of Commons, 16 February 1923

A platitude is simply a truth repeated until people get tired of hearing it.

29 May 1924

There are three classes which need sanctuary more than others – birds, wild flowers and Prime Ministers.

The Observer, 24 May 1925

Safety First does not mean a smug self-satisfaction with everything as it is. It is a warning to all persons who are going to cross a road in dangerous circumstances.

1929

Had the employers of past generations all of them dealt fairly with their men there would have been no unions.

1931

There are three groups that no British Prime Minister should provoke: the Vatican, the Treasury and the miners.

Attributed

I think it is well also for the man in the street to realise that there is no power on earth that can protect him from being bombed. Whatever people may tell him, the bomber will always get through … The only defence is offence, which means that you have to kill more women and children more quickly than the enemy if you want to save yourselves.

10 November 1932

Let us never forget this; since the day of the air, the old frontiers are gone. When you think of the defence of England you no longer think of the chalk cliffs of Dover, you think of the Rhine.

30 July 1934

He spent his whole life in plastering together the true and the false and therefrom manufacturing the plausible.

On Lloyd George

I give you my word there will be no great armaments.

To the International Peace Society, 1935

If there is going to be a war – and no one can say that there is not – we must keep him fresh to be our war Prime Minister.

On the main reason for excluding Winston Churchill from his Cabinet, November 1935

You will find in politics that you are much exposed to the attribution of false motive. Never complain and never explain.

Quoted by Harold Nicolson

The intelligent are to the intelligentsia what a gentleman is to a gent.

Attributed

Arthur Balfour

1848–1930; Prime Minister 1902–05

Conservative prejudices are rooted in a great past and Liberal ones in an imaginary future.

Attributed

It is unfortunate, considering that enthusiasm moves the world, that so few enthusiasts can be trusted to speak the truth.

19 May 1891

I am a Conservative because I am absolutely certain that no community in this world has ever flourished, or could ever flourish, if it was faithless to its own past.

Attributed

The energies of our system will decay, the glory of the sun will be dimmed, and the earth, tideless and inert, will no longer tolerate the race which, for a moment disturbed its solitude. Man will go down into the pit, and all his thoughts will perish.

The Foundations of Belief (1895)

I thought he was a young man of promise but it turns out he was a young man of promises.

On Winston Churchill, 1899

World Crisis – Winston has written four volumes about himself and called it World Crisis.

Attributed

Biography should be written by an acute enemy.

1927

I never forgive but I always forget.
    Attributed

Douglas Bandow
b. 1954; aide to Ronald Reagan

... the most interesting form of welfare institution in the West, at least to those concerned about individual liberty and personal independence, is collective self-help, or mutual aid as it is more commonly called.
    Welfare Reform has become a Forgotten Issue, 1992

Claude Frederic Bastiat
1801–50; French statesman and economist

Try to imagine a regulation of labour imposed by force that is not a violation of liberty; a transfer of wealth imposed by force that is not a violation of property. If you cannot reconcile these contradictions, then you must conclude that the law cannot organise labour and industry without organising injustice.
    The Law, 1850

Lord Beaverbrook
1879–1964; newspaper magnate and Conservative MP

Mr Baldwin, a well-meaning man of indifferent judgement who, whether he did right or wrong, was always sustained by a belief that he was acting for the best.
    1931

His [Stanley Baldwin] successive attempts to find a policy remind me of a chorus of a third-rate review. His evasions reappear in different scenes and in new dresses, and every time they dance with renewed and despairing vigour. But it is the same old jig.

Attributed

He didn't care in which direction the car was travelling, so long as he remained in the driver's seat.

On Lloyd George

Daniel Bell

1919–2011; American sociologist

… equality of opportunity is a zero-sum game in which individuals can win in different ways. But equality of result, or redistributive polices, essentially is a zero-sum game, in which there are distinct losers and winners. And inevitably these conditions lead to more open political competition and conflict.

The Winding Passage (1980)

Distributive justice is one of the oldest and thorniest problems for political theory. What has been happening in recent years is that entitlement, equity, and equality have become confused with one another, and the source of rancorous political debate. Yet they are also the central value issues of the time.

Ibid.

William Bennett

b. 1943; American Republican politician

Discrimination on the basis of race is illegal, immoral, and unconstitutional, inherently wrong and destructive of democratic society.

Counting by Race (1979)

It is bad enough that so much of what passes for art and entertainment these days is the rampant promiscuity and the casual cruelty of our popular culture. To ask us to pay for it is to add insult to injury. We will not be intimidated by our cultural guardians into accepting either the insult or the injury.

Speech to the Republican National Convention, 19 August 1992

It is hard to fight a war when you've got to debate the worthiness of fighting it.

CNN, 16 December 1989

If we believe that good art, good music and good books will elevate taste and improve the sensibilities of the young – which they most certainly do – then we must also believe that bad music and bad books will degrade. As a society, as communities, as policy makers, we must come to grips with the truth.

The Devaluing of America (1992)

Conservatism as I understand it is not essentially theoretical or ideological, but is rather a practical matter of experience. It seeks to conserve the best elements of the past.

Ibid.

Conservatives are interested in pursuing policies that will better reinforce and encourage the best of our people's common culture, habits and beliefs.

Ibid.

Conservatism ... is based on the belief that the social order rests upon a moral base, and that what ties us together as a people ... is in constant need of support.

Ibid.

The problem is that some people tend to regard anyone who would pronounce a definitive judgement as an unsophisticated Philistine or a closed-minded 'elitist' trying to impose his view on everybody else.

Ibid.

Arthur Benson

1862–1922; essayist, poet and author

Land of Hope and Glory, mother of the free,
How shall we extol thee, who are born of thee?
Wider still and wider shall they bounds be set,
God, who made thee mighty, make thee mightier yet.

Land of Hope and Glory (1902)

Brigitte Berger

b. 1928; American sociologist

[T]he family, and specifically the bourgeois family, is the
necessary social context for the emergence of autonomous
individuals who are the empirical foundation of political
democracy. This has been so historically. There is every reason
to think that it continues to be so today.

The War Over the Family (1983)

No amount of legislation and court decisions can produce in the
individual such basic moral ideas as the inviolability of human
rights, the willing assent to legal norms, or the notion that
contractual agreements must be respected.

Ibid.

Public policy with regard to the family should primarily be
concerned with the family's capacity to take care of its children,
its sick and handicapped, and its aged. The basic principle here
should be that, whenever possible, these needs are best taken
care of *within* the family, *any family* ... regardless of social or
cultural type. This means that the overriding concern of public
policy should be to provide support for the family to discharge
these caring tasks, rather than to relieve the family of these
tasks.

Ibid.

[I]f one wants to foster the bourgeois family, the best course to take is to give people freedom of choice. Most of them will choose bourgeois values and bourgeois lifestyles – especially people in the 'targeted' groups of the poor and disadvantaged.
Ibid.

Peter Berger
b. 1929; American political philosopher

Modern capitalism ... has been a liberating force. The market in and of itself liberates people from the old confines of subsistence economies.
The Capitalist Revolution (1986)

Kapitalistische luft macht frei [the air of capitalism liberates]
Ibid., adaptation of traditional German adage 'the city air liberates'

[The liberating qualities of capitalism] is the empirical justification of the ideological position that there is an intrinsic connection between the economic freedom and all other liberties ... However, it does not follow from this that their liberating forces of capitalism are inevitable or irreversible.
Ibid.

Isaiah Berlin
1909–97; philosopher

Liberty is liberty, not equality or fairness or justice or human happiness or a quiet conscience.
Two Concepts of Liberty (1958)

The fundamental sense of freedom is freedom from chains, from imprisonment, from enslavement by others. The rest is extension of this sense, or else metaphor.
Four Essays on Liberty (1969)

The Bible
In the sweat of thy face shall thy cut bread.
  Genesis 3:10

Eye for Eye, tooth for tooth, hand for hand, foot for foot.
  Exodus 21:24

He that smiteth a man, so that he die, shall be surely put to death.
  Exodus 23:20

Neither shalt thou favour a poor man in his cause.
  Exodus 23:12

Thou art a God ready to pardon, gracious and merciful, slow to anger and of great kindness.
  Nehemiah

Where your treasure is, there shall your heart be also.
  Matthew 6:21

John Biffen
1930–2007; Conservative MP 1961–97, Cabinet minister

She was a tigress surrounded by hamsters.
  On Margaret Thatcher, December 1990

He was the sewer and not the sewage.
  On Bernard Ingham

John Biggs-Davison
1918–88; Conservative MP 1955–88

I have never conceived it my duty as a Member of Parliament to seek to amend the Ten Commandments.
  November 1976

Nigel Birch
1906–81; Conservative MP 1945–70

My God, they've shot our fox!
  On hearing of the Chancellor Hugh Dalton's resignation in 1947

For the second time the Prime Minister has got rid of a Chancellor of the Exchequer who tried to get expenditure under control. Once is more than enough.
  Following Macmillan's replacement of Selwyn Lloyd with Reginald Maudling, 1963

Lord Birkenhead (F. E. Smith)
1872–1930; Conservative MP 1906–18, Cabinet minister 1915–23, 1924–28

Austen always played the game and always lost it.
  On Austen Chamberlain

I think Baldwin has gone mad. He simply takes one jump in the dark; looks round; and then takes another.
  1923

Otto von Bismarck
1815–98; German Chancellor

Politics is the art of the possible.
> 1867

The politician has not to revenge what has happened but to ensure that it does not happen again.
> Ibid.

The less people know about how sausages and laws are made, the better they'll sleep at night.
> Attributed

Politics is not an exact science.
> Addressing the Prussian Parliament, 18 December 1863

Whoever speaks of Europe is wrong. It is a geographical concept.
> 1876

I have always found the word Europe on the lips of those politicians who wanted something from other Powers which they dared not demand in their own names.
> 1878

A lath of wood painted to look like iron.
> On Lord Salisbury at the Congress of Berlin, 1878

The old Jew! That is the man.
> On Disraeli, at the Congress of Berlin, 1878

If reactionary measures are to be carried, the Liberal Party takes the rudder, from the correct assumption that it will not overstep the necessary limits; if liberal measures are to be carried, the Conservative Party takes office in its turn for the same consideration.
> Attributed

William Blackstone
1723–80; lawyer

And, lastly, to vindicate these rights, when actually violated
and attacked, the subjects of England are entitled, in the first
place, to the regular administration and free course of justice in
the courts of law; next to the right of petitioning the king and
parliament for redress of grievances; and, lastly, to the right of
having and using arms for self-preservation and defence.

Commentaries on the Laws of England (1765–69)

That the king can do no wrong is a necessary and fundamental
principle of the English constitution.

Ibid.

The Royal Navy of England hath ever been its greatest defence
and armament; it is its ancient and natural strength; the
floating bulwark of our island.

Ibid.

It is better that ten guilty persons escape than one innocent
one suffer.

Ibid.

Lord (Robert) Blake
1916–2003; historian

It is too often said that Thatcherism is a departure from
Conservative tradition. She proclaims herself to be radical.
In one sense she is; but in another sense she is harking back
to an older set of policies. After all, for most of the time
since 1846 Conservatives have been in favour of low taxation,
an enterprise culture, a stable currency, and minimal state
intervention; and, apart from a curious aberration by Disraeli,

have viewed what was quaintly called the trade union movement with a frosty eye.

The Times, 1989

Allan Bloom

1930–92; American political philosopher

Affirmative action now institutionalises the worst aspects of separatism.

On black militancy in American universities; *The Closing of the American Mind* (1987)

Democratic society cannot accept any principle of achievement other than merit.

Ibid.

David Boaz

b. 1953; libertarian

A key point to keep in mind is that non-government schools, which have to offer a better product to stay in business, do a better job of educating children.

Liberating Schools (1991)

Henry St John, Viscount Bolingbroke

1678–1751; High Tory

The constitution will be reverenced by him [the patriot king] as the law of God and of man; the force of which binds the king as much as the meanest subject, and the reason of which binds him much more.

'The Idea of a Patriot King', in *The Works of the Late Right Honourable Henry St John, Lord Viscount Bolingbroke*

Napoleon Bonaparte
1769–1821; Emperor of France 1804–15

A form of government that is not the result of a long sequence of shared experiences, effort and endeavours, can never take root.
1803

He who saves his country violates no law.
Maxims (1948)

My maxim was, *la carrière est ouverte aux talents*, without distinction of birth or fortune.
1817

Andrew Bonar Law
1858–1923; Prime Minister 1922–23

If, therefore, war should ever come between these two countries [Britain and Germany], which Heaven forbid! It will not, I think be due to irresistible natural laws, it will be due to want of human wisdom.
House of Commons, 27 November 1911

If I am a great man then a good many great men of history are frauds.
Letter to Max Aitken, 13 November 1911

A man with the vision of an eagle but with a blind spot in his eye.
On F. E. Smith, Lord Birkenhead, 1917

I am afraid I shall have to show myself very vicious, Mr Asquith, this session. I hope you will understand.
To Asquith at the beginning of the 1912 session of Parliament

They [the Liberal government] have turned the House of Commons into an exchange where everything is bought and sold. In order to retain for a little longer the ascendancy of their Party, to remain a few months longer in office, they have sold the Constitution, they have sold themselves.

Speech in Belfast

In war it is necessary not only to be active but to seem active.

1916

I must follow them. I am their leader.

Going along with backbench Tory MPs in the 1922 rebellion against a Conservative–Liberal coalition

Christopher Booker
b. 1937; journalist

In the life of any government, however safe its majority, there comes a moment when the social movements of which it had once been the expression, turn inexorably against it. After that moment, every mistake it makes becomes magnified; indeed blunders multiply as if feeding on themselves; and both outwardly and inwardly the government appears to be at the mercy of every wind.

The Neophiliacs (1969)

Our government has recently unleashed the greatest avalanche of regulations in peacetime history; and wherever we examine their working we see that they are using a sledgehammer to miss a nut.

1995

Daniel Boorstin
1914–2004; American historian

[W]e must abandon the prevalent belief in the superior wisdom of the ignorant. Unless we give up the voguish reverence for youth and for the 'culturally deprived,' unless we cease to look to the vulgar community as arbiters of our art and literature, and of all our culture, we will never have the will to de-provincialise our minds.

Democracy and its Discontents (1971)

Education is learning what you didn't even know you knew.

Ibid.

We must recognise that many of the acts committed in the name of equal opportunity are in fact acts of discrimination.

Ibid.

We must not allow ourselves to become the Quota States of America.

Ibid., on the tendency for minority education agendas

Robert Bork

1927–2012; US judge

In a constitutional democracy the moral content of law must be given by the morality of the framer or legislator, never by the morality of the judge.

American Enterprise Institute, 1977

Those who made and endorsed our Constitution knew man's nature, and it is to their ideas rather than to the temptations of utopia, that we must ask that our judges adhere.

The Tempting of America (1990)

Peter Bottomley

b. 1944; Conservative MP 1975–

When [The IRA] plant such bombs, it proves they can scare people, it proves they can kill people, it proves nothing.

1990

Virginia Bottomley

b. 1948; Conservative MP 1984–2005, Cabinet minister 1992–97

Suicide is a real threat to health in a modern society.
> As Health Secretary, 1993

Smoking is a dying habit.
> Ibid.

Edward Boyle

1923–81; Conservative MP 1950–70

Nothing in politics is ever as good or bad as it first appears.
> Quoted in *The Whitelaw Memoirs* (1989)

Rhodes Boyson

1925–2012; Conservative MP 1974–97

Politically there is no record of the continuance of political freedoms when economic freedoms have died.
> Cited in *Total Politics*

The militants in Liverpool spend money as if it came from outer space.
> 1987

Lord Brabazon of Tara

b. 1946; Conservative MP 1984–2001, Parliamentary Under-Secretary of State for Transport 1986–89, Minister of State (FCO) 1989–90, Minister of State for Transport 1990–92 ; Chairman of Committees 2002–12

Make no mistake about it, the repercussions of this new invention [television] are going to be ... very wholesome

because they tend to keep the home together … It does mean that people stay at home.
  1950

Gyles Brandreth
b. 1948; Conservative MP 1992–97

At the House of Commons sword-fighting is strictly taboo. Back-stabbing, on the other hand, is quite a different matter.
  Breaking the Code (2000)

In the Members' Dining Room, the Conservatives eat at one end, the Labour Party at the other, while the Liberals wait at table.
  Ibid.

Sir Leon Brittan
b. 1939; Conservative MP 1974–88; Cabinet minister 1983–86, European Commissioner 1988–99

The two offences of which people of all ages are most fearful are violent street crimes and burglary. Efforts against these two crimes must be targeted to make the best possible use of the available intelligence and skilled detective powers.
  As Home Secretary, 1985

D. W. Brogan
1900–74; historian

Political corruption breeds infection. The best safeguard is the fresh air of publicity.
  The Free State (1944)

Peter Brooke

b. 1934; Conservative MP 1977–2001, Cabinet minister, 1987–94

Clearly, the future is still to come.
   1986

Lord Brookeborough

1888–1973; Member of Northern Ireland Parliament 1929–68, Prime
Minister of Northern Ireland 1943–63

If it weren't for these troubles, Ireland would be a very happy
place.
   As Ulster minister with special responsibility for tourism, 1970

Warren Brookes

1929–91; American journalist and economist

[T]he whole notion of using the tax system as a method of
redistributing wealth rests on a fallacy – namely that wealth
is money, and that all one has to do to transfer wealth is
transfer money. The trouble with that hypothesis is that money
is nothing more than a medium of exchange. Real wealth is the
total productive output of the economy in the form of services
and goods, which are in turn the products of the energy,
resources and talents of the people who produce them. Thus
merely passing money around does little to change a nation's
real productive output or wealth, nor does it change the
inherent 'wealth capacity' of individual citizens. All it does is to
reduce the real value of the money itself through inflation.
   The Economy in Mind (1982)

The attempt to redistribute wealth by redistributing money
through the progressive tax tables only winds up keeping the

poor, the rich, and the middle classes struggling even harder to keep up with taxation.
Ibid.

In [America], it is still safe to say that 80–90 per cent of the new jobs and economic growth is contributed by the efforts, imagination, energy and initiative of less than 5–10 per cent of all individuals.
Ibid.

In the process [of wealth creation, the] top 5–10 per cent has become very rich, and not always very nice; but genius seldom seems to equate with meekness and charity.
Ibid.

... without those well-rewarded individuals who often have risked everything to create the one new enterprise in ten that succeeds, our economy would become stagnant and trickle-down would quickly be replaced by dole-out as it has in Poland, Russia, China, Cuba, or even England.
Ibid.

Inflation itself has its fundamental roots in the politics of envy.
Ibid.

Is it really any wonder that the money they print is *green*?
Ibid., on the use of inflationary measures to pay for wealth redistribution

Instead of genuine breakthroughs, we are seeing more and more in consumer products what we have seen on television shows: safe spin offs, frequent rip-offs, and modest variations on past success models.
Ibid., on the dangers of Corporations losing their entrepreneurial touch

Michael Brotherton

Conservative MP 1979–83

Social security scroungers should be made to give a pint of blood every six months.
1979

Lord Brougham

1778–1868; Lord Chancellor 1830–34

What is valuable is not new, and what is new is not valuable.
Edinburgh Review, 1880

Education makes a people easy to lead, but difficult to drive; easy to govern, but impossible to enslave.
Speech to the House of Commons, 29 January 1828

Andrew Brown

b. 1955; British journalist

Thatcherism is not an ideology, but a political style: a trick of presenting reasonable, rather pedestrian ideas in a way that drives reasonable men into a frothing rage.
The Spectator, 1984

Michael Brown

b. 1951; Conservative MP 1979–97, sketchwriter for *The Independent* 1998–

It was like losing my mother. My mother is still alive but one day she won't be, and when that occurs it will, I suspect, be exactly like the day that Margaret Thatcher resigned.
Daily Telegraph, 25 October 1993

Angela Browning

1946; Conservative MP for Tiverton and Honiton 1992–2010, shadow Minister of State of Employment and Education 1997–98, shadow Secretary of State for Trade and Industry 1999–2000, shadow Leader of the House of Commons 2000–01, Minister for Crime Prevention and Anti-Social Behaviour Reduction 2011

The idea that there are women who run perfect homes and have delightful children who never get chicken pox without giving a month's notice is unrealistic.

   Attributed

Patrick Buchanan

b. 1938; American Republican politician

And from the ancient forests of Oregon, to the Inland Empire of California, America's great middle class has got to start standing up to the environmental extremists who put insects, rats and birds ahead of families, workers and jobs.

   Republican Convention speech, 17 August 1992

William Buckley Jr

1925–2008; American journalist

Knee-jerk liberals and all the certified saints of sanctified humanism are quick to condemn this great and much-maligned Transylvanian statesman.

   On Vlad the Impaler

I mean to live my life an obedient man, but obedient to God, subservient to the wisdom of my political ancestors; never to the authority of political truths arrived at yesterday at the voting booth.

   Up From Liberalism (1959)

The state is a divine institution. Without it we have anarchy, and the lawlessness of anarchy is counter to the national law; so we abjure all political theories which view the state as inherently and necessarily evil. But it is the state which has been in history the principal instrument of abuse of the people, and so it is central to the Conservative program to keep the state from accumulating any but the most necessary powers.

The Catholic World

What was wrong with Communism wasn't aberrant leadership, it was Communism.

30 June 1995

Ivor Bulmer-Thomas

1905–93; Labour and Conservative MP

If he ever went to school without any boots it was because he was too big for them.

On Harold Wilson, Conservative Party Conference 1949

Julie Burchill

b. 1959; journalist

Despite the Right-On hysteria, Mrs Thatcher has never been an old-fashioned girl. Voting for her was like buying a Vera Lynn LP, getting it home and finding 'Never Mind the Bollocks' inside the red white and blue sleeve … She basically doesn't believe that sex is such a big deal; this is why she has proved such a disappointment to Whitehouse, Gillick, Anderton and the sperm-ridden minds of the Right who wanted moral rearmament and got a 2p in the pound tax cut instead.

From the article 'Margaret Thatcher'

Mrs Thatcher is not trying to drag this country kicking and screaming into the nineteenth century. She's a brutal futurist, a

Conservative with no interest in conserving, especially ye olde England and its ye olde industries.

Ibid.

[Mrs Thatcher] is an internationalist – unlike Labour, who lash themselves into a sentimental tizzy every time Johnny Foreigner puts in a bid for a British sweet factory.

Ibid.

What people forget is that it was not easy, until very recently, being Margaret Thatcher. She is one of those strange socio-economic mutations, like Morrissey, who have nowhere to go but the top. She is the misfit who made it...

Ibid.

[Mrs Thatcher] has always had to take stick for being a woman; from the drunken Tory who asked her at a No. 10 luncheon while she was Edward Heath's Education Minister if there was any truth in the rumour that she was a woman, to the caring, anti-sexist Labour Party and their Ditch the Bitch campaign of 1983. (How would they react to a black Conservative leader – Dump the Coon?)

Ibid.

Mrs Thatcher is not uncaring or cruel, but she is naïve. She can't comprehend how many absolutely useless, helpless and hopeless a good many people are and is cursed with an incredible optimism and romanticism as to what the individual is capable of. If she kicks away the crutches, it's because she really does believe that everybody has the ability to walk without them.

Ibid.

Like Kennedy, Roosevelt and Stalin, [Mrs Thatcher] has reached that place between holiness and hologram where no one seriously expects the policies to work but no one can shake the symbolism and what it means to their sense of the nation.

Ibid.

I don't believe in Thatcherism but I do believe in Thatcher, given the options. It is to her, not her discredited policies, that there really is no alternative. Send her victorious, happy and glorious. Because it's either that or getting excited about making runner-up in the Eurovision Song Contest.

Ibid.

Edmund Burke

1729–97; statesman and political philosopher

The laws reach but a very little way. Constitute government how you please, infinitely the greater part of it must depend upon the exercise of powers which are left at large the prudence and uprightness of the ministers of the state. Even all the use and potency of the laws depend on them. Without them, your commonwealth is no better than a scheme upon paper; not a living active, effective constitution.

Thoughts on the Causes of the Present Discontents (1770)

When bad men combine, the good must associate; else they will fall, one by one, on an unpitied sacrifice in a contemptible struggle.

Ibid.

The greater the power, the more dangerous the abuse.

Speech on the Middlesex election, 1774

Your representative owes you, not his industry only, but his judgement; and he betrays instead of serving you if he sacrifices it to your opinion.

Speech to the electors of Bristol, November 1774

All government indeed, every human benefit and enjoyment, every virtue and every prudent act is founded on compromise and barter.

'Second speech on conciliation with America: The Thirteen Resolutions', 22 March 1775

It is not what a lawyer tells me I may do; but what humanity, reason, and justice tell me I ought to do.
Ibid.

The concessions of the weak are the concessions of fear.
Ibid.

Abstract liberty, like other mere abstractions, is not to be found.
Ibid.

Freedom and not servitude is the cure of anarchy; as religion and not atheism, is the true remedy for superstition.
Ibid.

The use of force alone is but temporary; it may subdue for a moment; but it does not remove the necessity of subduing again: and a nation is not governed which is perpetually to be conquered.
Ibid.

I do not know the method of drawing up an indictment against a whole people. Magnanimity in politics is not seldom the truest wisdom; and a great empire and little minds go ill together.
Ibid.

The power of perpetuating our property in our families is one of the most valuable and interesting circumstances belonging to it, and that which tends the most to the perpetuation of society itself.
Attributed

History is a preceptor of prudence, not of principles. The principles of true politics are those of morality enlarged; and I neither now do, nor ever will admit of any other.
Attributed

Liberty must be limited in order to be possessed.
1777

We are afraid to put men to live and trade each upon his own
private stock of reason; because we suspect that the stock in
each man is small, and that the individuals would do better to
avail themselves to the general bank and capital of nations and
of ages … Prejudice is of ready application in the emergency,
it previously engages the mind in steady course of wisdom, and
virtue, and does not leave the man hesitating in the moment of
decision, sceptical, puzzled and unresolved. Prejudice renders
a man's virtue his habit; and not a series of unconnected acts.
Through just prejudice, his duty becomes part of his nature.
Reflections on the Revolution in France, 1790

Government is a contrivance of human wisdom to provide
for human wants. Men have a right that these wants should be
provided for by this wisdom.
Ibid.

To make us love our country, our country ought to be lovely.
Ibid.

People will not look forwards to posterity who never look
backward to their ancestors.
Ibid.

A state without the means of change is without the means of
conservation.
Ibid.

A nation without the means of reform is without the means of
survival.
Ibid.

A nation is not an idea only of local extent and individual
momentary aggregation, but it is an idea of continuity, which

extends in time as well as in numbers and in space. By the unbridled facility of changing the state as often and as much and in as many ways as their floating fancies or fashions, the whole chain and continuity of the commonwealth would be broken. No generation could link with the other. Men would become little better than the flies of a summer.

Ibid.

To be attached to the subdivision, to love the little platoon we belong to in society, is the first principle of public affections. It is the first link in the series by which we proceed towards a love of our country and mankind.

Ibid.

Manners are more important than laws. Upon them, in great measure, the law depends.

Ibid.

Party division, whether on the whole operating for good or evil, are things inseparable from free government.

Ibid.

He was not merely a chip off the old block, but the old block itself.

On William Pitt the Younger

There is a boundary to men's passions when they act from feelings; but none when they are under the influence of imagination.

Appeal from the New to the Old Whigs (1791)

You can never plan the future by the past.

Letter, 1791

Whenever a separation is made between liberty and justice, neither, in my opinion, is safe.

Letter, October 1789

There is but one law for all, namely that law that governs
all law, the law of our Creator, the law of humanity, justice,
equity, the law of nature and nations.

Trial of Warren Hastings, 1794

A thing may look specious in theory, and yet be ruinous in
practice; a thing may look evil in theory, and yet be in practice
excellent.

Ibid.

All that is necessary for the triumph of evil is that good men do
nothing.

1795 (attributed)

Mere parsimony is not true economy ... Expense and great
expense, may be an essential part of true economy.

Letter to a Noble Lad (1796)

Conor Burns

b. 1972; Conservative MP 2010–

On one occasion, I took a taxi from here to Chester Square
to see Lady Thatcher on a particularly wet and awful evening.
The taxi driver said, 'Which end of the square do you want,
guv?' I said, 'The house with the policeman outside.' 'Maggie
Thatcher's, guv?' 'That's right.' 'What you doin' there, then?'
'I'm going to have a drink with her – she's a friend of mine.'
'What d'you do then?' 'I'm a Tory MP.' As we pulled up, I went
to pay the driver, but he refused to take the fare. I apologise in
advance to the Prime Minister for repeating this story, but the
driver said, 'Your fare tonight, guv, is you go in there and you
tell 'er from me that we ain't had a good'un since!' I imparted
that message to Margaret, who looked at me and said, 'Well,
he's quite right.' I was then on the receiving end of a lecture

about how he probably had a wife and child to support, how I should have paid him and how it was monstrous that I had not.

House of Commons, 10 April 2013

George H. W. Bush

b. 1924; US President 1988–92

Read my lips: no new taxes.

Republican National Convention, 1988

We are a nation of communities, of tens and tens of thousands of ethnic, religious, social, business, labour unions, neighbourhoods, regional and other organisations, all of them varied, voluntary and unique ... a brilliant diversity spread like stars, like a thousand points of light in a broad and peaceful sky.

Ibid.

Use power to help people. For we are given power not to advance our own purposes, not to make a real show in the world, nor a name. There is but one just use of power and it is to serve the people.

Attributed

The power of America rests in a stirring but simple idea – that people will do great things if you only set them free.

Ibid.

Drug dealers need to understand a simple fact. You shoot a cop and you're going to be severely punished – fast. And if I had my way, with your life.

Washington Post, 10 March 1989

Boy, they were big crematoriums weren't they?

On a visit to Auschwitz

Giving peace a chance does not mean taking a chance with peace.

August 1990

Much good can come from the prudent use of power.

January 1992

I don't want to run the risk of ruining what is a lovely recession.

(Meaning 'reception'), 1992

John Butcher

1946–2006; Conservative MP 1979–97

We can beat them in the 1980s and 1990s. We have beaten them in other respects and we can do it again.

As Junior Trade and Industry Minister, on Japan, 1984

R. A. Butler

1902–82; Conservative MP 1932–66, Cabinet minister 1941–5, 1951–64

Politics is the art of the possible.

Attributed; see also Bismarck

The civil service machine is a bit like a Rolls Royce. You know it's the best machine in the world, but you're not quite sure what to do with it.

On the civil service

In politics you must always keep running with the pack. The moment that you falter and they sense that you are injured, the rest will turn on you like wolves.

Quoted by Dennis Walters

I think a Prime Minister has to be a butcher and know the joints. That is perhaps where I have not been quite competent – in knowing all the ways that you can cut up the carcass.

1966

Politics is largely a matter of the heart.

Attributed

Stuart Butler and Anna Kondratas

Butler: b. 1947; Director of the Center for Policy Innovation, Washington DC; Kondratas: DOB unknown; policy adviser and analyst

The secret to making real progress against poverty and distress is to realise that it will come from a 'bottom up' and not a 'top down' process ... Rather than try to stamp out diversity in an effort to find the unitary solution to welfare and social problems, we should be nurturing diversity, recognising that it is the key to success and progress in all fields.

Out of the Poverty Trap (1987)

C

David Cameron
b. 1966; Member of Parliament 2001–, Leader of the Conservative
Party 2005–, Prime Minister 2010–

I joined this party because I believe in freedom. We are the
only party believing that if you give people freedom and
responsibility, they will grow stronger and society will grow
stronger.
    Leadership contest speech, 2005

Some say that we should move to the right. I say that will turn
us into a fringe party, never able to challenge for government
again. I don't want to let that happen to this party. Do you?
    Ibid.

We don't just need new policies or presentation or organisation,
or even having a young, passionate, energetic leader – though
come to think of it, that might not be such a bad idea.
    Ibid.

I want us to give this country a modern compassionate
Conservatism that is right for our times and right for our country.
    Leadership acceptance speech, 2005

We will change the way we look. Nine out of 10 Conservative
MPs, like me, are white men. We need to change the
scandalous under-representation of women in the Conservative
party and we'll do that.
    Ibid.

I am the heir to Blair.
    Remarks to newspaper executives, 3 October 2005

I want to talk about the future. He was the future once.

His first Prime Minister's Questions against Tony Blair, 2005

I think it was right to remove Saddam Hussein. I think it was the right decision then and I still think it was right now.

BBC Radio 5 Live *Breakfast*, 21 October 2005

I think the prospect of bringing back grammar schools has always been wrong and I've never supported it. And I don't think any Conservative government would have done it.

BBC *Sunday AM*, 15 January 2006

Tony Blair says it's all style and no substance. In fact he wrote me a letter about it.
Dear Kettle … You're black. Signed, Pot.
What a nerve that man has got.

Leader's speech, Bournemouth, 2006

Our Party's history tells us the ground on which political success is built. It is the centre ground.

Ibid.

The centre ground is where you find the concerns, the hopes and the dreams of most people and families in this country.

Ibid.

Some people want me to flash up some pie in the sky tax cuts to show what we stand for. Let me tell you straight. That is not substance. And that is not what we stand for. Do you know what I think? I think that when some people talk about substance, what they mean is they want the old policies back. Well they're not coming back. We're not going back.

Ibid.

Tony Blair once explained his priority in three words: education, education, education. I can do it in three letters. NHS.

Ibid.

Not everything that Labour have done since 1997 is bad. People don't want us to turn the clock back. They want us to improve the bad things, yes. But they also want us to keep the good things.

Ibid.

I am Conservative to the core of my being, as those who know me best will testify.

Daily Telegraph, 23 January 2006

Issues that once divided Conservatives from Liberal Democrats are now issues where we both agree. Our attitude to devolution and localisation of power. Iraq. The environment. I'm a liberal Conservative.

Letter to constituents in Dunfermline and West Fife by-election, 7 February 2006

We have a philosophy – liberal Conservatism – which has the answers to the great questions our country faces. For anyone who believes in this philosophy, there is a home waiting for them in the modern, moderate Conservative Party.

Speech in Bath, 2007

What do I believe? I am by nature an optimist. I think if we give people more power and control over their lives, I think they'll take the right decisions, they will grow stronger and society will grow stronger too. I don't believe in an ever larger state doing more and more, I believe in trying to make people do more themselves for their families and with society as well.

Leader's speech, Blackpool, 2007

I think this country has benefited immeasurably from immigration. People who want to come here and work hard and contribute to our country. I think our diverse and multi-racial society is a huge benefit for Britain.

Ibid.

So, Mr Brown, what's it going to be? Why don't you go ahead and call that election? Let the people pass judgement on ten years of broken promises, let people decide who's really making the arguments about the future of our country. Let people decide who can make the changes that we really need in our country. Call that election. We will fight. Britain will win.
　　Ibid.

Refusing to use these words – right and wrong – means a denial of personal responsibility and the concept of a moral choice.
　　'Broken Society' speech, Glasgow, 2008

The values we need to repair our broken society and to build a strong society are values that should be taught in the home, in the family.
　　Ibid.

Many people wrongly believe that the Conservative Party is all about freedom. Of course we care passionately about freedom from oppression and state control. But freedom can too easily turn into the idea that we all have the right to do whatever we want, regardless of the effect on others. That is libertarian, not Conservative – and it is certainly not me.
　　Leader's Conference speech, Birmingham, 2008

Social responsibility, not state control.
　　Ibid.

I am not an ideologue.
　　Ibid.

The central task I have set myself and this Party is to be as radical in social reform as Margaret Thatcher was in economic reform.
　　Ibid.

Some say our society isn't broken. I wonder what world they live in.

Ibid.

We are not an anti-state party.

Ibid.

The election of a Conservative government will bring – and I mean this almost literally – a declaration of war against those parts of the educational establishment who still cling to the cruelty of the 'all must win prizes' philosophy.

Ibid.

Progressive ends; Conservative means. That is a big argument about the future. That is a big change.

Ibid.

Too many tweets make a twat.

Interview on Absolute Radio, 29 July 2009

The clearest sign of big government irresponsibility is the enormous size of our debt.

Leader's Conference speech, Manchester, 2009

I say to the Labour Party and the trades unions just tell me what is compassionate, what is progressive about spending more on debt interest than on helping the poorest children in our country?

Ibid.

On Monday, when we announced our plan to Get Britain Working you know what Labour called it? 'Callous.'
Excuse me? Who made the poorest poorer? Who left youth unemployment higher? Who made inequality greater? No, not the wicked Tories… you, Labour: you're the ones that did this to our society. So don't you dare lecture us about poverty. You

have failed and it falls to us, the modern Conservative Party to
fight for the poorest who you have let down.
    Ibid.

This is going to be hard and difficult work. A coalition will
throw up all sorts of challenges. But I believe together we can
provide that strong and stable government that our country
needs based on those values – rebuilding family, rebuilding
community, above all, rebuilding responsibility in our country.
    General election victory speech, 2010

We have been sleepwalking our way to an economy that is
unsustainable, unstable, unfair and, frankly, uninspiring.
    Coalition strategy for economic growth, Shipley, 2010

Dealing with this deficit is not an alternative to economic
growth – the two go hand-in-hand. What's more, without
sound finances, none of our ambitions will be deliverable.
    Ibid.

Cutting tax and red tape is all about understanding the
limitations of government – where we need to get out of the
way. But at the same time, we should never be limited in our
aspirations for government – where we need to get involved.
    Ibid.

Some people have said that our coming together will feature
in the history books. But I don't want this to be an historic
government because we are a coalition, I want us to be an
historic government because of what this coalition achieves.
    Ibid.

There are the things you do because it's your passion. The things
that fire you up in the morning, that drive you, that you truly
believe will make a real difference to the country you love. And
my great passion is building the Big Society.
    'Big Society' speech, Liverpool, 2010

Nick and I didn't agree about everything. He wanted clearer pledges on PR. I wanted them on the family. When I told him what I really thought of the European parliament, he said: 'My God, it's worse than I thought.'

Leader's Conference speech, Birmingham, 2010

The Big Society spirit means facing up to this generation's debts, not shirking responsibility. And here I want to say something to the people who got us into this mess. The ones who racked up more debt in thirteen years than previous governments did in three centuries. Yes you, Labour. You want us to spend more money on ourselves, today, to keep racking up the bills, today and leave it to our children – the ones who had nothing to do with all this – to pay our debts tomorrow? That is selfish and irresponsible.

Ibid.

Society is not a spectator sport. This is your country. It's time to believe it. It's time to step up and own it. So mine is not just a vision of a more powerful country. It is a vision of a more powerful people.

Ibid.

My question right now would be to Colonel Gaddafi, which is: 'What on earth do you think you are doing? Stop it.'

24 February 2011

I know only one person here who has knifed a Foreign Secretary – and I'm looking at him.

Prime Minister's Questions, 9 March 2011

Picture by picture, these criminals are being identified and arrested, and we will not let any phony concerns about human rights get in the way of the publication of these pictures and the arrest of these individuals.

On the 2011 England riots, August 2011

Conservatives believe in the ties that bind us; that society is strong when we make vows to each other. So I don't support gay marriage in spite of being a Conservative. I support it because I am a Conservative.

Leader's Conference speech, October 2011

Under the doctrine of state multiculturalism, we have encouraged different cultures to live separate lives, apart from each other and apart from the mainstream. We've failed to provide a vision of society to which they feel they want to belong. We've even tolerated these segregated communities behaving in ways that run completely counter to our values.

Speech at Munich Security Conference, Munich, 2011

When a white person holds objectionable views, racist views for instance, we rightly condemn them. But when equally unacceptable views or practices come from someone who isn't white, we've been too cautious frankly – frankly, even fearful – to stand up to them.

Ibid.

The extremism we face is a distortion of Islam, so these arguments, in part, must be made by those within Islam.

Ibid.

People have very clear instructions for this government: 'Lead us out of this economic mess.'

Leader's Conference speech, Manchester, 2011

No, Britain never had the biggest population, the largest land mass, the richest resources, but we had the spirit. Remember: it's not the size of the dog in the fight – it's the size of the fight in the dog. Overcoming challenge, confounding the sceptics, reinventing ourselves, this is what we do. It's called leadership.

Ibid.

We are a Christian country. And we should not be afraid to say so.

'King James Bible' speech, Oxford, 2011

Put simply, for too long we have been unwilling to distinguish right from wrong. 'Live and let live' has too often become 'do what you please'. Bad choices have too often been defended as just different lifestyles.

Ibid.

They're tweeting, blogging and poking for all they're worth, but they still haven't got a policy.

On the Labour Party, 12 December 2011

No one in this House is going to be surprised that Conservatives and Liberal Democrats don't always agree about Europe, but let me reassure him he shouldn't believe everything he reads in the papers. It's not that bad, it's not like we're brothers or anything!

Prime Minister's Questions, 14 December 2011

I've seen it, yes, it's a fantastic piece of acting by Meryl Streep, but I just, you can't help wondering, why do we have to have this film right now, it is a film much more about ageing and elements of dementia rather than an amazing Prime Minister, and my sort of sense was a great piece of acting, really staggering piece of acting, but a film I wish they could have made another day.

On *The Iron Lady*, 6 January 2012

As I put it – those who can, should; and those who can't, we will always help.

Speech on welfare, Bluewater, Kent, 2012

Governing is not a popularity contest.

Ibid.

Unless we act, unless we take difficult, painful decisions, unless we show determination and imagination, Britain may not be in the future what it has been in the past.
   Leader's Conference speech, Birmingham, 2012

Aspiration is the engine of progress. Countries rise when they allow their people to rise. In this world where brains matter more, where technologies shape our lives, where no one is owed a living ... the most powerful natural resource we have is our people.
   Ibid.

This party has a heart but we don't like wearing it on our sleeve. Conservatives think: let's just get on with the job and help people and not bang on about it. It's not our style.
   Ibid.

When they were in office, their answer was always: Borrow more money. Now they're out of office it's: Borrow more money. Whatever the day, whatever the question, whatever the weather it's: borrow more money. Borrow, borrow, borrow. Did you hear what Ed Miliband said last week about taxes? He described a tax cut as the government writing people a cheque. Ed ... Let me explain to you how it works. When people earn money, it's their money. Not the government's money: their money. Then, the government takes some of it away in tax. So, if we cut taxes, we're not giving them money – we're taking less of it away. OK?
   Ibid.

Here in this government, together in this country make this pledge – let's build an aspiration nation, let's get Britain on the rise.
   Ibid.

What you call austerity is what I might call efficiency.
   8 May 2012

The only little red pests I pursue these days are in this House.
Hitting back on fox-hunting at Prime Minister's Questions,
January 2013

I never want us to pull up the drawbridge and retreat from the world. I am not a British isolationist.
Bloomberg speech, January 2013

It is time for the British people to have their say. It is time to settle this European question in British politics.
Ibid.

When I stood on the steps of Downing Street for the first time I said I believed the best days for Britain lie ahead of us, not behind us. I still believe that. And by sticking to the plan we can prove it to be true. By sticking to the plan, we can – together – make Britain a great success story in the global race.
Speech on the economy, March 2013

I think we should think about it like this – that there will be young boys in schools today who are gay, who are worried about being bullied, who are worried about what society thinks of them, who can see that the highest Parliament in the land has said that their love is worth the same as anybody else's love and that we believe in equality. I think they will stand that bit taller today and I'm proud of the fact that that has happened.
On the *Today* programme, 22 May 2013

It was an amazing performance from Andy Murray, but also an amazing day for British tennis and for Britain. He never gave up and it was magnificent. It was a privilege to watch Andy Murray making history.
Congratulating Andy Murray on winning the 2013 Wimbledon championship, 7 June, 2013

My daughter is nine years old, she's just started to read all the Harry Potter books so I'm sort of rediscovering them all over again. I can think of all sorts of characters you don't want to be and I suppose in the end you know if you've got any sense you want to be Harry Potter.

Q&A session with students in Kazakhstan, July 2013

I don't want to be Prime Minister of England, I want to be Prime Minister of the whole of the United Kingdom.

Attributed

Albert Camus
1913–60; French novelist

What is a rebel? A man who says no.
1951

A free press can, of course, be good or bad, but most certainly, without freedom it will never be anything but bad … Freedom is nothing else but a chance to be better, whereas enslavement is a certainty of the worst.

Resistance, Rebellion & Death (1960)

George Canning
1770–1827; Prime Minister 1827

The happiness of constant occupation is infinite.
Letter to Lord Boringdon, 1796

I do not think it would be politic or for the interests of the country to have this House quite subject to popular control.
1810

I consider it to be the duty of a British statesman in internal as well as external affairs, to hold a middle course between extremes; avoiding alike extravagancies of despotism or the licentiousness of unbridled freedom.

Speech in the House of Commons, 1826

The whips' duty is to make a House and keep a House and cheer the minister.

On whips

Thomas Carlyle
1795–1881; historian

The great law of culture is: Let each become all that he was created capable of being.

Critical and Miscellaneous Essays (1827)

Not what I have, but what I do is my kingdom.

Sator Resartus (1836)

Adversity is sometimes hard upon a man; but for one man who can stand prosperity, there are a hundred that will stand adversity.

Heroes and Hero Worship (1841)

The history of the world is but the biography of great men.

Ibid.

All work, even cotton spinning, is noble; work is alone noble.

Past and Present (1843)

Truth and justice alone are capable of being 'conserved' and preserved. The thing which is unjust, which is not according to God's law, will you in a God's universe try to conserve that? It is so old, say you? Yes, and the hotter haste ought you of all others to be in to let it grow no older! If but the faintest whisper in your hearts intimate to you that it is not fair – hasten, for the sake of Conservatism itself, to probe it rigorously, to cast it forth at once and for ever if guilty.

    Ibid.

Andrew Carnegie

1835–1919; American industrialist and philanthropist

Surplus wealth is a sacred trust which its possessor is bound to administer in his lifetime for the good of the community.

    Wealth (1889)

Upon the sacredness of property civilisation itself depends – the right of the labourer to his hundred dollars in the savings bank, and the right of the millionaire to his millions.

    Ibid.

Lord Carrington

b. 1919; Cabinet minister 1970–74, 1979–82

If you're at the summit, you're trying to climb a mountain.

    Former Foreign Secretary on the finer points of international diplomacy, 1986

Lewis Carroll

1832–98; author

If everybody minded their own business, the Duchess said in a hoarse growl, the world would go round a deal faster than it does.

    Alice in Wonderland (1865)

The rule is, jam tomorrow and jam yesterday, but never jam today.

    Through the Looking Glass (1871)

Douglas Carswell
b. 1971; Conservative MP 2005–

It's the latest trendy thinking by the Ministry of Justice, and it will look like justice on the cheap. Restorative justice is a fad. I've never met a victim of crime who wants this.

On Kenneth Clarke's plan to end jail sentences for shoplifters, 1 March 2011

Dame Barbara Cartland
1901–2000; British novelist

If you vote for Kinnock, you are voting against Christ.

1992

Thomas Nixon Carver
1865–1961; American Conservative

The trouble with radicals is that they only read radical literature, and the trouble with Conservatives is that they don't read anything.

Quoted by J. K. Galbraith

Cato (the Elder)
234–149 BC; Roman statesman

He approaches nearest to the gods who knows how to be silent even though he knows he is right.

Attributed

By Liberty I understand the power which every man has over his own actions, and his right to enjoy the fruits of his labour, art, and industry, as far as by it he hurts not the society, or any members of it, by taking from any member, or by hindering him from enjoying what he himself enjoys. The fruits of a man's honest industry are the just rewards of it, ascertained to him by natural and eternal equity, as is his title to use them in the manner which he thinks fit: and thus, with the above limitations, every man is sole lord and arbiter of his own private actions and property.

Ibid.

Lord Hugh Cecil

1869–1956; Conservative politician

What brought Conservatism into existence was the French Revolution.

Conservatism (1912)

It is often assumed that Conservatism and Socialism are directly opposed. But this is not completely true. Modern Conservatism inherits the traditions of Toryism which are favourable to the activity and authority of the state.

Ibid.

That authority should relieve suffering, that it should control and regulate trade; that it should restrain luxury; that it should suppress vice; that it should maintain religious truth – these were the principles which appealed to our forefathers as reasonable and especially to those among them who were Tories.

Ibid.

The Socialist believes that it is better to be rich than poor, the Christian that it is better to be poor than rich.

Ibid.

Voting is not a right; voting is a public function. No one has any more right to be a voter than he has to be … a policeman, or a judge, or Prime Minister.

1931

Joseph Chamberlain

1836–1914; civic leader and Liberal imperialist

In almost every instance in which the rule of the Queen has been established and the great Pax Brittanica has been enforced, there has come with it greater security to life and property, and a material improvement in the condition of the bulk of the population.

Speech at Royal Colonial Institute, 1897

The day of small nations has long passed away. The day of Empire has come.

As former Colonial Secretary, 1904

Neville Chamberlain

1869–1940; Prime Minister 1937–40

In war, whichever side may call itself the victor, there are no winners, but all are losers.

Speech in Kettering, 4 July 1938

It is no part of a Prime Minister's duty to take a country into a war which he thinks you can't win.

Attributed

However much we may sympathise with a small nation confronted by a big and powerful neighbour, we cannot in all circumstances undertake to involve the whole British Empire in a war simply on her account.

After Bad Godesberg, September 1938

How horrible, fantastic, incredible it is that we should be digging trenches and trying on gas masks here because of a quarrel in a faraway country between people of whom we know nothing.

Radio Broadcast on the Sudetenland crisis, 27 September 1938

In spite of the hardness and ruthlessness I thought I saw in his face, I got the impression that here was a man who could be relied upon when he had given his word.

Attributed

This morning, I had another talk with the German Chancellor, Herr Hitler, and here is the paper which bears his name upon it as well as mine...

Speech at Heston, 30 September 1938

This is the second time in our history that there has come back from Germany to Downing Street peace with honour. I believe it is peace for our time.

Speech in Downing Street, 1 October 1938

Our past experience has shown us only too clearly that weakness in armed strength means weakness in diplomacy, and if we want to secure a lasting peace ... diplomacy cannot be effective unless the consciousness exists ... that behind the diplomacy is the strength to give effect to it.

After Munich, 1939

I have to tell you now that no such undertaking has been received, and that consequently, this country is at war with Germany.

Radio speech, 3 September 1939

Whatever may be the reason – whether it was that Hitler thought he might get away with what he had got without fighting for it, or whether it was that after all the preparations were not sufficiently complete – however, one thing is certain: he missed the bus.

Speech at Central Hall, Westminster, 5 April 1940

G. K. Chesterton
1874–1936; novelist

All conservatism is based upon the idea that if you leave things alone you leave them as they are. But you do not. If you leave a thing alone you leave it to a torrent of change.

Orthodoxy (1908)

A progressive is always a Conservative; he conserves the direction of progress. A reactionary is always a rebel.

Introduction to Carlyle's *Past and Present* (1843)

The prophet and the quack are alike admired for a generation and admired for the wrong reasons.

Attributed

Tolerance is the virtue of a man without convictions.

On Christian values

Smile at us, pay us, pass us; but do not quite forget. For we are the people of England, that never have spoken yet.

The Secret People (1907)

The man who sees consistency in things is a wit, the man who sees the inconsistency in things is a humorist.

George Bernard Shaw (1909)

Why shouldn't we quarrel about a word? What is the good of words if they aren't important enough to quarrel over? Why do we choose one word more than another if there isn't any difference between them.

The Ball and the Cross (1910)

Lady Randolph Churchill

1854–1921; wife of Lord Randolph Churchill

I shall never get used to not being the most beautiful woman in
the room. It was an intoxication to sweep in and know every
man had turned his head. It kept me in form.

Attributed

Lord Randolph Churchill

1849–95; Conservative politician, Chancellor of the Exchequer, 1886

If you want to gain the confidence of the working-classes, let
them have a share, and a large, a real share, not a sham share, in
your party councils and your party government.

Conservative Party Conference, 1883

We do not defend the Constitution from mere sentiment for
the past, or from any infatuated superstition about divine right
or hereditary excellence. We defend the Constitution solely
on the grounds of its utility to the people. It is on the grounds
of utility alone that we go forth to meet our foes, and if we fail
to make good our ground with utilitarian arguments and for
utilitarian ends, then let the present combination of Throne,
Lords and Commons be forever swept away…

'Trust the People', Birmingham, 16 April 1884

To tell the truth I don't know myself what Tory democracy is.
But I believe it is principally opportunism.

1885

An old man in a hurry.

On Gladstone, 1886

Ulster will fight. Ulster will be right.

1886

He never believed in doing something that he could get someone else to do for him.

On Stanley Baldwin

Winston Churchill

1874–1965; Prime Minister 1940–45, 1951–55

The maxim of the British people is 'Business as usual'.

1914

Don't talk to me about naval tradition. It's nothing but rum, sodomy and the lash.

On the navy

... a party of great vested interests ... corruption at home, aggression to cover up abroad ... sentiment by the bucket-load, patriotism by the imperial pint.

On the Tory Party while a Liberal MP

They told me how Mr Gladstone read Homer for fun, which I thought served him right.

My Early Life (1930)

It is a good thing for an uneducated man to read books of quotations.

Ibid.

India is no more a political personality than Europe. India is a geographical term. It is no more a united nation than the equator.

1931

We know that he has, more than any other man, the gift of compressing the largest amount of words into the smallest amount of thought.

On Ramsay MacDonald, 1933

I have waited fifty years to see the Boneless Wonder sitting on the Treasury bench.

Ibid.

Criticism may not be agreeable, but it is necessary. It fulfils the same function as pain in the body. It calls attention to an unhealthy state of things.

On criticism

The power of man has grown in every sphere, except over himself.

Banquet speech, on receiving the Nobel Prize in Literature, 1953 (read by Lady Churchill on her husband's behalf)

Mr [Joe] Chamberlain loves the working man. He loves to see him work.

On Joseph Chamberlain

He looked at foreign affairs through the wrong end of a municipal drainpipe.

On Neville Chamberlain

He occasionally stumbled over the truth, but hastily picked himself up and hurried on as if nothing had happened.

On Stanley Baldwin (attributed)

I am certainly not one of those who need to be prodded. In fact, if anything, I am the prod.

Attributed

Some regard private enterprise as if it were a predatory tiger to be shot. Others look upon it as a cow that they can milk. Only a handful see it for what it really is – the strong horse that pulls the whole cart.

On private enterprise

I would say to the House, as I said to those who have joined this government: I have nothing to offer but blood, toil, tears and sweat.

First speech as Prime Minister, House of Commons, 13 May 1940

Victory at all costs, victory in spite of all terror, victory however long and hard the road may be; for without victory there is no survival.

Ibid.

Upon this battle [of Britain] depends the survival of Christian civilisation ... Hitler knows that he will have to break us in this Island or lose the way. If we can stand up to him, all Europe may be free and the life of the world may move forward into broad, sunlit uplands...

Speech to the House of Commons, 1940

Arm yourselves, and be ye men of valour, and be in readiness for the conflict; for it is better for us to perish in battle than to look upon the outrage of our nation and our altar.

Broadcast on the BBC, 19 May 1940

We shall defend our island, whatever the cost may be. We shall fight on the beaches. We shall fight on the landing grounds. We shall fight in the fields, and in the streets, we shall fight in the hills. We shall never surrender!

On Dunkirk, speech given in House of Commons, 4 June 1940

Let us therefore brace ourselves to our duties, and so bear ourselves that if the British Empire and Commonwealth last for a thousand years, men will still say, 'This was their finest hour'.

Speech delivered to the House of Commons 18 June 1940, following the collapse of France

Never in the field of human conflict was so much owed by so many to so few.

In the House of Commons as the Battle of Britain peaked, 20 August 1940

We shall show mercy, but we shall not ask for it.

Speech in the House of Commons, 14 July 1940

The greatest lesson in life is to know that even fools are right sometimes.

1941

We shall not fail or falter; we shall not weaken or tire ... Give us the tools and we will finish the job.

BBC radio broadcast, 9 February 1941

Today we may say aloud before an awestruck world: We are still masters of our fate. We are still captain of our souls.

On the war situation, House of Commons, 9 September 1941

I am a child of the House of Commons. I was brought up in my father's house to believe in democracy. Trust the people – that was his message ... I cannot help reflecting that if my father had been American and my mother British, instead of the other way around, I might have got here on my own ... I owe my advancement entirely to the House of Commons, whose servant I am. In my country, as in yours, public men are proud to be the servants of the state and would be ashamed to be its masters.

Speech made to a Joint Session of the American Congress, 26 December 1941

This is not the end. It is not even the beginning of the end. But it is, perhaps, the end of the beginning.

Speech given at the Lord Mayor's Luncheon, Mansion House, London, 10 November 1942

I have not become the King's First Minister in order to preside over the dissolution of the British Empire.
1942

The price of greatness is responsibility. Speech at Harvard, 6 September 1943

The empires of the future are the empires of the mind.
Ibid.

The crafty, cold-blooded, black-hearted Italian.
On Mussolini, 1944

A love of tradition has never weakened a nation, indeed it has strengthened nations in their hour of peril; but the new view must come, the world must roll forward.
Speech in the House of Commons, 29 November 1944

In the depths of that dusty soul is nothing but abject surrender.
On Neville Chamberlain

The Honourable Gentleman should not generate more indignation than he can conveniently contain.
On William Wedgwood Benn

The inherent vice of capitalism is the unequal sharing of blessings; the inherent virtue of Socialism is the equal sharing of miseries.
On socialism, 1945

There are few virtues that the Poles do not possess and there are few mistakes they have ever avoided.
In the House of Commons, after the Potsdam Conference, 1945

A sheep in sheep's clothing.
On Clement Attlee, 1945

A modest little man with much to be modest about.
    On Clement Attlee

I do not believe that a successful export trade can be founded on a starved home market.
    1947

A fanatic is one who can't change his mind and won't change the subject.
    On socialism, 1947

History will be kind to me for I intend to write it.
    Speech in the House of Commons, 23 January 1938

Socialism is the philosophy of failure, the creed of ignorance and the gospel of envy.
    1948

Trying to maintain good relations with the Communists is like wooing a crocodile. You do not know whether to tickle it under the chin or beat it over the head. When it opens its mouth you cannot tell whether it is trying to smile or preparing to eat you up.
    Speech to the House of Commons, 1949

The difference between our outlook and the Socialist outlook on life is the difference between the ladder and the queue. We are for the ladder. Let all try their best to climb. They are for the queue. Let each wait his place until his turn comes.
But we ask: 'What happens if anyone slips out of his place in the queue?' 'Ah,' say the Socialists, 'our officials – and we have plenty of them – come and put him back in it, or perhaps put him lower down to teach others.'
And when they come to us and say: we have told you what happens when anyone slips out of the queue, but what is your answer to what happens if anyone slips off the ladder? Our reply

is 'we shall have a good NHS and the finest social ambulance service in the world.'

1951

An appeaser is one who feeds a crocodile – hoping that it will eat him last.

Reader's Digest, 1954

There is nothing more exhilarating than to be shot at without result.

After a failed assassination attempt

For myself I am an optimist – it does not seem to be much use being anything else.

Speech at the Lord Mayor's banquet, London, 9 November 1954

It may well be that we shall, by a process of sublime irony, have reached a state in this story where safety will be the sturdy child of terror and survival the twin brother of annihilation.

On the nuclear deterrent, last speech to the House of Commons as Prime Minister, 1955

A Labour government is a government of the duds, by the duds and for the duds.

On the Labour Party

It is no use saying, 'We are doing our best.' You have got to succeed in doing what is necessary.

Attributed

Broadly speaking, the short words are the best, and the old words best of all.

Ibid.

Although prepared for martyrdom, I preferred that it be postponed.

Ibid.

Men stumble over the truth from time to time, but most pick themselves up and hurry off as if nothing happened.
    Ibid.

A pessimist sees the difficulty in every opportunity; an optimist sees the opportunity in every difficulty.
    Ibid.

To build may have to be the slow and laborious task of years. To destroy can be the thoughtless act of a single day.
    Ibid.

When the eagles are silent, the parrots begin to jabber.
    Ibid.

Success is the ability to go from one failure to another with no loss of enthusiasm.
    Ibid.

You can sum up what CND means in three words: trust the Kremlin.
    Ibid.

Cicero

106–43 BC; Roman statesman and writer

Laws are dumb in the midst of arms.
    Pro Milone speech (52 BC)

The good of the people is the chief law.
    De Legibus (52 BC)

So long as the Empire of the Republic was maintained not by injustice but by the benefits it conferred ... our government might have been called not so much Empire as a Protectorate of the whole world.

De Officiis (44 BC)

An army at home is of little use unless there are prudent counsels at home.

Ibid.

Alan Clark

1928–99; Conservative MP

Yesterday I travelled by train, and a plump young lady came into my compartment at Waterloo. She was not wearing a bra, and her delightful globes bounced prominently, but happily under a rope-knitted jersey. After a bit I moved over and sat beside her … She works as a shop assistant in Maidstone.

Alan Clark Diaries (1993–2002)

Everyone in politics ought to be arrested at least once. It's an education.

After being arrested in Piccadilly for allegedly trying to cross a police cordon

Bongo Bongo land.

On the origins of an African delegation, 1985

Might as well have a corncob up his arse.

On Douglas Hurd

Like most Chief Whips, he knew who the shits were.

On Michael Jopling, *Diaries*, 17 June 1987

There's nothing so improves the mood of the Party as the imminent execution of a senior colleague.

Diary, 13 July 1990

There are no friends in politics. We are all sharks circling and waiting for traces of blood to appear in the water.

Diary, 20 November 1990

As far as I am concerned, dirty tricks are part and parcel of effective government.

1993

The radiation and vitality was such that you felt electrified by it. But you also felt uncertain, you didn't know what was going to happen next. I never felt that with any other minister or any other member of the government; I couldn't give a damn what they wanted. But with her, I wished to please her, and nor for my own advancement. I wished to please her because she was such a remarkable individual.

On Margaret Thatcher

Give a civil servant a good case and he'll wreck it with clichés, bad punctuation, double negatives and convoluted apology.

Attributed

Gillian Clarke
Wife of Kenneth Clarke

A Cabinet minister's wife needs a good hobby. I don't think there is much for a Cabinet minister's wife to do in London. What should decide Ken's reputation is how he does his job, not anything else. I prefer to keep in the background.

1993

The lady may never have been for turning but she certainly turned heads. Everybody flirted with the Prime Minister. I think she took it as her due that you should flirt with her.

On Margaret Thatcher, 1993

Kenneth Clarke

b. 1940; Conservative MP, 1970–, Cabinet minister, 1985–97

Not only Celtic nationalists feel the need for a significant
shift of power away from the centre of British politics …
One practical answer could be the creation of new regional
parliaments. They could strengthen the working of democracy
in their areas. With some devolution of powers, they could also
take a lot of the workload off Parliament.

Birmingham Bow Group pamphlet, 1968

It is surprising that the present bitter controversy has arisen
between the government and, on the one hand, the Labour
Party – and to some extent the centre parties as well – and on
the other the British Medical Opposition – The British Medical
Association. That is certainly my most Freudian slip of the
tongue so far.

Debate on the NHS, 1989

All those people who say that there will never be a single
European Currency are trying to forecast history.

As Chancellor of the Exchequer, 1993

At Consett you have got one of the best steelworks in Europe.
It doesn't employ as many people as it used to because it is so
modern.

BBC Radio Newcastle, March 1995 (the works had closed in 1980)

I don't think the Conservative Party could win an election in
1,000 years on this ultra-right-wing programme.

On John Redwood's leadership bid against John Major, *The
Independent*, 27 June 1995

Tell your kids to get their scooters off my lawn.

To Tory Party Chairman Brian Mawhinney

I think [Consett] is also one of the major centres for disposable baby nappies; diapers as well.

c. March 1995 (the nappy factory had closed in 1991)

They are eighteen year-olds in the saloon bar trying every bottle on the shelf.

On the Labour Party's Treasury team, 24 May 1997

If the Conservative right brings in more of the sort of certain Republican right American politics to the politics of the Conservative Party they will be making a serious mistake.

Sunday AM, 18 September 2005

Xenophobic and legal nonsense.

On David Cameron's plans for a British Bill of Rights, 27 June 2006

I am certainly not a blogger. Quite a large proportion of them are nuts and extremists – with the honourable exception of the Culture Secretary.

17 January 2012

I usually agree with Nick Clegg and most of the Liberals on these things.

On justice and sentencing, 4 April 2012

George wants me in to keep an eye on Vince, and Vince wants me in to keep an eye on George.

Speech at the Carlton Club following his move from Justice Secretary to Minister Without Portfolio, 17 September 2012

Some of my best friends are human rights lawyers.

House of Commons, 4 March 2013

The idea that they are all demanding a referendum on the European Union would be regarded as ridiculous, it would be out of sight as a public priority. It is the demand of a few right-wing journalists and a few extreme nationalist politicians.

16 May 2013

William Cobbett

1763–1835; journalist

... in the whole body of the industrious and working people of England, there was scarcely a single man to be found that had ever entertained the slightest thought of envying his richer neighbour, or wishing to share his property, or wishing all men pulled down to a level – I could never gather from one single working man, during the whole course of my communication with them, that he wished for anything beyond – that he wished for change other than – that which would leave him the enjoyment of the fair fruit of his earnings.

Rural Rides (1830)

Samuel Taylor Coleridge

1772–1834; poet, critic and social philosopher

The true patriot will reverence not only whatever tends to make the component individuals more happy, and more worthy of happiness; but likewise whatever tends to bind them together more closely as a people.

The Friend (1809–10)

In politics, what begins in fear usually ends in folly.

1830

It is a good people and not a gabbling people that is wanted in the country, and this smattering of education will only raise the labourers of this country above the situations best suited to their own interests … It will put into their heads that they were not born to labour but to get their living without it.

1834

No man does anything from a single motive.

Attributed

Confucius

c.551–479 BC; Chinese teacher, editor, politician and philosopher

If a man takes no thought about what is distant, he will find sorrow near at hand.

Attributed

The strength of a nation is derived from the integrity of its homes. Whoever serves his country well has no need of ancestors.

Ibid.

Joseph Conrad

1857–1924; writer

Efficiency of a practically flawless kind may be reached naturally in the struggle for bread. But there is something beyond, a higher point, a subtle and unmistakable touch of love and pride beyond mere skill; almost an inspiration which gives to all work that finish which is almost art – which is art.

The Mirror of the Sea (1906)

Conservative Party

Forewords from party leaders

We seek the good of the whole nation, not that of one section or one faction. We believe in the living unity of the British people, which transcends class or party differences. It was this living unity which enabled us to stand like a rock against Germany when she over-ran Europe.

Winston Churchill, *Mr Churchill's Declaration of Policy to the Electors*, 1945

Upon our power to retain unity, the future of this country and of the whole world largely depends.

Ibid.

This is the time for freeing energies, not stifling them. Britain's greatness has been built on character and daring, not on docility to a state machine.

Ibid.

At all costs we must preserve that spirit of independence and that right to live by no man's leave underneath the law.

Ibid.

All who cherish the cause of our country at this fateful moment must cast their vote after hard and long thought, and make sure they cast it effectively.

Winston Churchill, *This Is the Road*, 1950

As for peace, it is of course the supreme purpose of all policy. I have lived through two wars and all my efforts are directed to prevent a third. Events of the last few months give me hope that we may be moving into a more constructive period. Vital international negotiations lie ahead and I ask you to continue to entrust them to a Conservative government.

Harold Macmillan, *The Next Five Years* (1959)

Only by trusting the individual with freedom and responsibility shall we gain the vitality to keep our country great.

Alec Douglas-Home, *Prosperity with a Purpose* (1964)

Decisions lightly entered into have been as lightly abandoned.
Edward Heath, *A Better Tomorrow* (1970)

It is not surprising that when I have travelled abroad in recent years friends of Britain have told me of their sadness at the way in which our reputation has shrunk. It is not surprising that young people in this country looking at politics for the first time should be suspicious and cynical.
Ibid.

Once a decision is made, once a policy is established, the Prime Minister and his colleagues should have the courage to stick to it. Nothing has done Britain more harm in the world than the endless backing and filling which we have seen in recent years.
Ibid.

Courage and intellectual honesty are essential qualities in politics, and in the interest of our country it is high time that we saw them again.
Ibid.

[L]et no one suppose that as a nation we can deal with the immediate problem without hardship and sacrifice.
Edward Heath, *Firm Action for a Firm Britain*, February 1974

What could destroy, not just our present standard of living but all our hopes for the future, would be inflation we brought upon ourselves.
Ibid.

[Prosperity] has now, for the time being, been blighted by the effects of the three-day week, forced upon us by the need to ration electricity so as to prevent our power stations from running out of coal altogether as a consequence of the industrial action taken by the National Union of Mineworkers.
Ibid.

A Britain united in moderation, not divided by extremism.
A society in which there is change without revolution. A
government that is strong in order to protect the weak. A
people who enjoy freedom with responsibility. A morality of
fairness without regimentation. A nation with faith in itself,
and a people with self-respect.
    Ibid.

If we do not solve our economic problems, our political
difficulties will be made worse. And if we do not tackle our
political problems, our economic difficulties will be insoluble.
    Edward Heath, *Putting People First*, October 1974

They [trade unions] are not the government of the country.
    Ibid.

Our nation still possess great moral reserves. Our patriotism,
our knowledge that what unites us is far more significant than
what divides us, our idealism, our wish to make our country
better and to improve the lot of our fellow citizens – all these
feelings and beliefs remain strong in Britain. But they can
only by properly summoned to the service of our nation by
a government that commands the confidence of the country
because it puts the country first.
    Ibid.

For me, the heart of politics is not political theory, it is people
and how they want to live their lives.
    Margaret Thatcher, Conservative Party manifesto, 1979

No one who has lived in this country during the last five years
can fail to be aware of how the balance of our society has
been increasingly tilted in favour of the state at the expense of
individual freedom.
    Ibid.

The things we have in common as a nation far outnumber those that set us apart.

Ibid.

Every thinking man and woman wants to get rid of nuclear weapons. To do this we must negotiate patiently from a position of strength, not abandon ours in advance.

Margaret Thatcher, *The Challenge of Our Times* (1983)

The universal problem of our time, and the most intractable, is unemployment.

Ibid.

The answer [to unemployment] is not bogus social contracts and government overspending. Both, in the end, destroy jobs. The only way to a lasting reduction in unemployment is to make the right products at the right prices, supported by good services. The government's role is to keep inflation down and offer real incentives for enterprise. As we win back customers, so we win back jobs.

Ibid.

Only if we create wealth can we continue to do justice to the old and the sick and the disabled. It is economic success which will provide the surest guarantee of help for those that need it most.

Ibid.

Our history is the history of a free people – a great chain of people stretching back into the past and forward into the future.

Ibid.

Britain has come right by her own efforts. We trusted in the character and talents of our people. The British instinct is for choice and independence. Given the opportunities provided by

Conservative policies, many more families now enjoy the pride of ownership – of homes, of shares, of pensions.

Margaret Thatcher, *The Next Moves Forward* (1987)

Together we are building One Nation of free, prosperous and responsible families and people. A Conservative dream is at last becoming a reality.

Ibid.

At the end of this Parliament a new Millennium will be in view. We must raise our sights high. This Manifesto is about making our country respected and secure, and helping you to achieve a better, safer and more prosperous future. For I believe – strongly – that you, not the government, should be in charge of your life. That's what Conservatism stands for. That principle underlies all the policies in this Manifesto.

John Major, Conservative Party manifesto, 1992

Why ... do we still need a Conservative government? Because resting on what we have achieved is not enough. To stand still is to fall back. Our goal must be for Britain to be the best place in the world to live.

John Major, *You Can Only be Sure with the Conservatives* (1997)

If we relax for one moment, our hard won success will slip away again.

Ibid.

Conservative Party
On Socialism and the Labour Party

There is no foundation for the Socialist claim to have brought us prosperity and security. Ministers themselves have declared that but for American Aid there would have been two million people unemployed.

Conservative Party manifesto, 1945

During these bleak years [1945–50] Britain has lurched from crisis to crisis and from makeshift to makeshift.
Ibid.

In 1945, the Socialists promised that their methods of planning and nationalisation would make the people of Britain masters of their economic destiny. Nothing could be more untrue.
Ibid.

Until the Socialist government is removed neither Scotland nor Wales will be able to strike away the fetters of centralisation and be free to develop their own way of life.
Ibid.

The attempt to impose a doctrinaire Socialism upon an Island which has grown great and famous by free enterprise has inflicted serious injury upon our strength and prosperity.
Ibid.

A vote for Socialism is a vote for the policy which was tried and which failed.
Conservative Party manifesto, 1955

Under Conservative administration a working population of record peace-time size has been kept fully employed, without Socialist controls and without continual inflation.
Ibid.

[The Socialists] still cling to the broken reed of nationalisation; we work for a property-owning democracy.
Ibid.

On examination, what the Labour Party have to offer is not a 'New Britain', but a camouflaged return to the dreary doctrines which had already proved a failure when they were last dismissed from office.
Conservative Party manifesto, 1964

Labour's policies for the future are their policies of the past.

Conservative Party manifesto, 1970

By practising the politics of envy and by actively discouraging the creation of wealth, [the Labour Party] have set one group against another in an often bitter struggle to gain a larger share of a weak economy.

Conservative Party manifesto, 1979

Labour's policy would mean not a secure Britain, but a neutralist Britain. And eventually, for there can be no trifling with Soviet power, a frightened and fellow-travelling Britain.

Conservative Party manifesto, 1987

The free market is winning the battle of ideas the world over. From Russia to Vietnam, from China to Romania, people are realising that the Socialist model has failed. This is not just an economic triumph. It is a triumph for human freedom. Britain helped to secure it. We should take pride in it.

Conservative Party manifesto, 1997

Conservative Party
Britain in the World

Movement of men and women within the Empire must be made easier. A two-way traffic should grow. Those who wish to change their homes should be enabled to carry their national insurance rights with them wherever they go. Imperial ties should be knit together by closer personal contact and understanding.

Conservative Party manifesto, 1945

Unless Britain can hold her place in the world, she cannot make her full contribution to the preservation of peace, and peace is our supreme purpose. Britain, wisely led, can bring together the Commonwealth and Empire, Western Europe and the

Atlantic Powers into a partnership dedicated to the cause of saving world peace and of preserving democratic freedom and the rule of law.

Conservative Party manifesto, 1950

Socialism abroad has been proved to be the weakest obstacle to Communism and in many countries of Eastern Europe has gone down before it. We are not prepared to regard those ancient states and nations which have already fallen beneath the Soviet yoke as lost forever.

Ibid.

A Conservative government will go forward resolutely to build, within the framework of the United Nations, a system of freedom based upon the rule of law.

Ibid.

Above all we seek to work in fraternal association with the United States to help by all means all countries, in Europe, Asia or elsewhere, to resist the aggression of Communism by open attack or secret penetration.

Ibid.

… banning the bomb alone would make the risks of war not smaller but greater, as long as the Communists retained their superiority in all other arms and in manpower.

Conservative Party manifesto, 1955

We should be wrong to minimise the fundamental issues of principle that divide us from the Communist world. We cannot ignore the post-war record of Communist subversion and attack, or their world-wide conspiracy to undermine free institutions and to divide and confuse the free peoples. We cannot excuse their denial of the rights of free worship and free expression. Whatever the origins of Communist theory, its practice has led to the extinction of freedom and the enthronement of tyranny wherever it has spread. Only if we are

firm in faith and spirit, and united in common purpose with
our allies, can we hope to achieve in time something better
than a state of cold war.

Ibid.

The British Commonwealth and Empire is the greatest force for
peace and progress in the world today. It comprises a quarter
of the world's population. It contains peoples of every race, of
every religion, of every colour, and at every stage of political
and economic advance. It represents the most fascinating and
successful experiment in government and in international
relations ever known.

Ibid.

We shall work to raise living standards and to guide Colonial
peoples along the road to self-government within the
framework of the Commonwealth and Empire.

Ibid.

Like all countries of advanced development and democratic
tradition, we have responsibilities towards the less fortunate
peoples of the world.

Ibid.

It is our responsibility to see that the rights of minorities are
fully safeguarded, and self-government can be granted only
when we are certain of this.

Ibid.

Whilst one hundred million people in Europe alone have, since
the war, been forcibly absorbed into the Communist bloc and
system, six times that number have been helped to nationhood
within the British Commonwealth. It is our duty to ourselves
and to the cause of freedom everywhere to see that the facts are
known, and that misrepresentation about British 'colonialism'

does not go unchallenged. Progressive expansion of overseas information services will remain our policy.

Conservative Party manifesto, 1959

Further British capital will be made available through loans and grants for sound Commonwealth development.

Ibid.

This historic evolution [of colonies to nationhood] is now reaching its final stages. Of our remaining dependencies many are well on the road to sovereignty. A number have multi-racial populations presenting special problems. Others are too small to bear the burdens of separate statehood. In each case we shall work for a fair and practical solution which will protect the interests of the peoples concerned.

Conservative Party manifesto, 1964

We have acted so that people might live in freedom and justice. The bravery, skill and determination with which Britain's task force recaptured the Falklands reverberated around the world. Many small nations gave thanks for that stand; and our allies in the North Atlantic are heartened by what Britain achieved in the South Atlantic.

Conservative Party manifesto, 1983

Labour's support for gestures of one-sided disarmament is reckless and naïve. There is no shred of evidence to suggest that the Soviet bloc would follow such an example.

Ibid.

Labour would give up Britain's nuclear deterrent and prevent the United States from using its bases in Britain which are part of its nuclear shield over Europe. That would shatter the NATO Alliance, and put our safety in the greatest jeopardy.

Ibid.

Britain is a world leader as well as a European nation. Our economic strength, our history and our language make us a global trading nation with links right around the world. Only the United Kingdom is a member of the European Union, the United Nations Security Council, the Commonwealth, NATO and the Group of Seven leading industrial nations.

Conservative Party manifesto, 1997

Conservative Party
Britain and European Integration

Entry into the European Economic Community is not open to us in existing circumstances, and no question of fresh negotiations can arise at present. We shall work, with our EFTA partners, through the Council of Europe, and through Western European Union, for the closest possible relations with the Six consistent with our Commonwealth ties.

Conservative Party manifesto, 1964

We are about to join an economic association of Seven European countries; our aim remains an industrial free market embracing all Western Europe.

Conservative Party manifesto, 1966

We are determined to give Britain a respected place in the world again and lead her into the European Community.

Ibid.

If we can negotiate the right terms, we believe that it would be in the long-term interest of the British people for Britain to join the European Economic Community, and that it would make a major contribution to both the prosperity and the security of our country.

Conservative Party manifesto, 1970

By far the most historic achievement of the last Conservative government was to bring about British entry into the European Community. Membership of the EEC brings us great economic advantages, but the European Community is not a matter of accountancy. There are two basic ideas behind the formation of the Common Market; first, that having nearly destroyed themselves by two great European civil wars, the European nations should make a similar war impossible in future; and, secondly, that only through unity could the Western European nations recover control over their destiny – a control which they had lost after two wars, the division of Europe and the rise of the United States and the Soviet Union.

Conservative Party manifesto, October 1974

British withdrawal [from the Common Market] would mean the abandonment of export opportunities, the decline of industrial development in this country and the loss of jobs. Withdrawal would give us less power and influence in the world not more. Withdrawal would confront us with the choice of almost total dependence on others or retreat into weak isolation. We reject such a bleak and impotent future for Britain.

Ibid.

Europe gives us the opportunity to reverse our political and economic decline. It may be our last.

Ibid.

The Labour Party wants Britain to withdraw from the Community, because it fears that Britain cannot compete inside and that it would be easier to build a Socialist siege economy if we withdrew.

Conservative Party manifesto, 1983

The European Community is the world's largest trading group. It is by far our most important export market. Withdrawal would be a catastrophe for this country.

Ibid.

Being good Europeans does not prevent us from standing up for British interests.

Conservative Party manifesto, 1987

The Maastricht Treaty was a success both for Britain and for the rest of Europe.

Conservative Party manifesto, 1992

The Treaty negotiated at Maastricht laid down the process under which the Community can, if its members meet certain economic conditions, create a monetary union with a single currency for some or all of them.

Ibid.

The government has a positive vision for the European Union as a partnership of nations. We want to be in Europe, but not run by Europe.

Conservative Party manifesto, 1997

Conservative Party
Liberating the Economy

Our war Budget has been rendered possible only by the severest taxation pressing heavily on everybody, by borrowing on a vast scale to meet the passing crisis, by huge Lend-Lease supplies from the United States and by generous gifts from Canada and elsewhere. All this cannot go on.

Conservative Party manifesto, 1945

The state has no resources of its own. It can only spend what it takes from the people in taxes or borrowing. Britain is now a nation of taxpayers. Its record of providing more than half of the national expenditure during the last years of the war from taxation is unsurpassed. The willingness of this generation to bear their fair share of sacrifices must, though we hope for relief, be continued. Our future needs for the war against

Japan, for winding up the German war, and the plans for social progress which we are determined to carry out, cause and require a much higher rate of national expenditure than before the war.

Ibid.

Where all benefit, all will have to contribute. The revenue is not created by waving a magic wand. It is drawn from the fruits of the nation's industry, agriculture and commerce. It is won by work and paid in taxes. The present level of taxation drastically restricts the ability of the ordinary citizen to satisfy his personal desires. It is discouraging to his enterprise and his efforts to better himself by doing the bit extra, for so large a part of anything he gains to be removed by the tax-collector.

Ibid.

We must guard against abuses to which monopolies may give rise.

Ibid.

We intend to guard the people of this country against those who, under guise of war necessity, would like to impose upon Britain for their own purposes a permanent system of bureaucratic control, reeking of totalitarianism.

Ibid.

Britain can resolve her economic difficulties not only by reviving her native strength but by fortifying every link with the nations of our Empire and Commonwealth.

Conservative Party manifesto, 1950

Conservatives believe in enterprise. We believe that the quality of daring was never more needed than today.

Ibid.

The foundation of industrial endeavour must be good human relationships, not impersonal control from aloft and afar.

Ibid.

Almost every incident of daily life is bound by controls which Parliament has had little chance to debate. These controls shelter the sluggish from failure while holding back the adventurous from success.

Ibid.

We shall bring Nationalisation to a full stop here and now.

Ibid.

Devaluation was the offspring of wild, profuse expenditure, and the evils which we suffer today are the inevitable progeny of that wanton way of living.

Conservative Party manifesto, 1951

We believe that the British people have a real chance during the coming twenty-five years to double their standard of living. The future beckons to this generation with a golden finger.

Conservative Party manifesto, 1955

We live by world trade: the more world trade there is, the better we shall live. We share in it, we ship it, we insure it and we help finance it. We have been selling, and we shall have to go on selling, against fierce competition in the markets of the world. The first object of our policy must be to enable British industry to do this in what is likely to remain a buyer's market.

Ibid.

We must re-establish sterling in a position so strong and respected that it can play its full part as a major international currency.

Ibid.

Where they are suitable and desired, co-partnership and profit-sharing schemes should be encouraged. They give employees a stake in the prosperity of their firm and so contribute to our concept of a property-owning democracy. We shall continue to assist better training within industry.

Ibid.

... those sections of our economy that remain nationalised must be brought to a higher peak of efficiency. Here again, investment is an important factor.

Ibid.

Conservative policy is to double the British standard of living in this generation and ensure that all sections of society share in the expansion of wealth.

Ibid.

Sterling is the currency in which nearly half the world's trade is done. Our paramount aim will be to maintain international confidence in it as a sound and stable medium of exchange.

Ibid.

The long-term problem of the balance of payments can only be solved by bringing our trading economy to the highest pitch of competitiveness and modern efficiency.

Conservative Party manifesto, 1964

Our aim is an economy in which earnings rise in step with productivity and do not outpace it.

Ibid.

... the rapidly changing world of industrial technology is the last place for Socialism. It calls for a flexibility, and a response to new ideas and requirements, which a system of free competitive enterprise is best suited to provide.

Ibid.

We will reduce taxation. We will simplify the tax system.

Conservative Party manifesto, 1970

Other countries achieve a low-cost high-wage economy. So can we.

Ibid.

There is no majority for a massive extension of nationalisation. There is no majority for the continued harrying of private enterprise. There is no majority for penalising those who save, own property or make profits.

Conservative Party manifesto, October 1974

The first priority for any government must be to defend the value of the currency and to bring inflation down from the present ruinous rates. This cannot be done overnight; it cannot be done by using only one weapon; and it cannot be done without united effort. If it is not done, the effects on every family will be calamitous.

Ibid.

Every reasonable person knows that if we pay ourselves higher wages than we can afford, sooner or later we shall have to pay higher bills than we can afford.

Ibid.

What we do oppose are ill-considered and damaging additional burdens piled on top of existing penal and comprehensive taxes. Britain already has higher taxes on both capital and income than other countries – with a top rate for income tax of 98 per cent. Tax on tax on tax: this is a prescription, not for a fairer society, but for a poorer and more bitter one.

Ibid.

Even in the depression of the 1930s the British economy progressed more than it has under this Labour government.

Ibid.

Profits are the foundation of a free enterprise economy. In Britain profits are still dangerously low.

Ibid.

Too much emphasis has been placed on attempts to preserve existing jobs. We need to concentrate more on the creation of conditions in which new, more modern, more secure, better paid jobs come into existence.

Ibid.

Just as we reject nationalisation, so we are opposed to the other Socialist panacea-import controls. They would restrict consumer choice, raise prices and invite damaging retaliation against British goods overseas.

Ibid.

In the next Parliament, we shall endeavour to bring inflation lower still. Our ultimate goal should be a society with stable prices.

Conservative Party manifesto, 1983

There has been a rapid shift of jobs from the old industries to the new, concentrated on services and the new technologies. Tragically, trade unions have often obstructed these changes. All too often this has delayed and reduced the new and better-paid jobs which could replace those that have been lost.

Ibid.

Most decisions worth taking are difficult.

Ibid.

There is no better yardstick of a party's fitness to govern than its attitude to inflation. Nothing is so politically immoral as a party that ignores that yardstick.

Conservative Party manifesto, 1987

We are the only party that believes in lower taxation.

Ibid.

Self-employment is the seedcorn of the new enterprises of tomorrow.

Ibid.

Like other sections of British industry ... the City was held back by restrictive practices until they were swept away in last year's 'big bang'. This has brought nearer the day when shares can be bought and sold over the counter in every high street.
   Ibid.

Curbing the power of the trade unions, opening up markets and cutting red tape, has given us a low-strike, lost-cost economy: and as a result Britain is the number one location for foreign investment in Europe.
   Conservative Party manifesto, 1997

Conservative Party
Domestic Concerns

In local government we favour more devolution to the boroughs and district councils to avoid the swarms of full-time organisers and supervisors like those who have sprung up in the health services.
   Ibid.

The peaceful uses of nuclear energy can make an incalculable contribution to the raising of living standards. A new industrial era may indeed be ushered in when the atom has been harnessed to bring everyday heat, light and power to factory, farm and home.
   Conservative Party manifesto, 1951

The Conservative Party gives a pledge to the farming community that so long as we are responsible there will be fair prices for good farming, orderly marketing of the main farm products, and no nationalisation of the land.
   Ibid.

We shall cherish local democracy.
   Ibid.

We shall root out the slums at an increasing pace, and aim to re-house at least 200,000 people a year from them.
Ibid.

Conservatives will continue to guarantee the present freedom of the Universities from government interference.
Ibid.

By raising living standards and by social reform we are succeeding in creating One Nation at home.
Conservative Party manifesto, 1959

We shall go ahead with a 'round-the-world' telephone cable in cooperation with the Commonwealth, and maintain our lead in telecommunications by building a new large cable-laying ship.
Ibid.

Two out of three families in the country now own TV, one in three has a car or motor-cycle, twice as many are taking holidays away from home – these are welcome signs of the increasing enjoyment of leisure. They are the fruits of our policies.
Ibid.

Our policy of opportunity will ... be extended. In particular, we propose to reorganise and expand the Youth Service. Measures will be taken to encourage youth leadership and the provision of attractive youth clubs, more playing fields and better facilities for sport. We shall do more to support the arts including the living theatre. Improvements will be made in museums and galleries and in the public library service. Particular attention will be given to the needs of provincial centres.
Ibid.

We intend to press ahead with negotiations for the Channel Tunnel so that an early start can be made.
Conservative Party manifesto, 1964

There is an enormous growth in the variety and richness of leisure-time activity. Appreciation of the arts, hobbies and handicrafts of every kind, physical sports, home and foreign travel – these and other pursuits are increasing year by year. They are a cheerful measure of rising prosperity. For the 'affluence' at which Socialists sneer is enabling people, not only to satisfy material wants, but to develop their interests and their feel for the quality of life.

Ibid.

We shall also seek to promote higher standards of architecture and civic planning, and commission works by contemporary artists for public buildings.

Ibid.

[We shall] ensure that all immigrants living in Britain are treated in all respects as equal citizens and without discrimination.

Conservative Party manifesto, 1966

Combine stricter control of entry with special help where necessary to those areas where immigrants are concentrated.

Ibid.

Farmers are frustrated and disgruntled.

Conservative Party manifesto, 1970

We will bring forward a sensible measure of local government reform which will involve a genuine devolution of power from the central government and will provide for the existence of a two-tier structure.

Ibid.

We will ensure that the natural beauty of our British countryside and seashore is conserved and wildlife is allowed to flourish.

Ibid.

We do not accept that, by becoming more prosperous, we will destroy the quality of our environment.

Conservative Party manifesto, October 1974

In the interests of good race relations, and for the benefit of immigrants already in Britain, as well as for the wider community, a Conservative government will follow a policy of strictly limited immigration.

Ibid.

We are utterly opposed to racial discrimination wherever it occurs, and we are determined to see that there is real equality of opportunity.

Conservative Party manifesto, 1983

We have to cure the disastrous mistakes of decades of town-hall Socialism by striking a better balance between public and private effort.

Ibid.

Conservatives are by instinct conservationists – committed to preserve all that is best of our country's past.

Conservative Party manifesto, 1987

A more prosperous Britain can afford to be ambitious. We can aspire to excellence in the arts, broadcasting and sport. We can use our increased leisure time, energy and money, to improve life for ourselves and our families. The National Lottery we propose to introduce can be used to restore our heritage and promote projects which will become a source of national pride.

Conservative Party manifesto, 1992

Britain is blessed with some of the most beautiful countryside in Europe. We have to strike a balance: our rural communities must not become rural museums, but remain vibrant places to live and work.

Conservative Party manifesto, 1997

Conservative Party
The Welfare State

The health services of the country will be made available to all citizens. Everyone will contribute to the cost, and no one will be denied the attention, the treatment or the appliances he requires because he cannot afford them.

Conservative Party manifesto, 1945

We propose to create a comprehensive health service covering the whole range of medical treatment from the general practitioner to the specialist, and from the hospital to convalescence and rehabilitation; and to introduce legislation for this purpose in the new parliament.

Ibid.

Our object is to provide education which will not produce a standardised or utility child, useful only as a cog in a nationalised and bureaucratic machine, but will enable the child to develop his or her responsible place, first in the world of school, and then as a citizen. Many parents will be able to choose the school they like and to play their part with the educational authorities in the physical and spiritual well-being of their children.

Ibid.

No system of education can be complete unless it heightens what is splendid and glorious in life and art. Art, science and learning are the means by which the life of the whole people can be beautified and enriched.

Ibid.

We regard social security, not as a substitute for family thrift, but as a necessary basis or supplement to it. We think of the National Health Service as a means, not of preventing anyone from paying anything for any service, but of ensuring that proper attention and treatment are denied to no one.

Conservative Party manifesto, 1955

We are anxious that the status and rewards of the teaching profession should continue to attract men and women of high attainment and character.

Ibid.

More and more [school children] who have the ability to benefit will stay on to 17 and 18 and go forward to higher education. This will be made possible by our plans for the universities, colleges of advanced technology, higher technical institutions and teacher training colleges. There will be places for 100,000 extra students by 1968, and for a steadily growing number after that.

Conservative Party manifesto, 1964

One family in every four is living in a new home built under the Conservatives.

Ibid.

In the towns and cities where most remaining slums are concentrated, clearance rates are being doubled. We aim to clear by 1973 virtually all the known slums.

Ibid.

A Royal Commission has been set up to report on sentencing policies and the most effective methods for the treatment of offenders. We have asked it to give urgent priority to the growing problem of crime among the young.

Ibid.

Much juvenile delinquency originates in broken or unhappy homes. We shall continue to support the work of marriage guidance.

Ibid.

The fundamental problem of all Britain's social services – education, health, provision for the old and those in need – is the shortage of resources.

Conservative Party manifesto, 1970

In forward planning for health, we will put more emphasis on community services.

Ibid.

We wish to move the debate away from the kind of school which children attend and concentrate on the kind of education they receive.

Conservative Party manifesto, February 1974

It must pay a man or woman significantly more to be in, rather than out of, work.

Conservative Party manifesto, 1979

We need more compulsory attendance centres for hooligans at junior and senior levels. In certain detention centres we will experiment with a tougher regime as a short, sharp shock for young criminals.

Ibid.

We will give greater emphasis to the prevention of avoidable illness and the promotion of good health to make the NHS more truly a health service and not merely a sickness service.

Conservative Party manifesto, 1983

To fight AIDS, the government has undertaken the biggest health education campaign ever seen in this country, one much admired abroad, and is fully supporting the Medical Research Council in a special programme of research towards treatments and vaccines.

Ibid.

Elderly, disabled, mentally ill and mentally handicapped people, should be cared for within the community whenever this is right for them.

Ibid.

The battle against drugs can and must be won. Already there are some signs that the heroin problem may have passed its peak. The cocaine explosion has never happened. It need never happen.

Ibid.

The origins of crime lie deep in society: in families where parents do not support or control their children; in schools where discipline is poor; and in the wider world where violence is glamorised and traditional values are under attack.

Ibid.

By the year 2000, one in three young people will follow full-time higher education courses. Meanwhile, the number of mature entrants to higher education has risen by 65 per cent since 1979. And our universities are attracting increasing numbers of foreign students.

Conservative Party manifesto, 1992

Despite this huge expansion, our students enjoy one of the most generous support systems in the world. The introduction of student loans has given students 30 per cent more money for their living costs than the former system of grants alone.

Ibid.

The public sector is being transformed the world over. Britain is in the vanguard. Everyone wants to learn from our vision of a smaller state doing fewer things and doing them better.

Conservative Party manifesto, 1997

Conservative Party
Industrial Relations

Conservatives should not hesitate to join Trade Unions as so many of our Party have already done, and to play their full part in their union affairs.

Conservative Party manifesto, 1950

The foundation of industrial endeavour must be good human relationships, not impersonal control from aloft and afar.
Ibid.

We must free ourselves from our impediments. Of all impediments the class war is the worst.
Conservative Party manifesto, 1951

We intend to reform both British management and British trade unions.
Conservative Party manifesto, 1959

Everyone is fed up with pointless strikes and outdated management.
Ibid.

It is manifestly unfair that those who do not go on strike are, in effect, obliged to subsidise those who do. It is no part of our policy to see the wives and children of men on strike suffering. But it is only right that the unions themselves, and not the taxpayer, should accept their primary responsibility for the welfare of the families of men who choose to go on strike; and after discussions with trade unions and employers, we will amend the social security system accordingly.
Conservative Party manifesto, February 1974

The Achilles heel of the British economy has long been, and continues to be, industrial relations.
Ibid.

We believe that the great majority of the trade union movement will be prepared to work with the democratically elected government of the country for the public good.
Conservative Party manifesto, October 1974

Much of the friction in our industrial relations is a symptom of the frustration and boredom found in many jobs in modern industry.

Ibid.

During the industrial strife of last winter, confidence, self-respect, common sense, and even our sense of common humanity were shaken. At times this society seemed on the brink of disintegration.

Ibid.

The trade union movement, which sprang from a deep and genuine fellow-feeling for the brotherhood of man, is today more distrusted and feared than ever before.

Ibid.

Does anyone suppose that the Labour Party would have resisted, let alone defeated, the violence and intimidation in the coal strike? Or that the Liberals or the Social Democrats would have fought so hard for our rebate from the European Community? Or that any of the opposition parties would have persevered through all these difficulties to break the back of inflation and restore honest money?

Conservative Party manifesto, 1987

Conservative Party
The Individual

It will be our aim and purpose to make an early reduction in taxation in a way that will stimulate energy and permit free individual choice.

Conservative Party manifesto, 1945

All possible encouragement will be given to the enterprise of individuals and firms to take advantage of export opportunities

of all kinds, and nothing must be done to paralyse the spirit of adventure.
Ibid.

The small man in trade or industry, who adventures all he has in the effort to make a success of the business he undertakes, must be given every chance to make good. His independence of spirit is one of the essential elements that made up the life of a free society. Many thousands of such men have been hit bitterly hard by war. Other men may have jobs to go back to, but the businesses of some of these men are gone, or hanging by a thread.
Ibid.

We intend to help all those who wish to own a house of their own or a smallholding. A true property-owning democracy must be based upon the wide distribution of private property, not upon its absorption in the state machine.
Conservative Party manifesto, 1950

It is certainly no proper function of the state in normal times to go into trade itself, to interfere in the day-to-day running of business, or to tell housewives how to do their shopping.
Conservative Party manifesto, 1955

[The Socialists] seem to think that the British housewife is incapable of deciding for herself; we are sure that it is the customer, and not 'the gentleman in Whitehall,' who knows best.
Ibid.

Our theme is that property, power and responsibility alike must not become absorbed into the state machine, but be widely spread throughout the whole of the community.
Ibid.

To this end, we shall encourage home ownership. We shall foster thrift. We shall stimulate a spirit of partnership in

industry. We shall maintain the independence of the small
trader and landowner and of the professional man.
    Ibid.

Small businesses have had a raw deal from Labour. They have
had to suffer higher and more complicated taxes, and waste
more time filling up forms.
    Conservative Party manifesto, 1970

Protection of the individual citizen is a prime duty of
government. Urgent action is needed to check the serious rise
in crime and violence.
    Ibid.

People feel increasingly frustrated and even oppressed by the
impact on their lives of remote bureaucracy, and of events
which seem to be entirely beyond their control or that of our
democratic institutions.
    Conservative Party manifesto, October 1974

People want to be helped to achieve, not encouraged to envy.
    Ibid.

We want also to help the small, often family-owned businesses
which form the backbone of British enterprise.
    Ibid.

An important part of the distinct Conservative policy on
education is to recognise parental rights. A say in how their
children are to be brought up is an essential ingredient in the
parental role.
    Ibid.

Through the centuries, the law in Britain has acted as the
defence of the small man against the great, of the weak against
the strong.
    Ibid.

By enlarging the role of the state and diminishing the role of the individual, [the Labour Party] have crippled the enterprise and effort on which a prosperous country with improving social services depends.

Conservative Party manifesto, 1979

We want to work with the grain of human nature, helping people to help themselves – and others. This is the way to restore that self-reliance and self-confidence which are the basis of personal responsibility and national success.

Ibid.

Freedom and responsibility go together. The Conservative Party believes in encouraging people to take responsibility for their own decisions.

Conservative Party manifesto, 1983

Of course, it is not possible to give people independence. That is something we must all achieve by our own efforts.

Conservative Party manifesto, 1987

In this way One Nation is finally reached not by a single people being conscripted into an organised Socialist programme but by millions of people building their own lives on their own.

Ibid.

We were determined to make share-ownership available to the whole nation. Just as with cars, television sets, washing machines and foreign holidays, it would no longer be a privilege of the few; it would become the expectation of the many.

Ibid.

Small businesses are the seedcorn of the economy

Conservative Party manifesto, 1992

Conservative Party

The Constitution

... we must guard the British way of life, hallowed by centuries of tradition. We have fought tyrants at home and abroad to win and preserve the institutions of constitutional Monarchy and Parliamentary government.

Conservative Party manifesto, 1951

We have cut back war-time powers and regulations which trespassed upon British liberties.

Conservative Party manifesto, 1955

The functions and powers of government have expanded so much in recent years that the traditional safeguards for the citizen no longer suffice. Although we will reduce government activity and interference, a better system of control and examination of decisions by civil servants, public bodies and local authorities which affect individual citizens is also needed. Parliament during recent years has often passed government legislation which has infringed individual rights and given wide discretionary powers to ministers and their civil servants. We will closely examine ways of safeguarding more effectively and equitably the rights and freedom of the individual citizen.

Conservative Party manifesto, 1970

We do not believe that the great majority of people want revolutionary change in society, or for that matter that the future happiness of our society depends on completely altering it.

Conservative Party manifesto, October 1974

At a time when there are too many people prepared to take the law into their own hands, a Conservative government, backed by public opinion, will uphold the rule of law. Without law, there can be no freedom.

Ibid.

By heaping privilege without responsibility on the trade unions, Labour have given a minority of extremists the power to abuse individual liberties and to thwart Britain's chances of success.

Conservative Party manifesto, 1979

We will see that Parliament and no other body stands at the centre of the nation's life and decisions, and we will seek to make it effective in its job of controlling the Executive.

Ibid.

Labour want not merely to abolish the House of Lords but to put nothing in its place. This would be a most dangerous step. A strong Second Chamber is necessary not only to revise legislation but also to guarantee our constitution and liberties.

Ibid.

The rule of law matters deeply to every one of us. Any concession to the thief, the thug or the terrorist undermines that principle which is the foundation of all our liberties. That is why we have remained firm in the face of the threats of hijackers and hunger strikers alike. The defeat of the occupation of the Iranian embassy is only one example of our determination to be patient but still unyielding.

Conservative Party manifesto, 1983

The British Constitution has outlasted most of the alternatives which have been offered as replacements. It is because we stand firm for the supremacy of Parliament that we are determined to keep its rules and procedures in good repair.

Ibid.

Cutting a clear path through the jungle of a modern bureaucracy is hard going.

Ibid.

Radical changes that alter the whole character of our constitutional balance could unravel what generations of our

predecessors have created. To preserve that stability in future
– and the freedom and rights of our citizens – we need to
continue a process of evolution, not revolution.

Conservative Party manifesto, 1997

Conservative Party
A Conservative Britain

Ours is a great nation and never in its history has it stood in
higher repute in the world than today. Its greatness rests not on
its material wealth, for that has been poured out in full measure,
nor upon its armed might, which other nations surpass. It has its
roots in the character, the ability, and the independence of our
people and the magic of this wonderful island. British virtues
have been developed under the free institutions which our fathers
and forefathers struggled through the centuries to win and to
keep. We of this generation are trustees for posterity, and the
duty lies upon us to hand down to our children unimpaired
the unique heritage that was bequeathed to us.

Conservative Party manifesto, 1945

Our programme is not based upon unproved theories or fine
phrases, but upon principles that have been tested anew in the
fires of war and not found wanting. We commend it to the
country not as offering an easy road to the nation's goal but
because, while safeguarding our ancient liberties, it tackles
practical problems in a practical way.

Ibid.

We shall make Britain once again a place in which hard work,
thrift, honesty and neighbourliness are honoured and win their
true reward in wide freedom underneath the law. Reverence for
Christian ethics, self-respect, pride in skill and responsibility, love
of home and family, devotion to our country and the British Empire
and Commonwealth, are the pillars upon which we base our faith.

Conservative Party manifesto, 1950

We Conservatives place our political faith in the unity of our country, in the neighbourliness of its spirit, in the vigour of its character, and in the liberties of its subjects.

Conservative Party manifesto, 1955

Conservatism is more than successful administration. It is a way of life. It stands for integrity as well as for efficiency, for moral values as well as for material advancement, for service and not merely self-seeking.

Conservative Party manifesto, 1959

In thirteen years of Conservative government the living standards of the British people have improved more than in the whole of the previous half-century.

Conservative Party manifesto, 1964

As a nation, we have been starved of achievement. We have become conditioned to failure.

Conservative Party manifesto, 1970

Conservatives are proud of yesterday's achievements. Angered by today's failures. Determined that tomorrow shall be better again.

Ibid.

Under a Conservative government, the gap between the politician's promise and government performance will be closed, so that people and government can be brought together again in one nation united in a common purpose – a better tomorrow.

Ibid.

What has happened to our country, to the values we used to share, to the success and prosperity we once took for granted?

Conservative Party manifesto, 1979

Our country's relative decline is not inevitable.
Ibid.

The Conservative government's first job will be to rebuild our economy and reunite a divided and disillusioned people.
Ibid.

The years of make-believe and false optimism are over. It is time for a new beginning.
Ibid.

We shall never lose sight of the British traditions of fairness and tolerance. We are also determined to revive those other British qualities – a genius for invention and a spirit of enterprise.
Ibid.

Remember the conventional wisdom of the day. The British people were 'ungovernable'. We were in the grip of an incurable 'British disease'. Britain was heading for 'irreversible decline'.
Conservative Party manifesto, 1987

Well, the people were not ungovernable, the disease was not incurable, the decline has been reversed.
Ibid.

In this election, only the Conservative Party is offering strong, decisive and united government. We intend to press on with the radical Conservative reform which we embarked upon in 1979, and which has already revived the spirit of our people and restored the reputation of our country.
Ibid.

In twenty years, privatisation has gone from the dream of a few Conservative visionaries to the big idea which is transforming decaying public sector industries in almost every country in the world. Britain has led the world with this new industrial revolution: we can be proud of what we have achieved.

Conservative Party manifesto, 1997

Conservative Party
Slogans

Safety First.
1929 general election slogan

This is the Road.
1950 general election manifesto

Britain Strong and Free.
1951 general election manifesto

United for Peace and Progress.
1955 general election manifesto

Life's Better with the Conservatives. Don't let Labour ruin it.
1959 general election manifesto

Prosperity with a Purpose.
1964 general election manifesto

Action Not Words.
1966 general election manifesto

A Better Tomorrow.
1970 general election manifesto

Who Governs Britain?
1974 general election manifesto

Labour isn't working.
1979 general election poster

Challenge of Our Times.
> 1983 general election manifesto

The Next Moves Forward.
> Conservative Party Conference, 1986

The Best Future for Britain.
> 1992 general election manifesto

You can only be sure with the Conservatives.
> 1997 general election manifesto

Calvin Coolidge
1872–1933; US President 1923–29

The business of America is business.
> 1925

Don't expect to build up the weak by pulling down the strong.
> Attributed

Ultimately property rights and personal rights are the same thing.
> Ibid.

Julian Critchley
1930–2000; Conservative MP 1959–64, 1970–97

> Humming, hawing and hesitation are the three Graces of contemporary parliamentary oratory. *The Times*, 1982

She cannot see an institution without hitting it with her handbag.
> On Margaret Thatcher, 1982

If she has a weakness it is for shopkeepers, which probably accounts for the fact that she cannot pass a branch of Marks & Spencer without inviting the manager to join her private office.

On Margaret Thatcher

The only safe pleasure for a parliamentarian is a bag of boiled sweets.

1982

Like Marxism, Thatcherism is, in fact, riddled with contradictions. Mrs Thatcher, on the other hand, is free of doubt. She is the label on the can of worms.

Palace of Varieties (1989)

Disloyalty is the secret weapon of the Conservative Party.

The Observer, November 1990

Mrs Thatcher is a woman of common views but uncommon abilities.

Attributed

As Margaret Thatcher came up in the world, so the Conservative Party came down.

BBC TV, *Julian Critchley*, 1991

He could not see a parapet without ducking beneath it.

On Michael Heseltine

Edwina Currie

b. 1946; Conservative MP 1983–97

I'm quite deliberate sometimes about getting into the tabloid press and on TV because I think that if responsible politicians don't do it, then irresponsible ones will.

1983

People in the north die of ignorance and crisps.
    As Junior Health Minister, 1986

Cervical cancer is the result of being far too sexually active —
nuns don't get it.
    As Junior Health Minister

Good Christian people ... will not catch AIDS.
    Ibid.

Take the wife.
    As Junior Health Minister on how businessmen travelling abroad
    should avoid AIDS

Buy long johns, check your hot water bottles, knit gloves and
scarves and get your grandchildren to give you a woolly night-
cap.
    As Junior Health Minister, advice to pensioners for keeping warm in
    winter

Most of the egg production in this country sadly is now
infected with salmonella.
    As Junior Health Minister, 1988 (she resigned two weeks later)

The strongest possible piece of advice I would give to any young
woman is: Don't screw around, and don't smoke.
    1988

There's no smoke without mud being flung around.
    1989

I have nothing to do with any aspects of advertising. I can't even
tell a Cinzano from a Martini. But I do trust the public to tell
the difference between real life and advertisements which is
more than better educated worthies seem willing to do.
    Denying that advertising on the BBC would be bad for the public,
    1989

Lord Curzon

1859–1925; Conservative MP 1886–98, Cabinet minister 1916–24

That strange, powerful, inscrutable and brilliant obstructive deadweight at the top.

On Robert Cecil, Lord Salisbury

Not even a public figure. A man of no experience. And of the utmost inexperience.

On Stanley Baldwin

When a group of Cabinet ministers begins to meet separately and to discuss independent action, the death tick is audible in the rafters.

November 1922

I think and hope that we have conveyed not merely the impression, but the conviction that, whatever other countries or governments may do, the British government is never untrue to its word, and is never disloyal to its colleagues or its allies, never does anything underhand or mean; and if this conviction be widespread – as I believe it to be – that is the real basis of the moral authority which the British Empire has long exerted and I believe will long continue to exert in the affairs of mankind.

As Foreign Secretary, 1923

D

Dante
1265–1321; poet

The hottest places in Hell are reserved for those who in time of great moral crisis maintain their neutrality.
    Attributed

David Davis
b. 1948; Conservative MP 1987–, Conservative Party Chairman 2001–02, shadow Home Secretary 2003–08

I want to see a Britain that is utterly blind to race or colour – that celebrates difference but that celebrates Britishness, too. And, let's face it, in recent years we haven't celebrated it enough.
    David Davis leadership contender speech, 2005

So I wasn't born a Conservative; I chose to be a Conservative. Because I came to realise something that every one of us here today knows: Labour always ends up letting people down. And they let down the poorest and weakest in society most of all.
    Ibid.

I became a Conservative because I believe that you don't make the weak strong by making the strong weak.
    Ibid.

Gordon Brown is rooted in the past. He's driven by a socialism that's out of date, out of time and out of place in today's world.
    Ibid.

I make no bones about it, I'm a product of my upbringing and of the time I was brought up, so I'm not going to pretend not to be.
The Guardian, 21 December 2012

UKIP has deliberately become more than a single-issue party. Since 2004 it has transformed itself into a Primary Colours Conservative Party.
Daily Telegraph, 3 May 2013

The British public are neither snobs nor inverted snobs, but they do expect the government to understand their problems and do something about it. That means more straight talking and fewer focus groups: more conventional Tory policies, not because they are Tory, but because they work: less pandering to metropolitan interest groups: and please, please, no more Old Etonian advisers.
Ibid.

Lord Denning
1899–1998; High Court judge

The Treaty of Rome is like an incoming tide. It flows into the estuaries and up the rivers. It cannot be held back.
1975

Earl of Derby
1799–1869; Prime Minister 1852, 1858–59, 1866–68

I am an advocate in a cause which I believe to be that of policy, of justice and humanity. I am an advocate for weakness against power, for perplexed and bewildered barbarism against the arrogant demands of overweening, self-styled civilisation. I am an advocate for the feeble defencelessness of China against the overpowering might of Great Britain.
Speech in the House of Lords attacking Palmerston's policy on China, 24 February 1857

The foreign policy of the Noble Earl may be summed up in two expressive words – meddle and muddle.

On Lord John Russell, speech in the House of Lords, February 1864

No doubt we are making a great experiment and taking a leap in the dark but I have the greatest confidence in the sound sense of my fellow countrymen, and I entertain a strong hope that the extended franchise which we are now conferring upon them will be the means of placing the institutions of this country on a firmer basis, and that the passing of this measure will tend to increase the loyalty and contentment of a great portion of Her Majesty's subjects.

After the Third Reading of the Reform Bill, 6 August 1867

Geoffrey Dickens
1931–95; Conservative MP 1979–95

I believe that people like myself should stand shoulder to shoulder with the homosexual fraternity ... but you're only going to get that support if you don't continue to flaunt your homosexuality and stuff it down other people's throats.

1988

Denis Diderot
1713–84; French philosopher

From fanaticism to barbarism is only one step.

Essay on the merits of virtue, 1745

Benjamin Disraeli
1804–81; Prime Minister 1868, 1874–80

There are three kinds of lies; lies, damned lies and statistics.

Attributed by Mark Twain

The wisdom of the wise and the experience of the ages are perpetuated by quotations.

Attributed

Mr Speaker, I withdraw. Half the Cabinet are not asses.

On being reprimanded by the Speaker for saying that 'half the Cabinet are asses'

I repeat that all power is a trust – that we are accountable for its exercise – that, from the people, and for the people, all springs, and all must exist.

Vivian Grey (1826)

There is no act of treachery or meanness of which a political party is not capable; for in politics there is no honour.

Ibid.

An arch-mediocrity presiding over a Cabinet of mediocrities.

On Lord Liverpool

Every man has a right to be conceited until he is successful.

Attributed

Though I sit down now, the time will come when you will hear me.

Maiden speech in the House of Commons, 7 December 1837

The Continent will [not] suffer England to be the workshop of the world.

House of Commons, 15 March 1838

The House of Commons is absolute. It is the State. L'Etat c'est moi.

Coningsby (1844)

The European talks of progress because, by the aid of a few scientific discoveries, he has established a society which has mistaken comfort for civilisation.

Attributed

Conservatism discards prescription, shrinks from Principle, disavows progress; having rejected all respect for antiquity, it offers no redress for the present, and makes no preparation for the future.

Ibid.

A sound Conservative government? I understand: Tory men and Whig measures.

Ibid.

Thus you have a starving population, an absentee aristocracy, and an alien church, and in addition the weakest executive in the world. That is the Irish question.

16 February 1844

No government can long be secure without a formidable opposition.

1844

I have not been ever of the opinion that revolutions are not to be evaded.

Attributed

This respect for precedent, this clinging to prescription, this reverence for antiquity which all too often ridiculed by conceited and superficial minds, and more the special contempt of the gentleman who admire abstract principles, appear to me to have their origin in a profound knowledge of human nature and in a fine observation of public affairs, and satisfactorily account for the permanent character of our liberties. Our constitution is a prescriptive constitution, it is a constitution whose sole authority is that it has existed time out of mind ... it is a constitution made by what is ten thousand times better than choice. It is made by the peculiar circumstances, occasions, tempers, dispositions and moral, social and civil habitudes of the people, which disclose themselves only in a long space of time.

Vindication of the English Constitution (1835)

A Conservative government is an organised hypocrisy.

Debate in the House of Commons on the Corn Laws, 17 March 1845

He never wrote an invitation to dinner without an eye on posterity.

On writer and politician, Edward Bulwer

His temper naturally morose, has become licentiously peevish. Crossed in his Cabinet, he insults the House of Lords, and plagues the most eminent of his colleagues with the crabbed malice of a maundering witch.

On the Earl of Aberdeen

Gladstone, like Richelieu, can't write. Nothing can be more unmusical, more involved or more uncouth than all his scribblement.

Attributed

That fatal drollery called a representative government.

Tancred (1847)

Justice is truth in action.

11 February 1851

England does not love coalitions.

House of Commons, 16 December 1852

If a traveller were informed that such a man was the Leader of the House of Commons, he might begin to comprehend how the Egyptians worshipped an insect.

On Lord John Russell

I doubt very much whether a democracy is a government that would suit this country.

1865

Individuals may form communities, but it is institutions alone that can create a nation.

Speech in Manchester, 1866

[The result of widening the franchise would be] a parliament of no statesmanship, no eloquence, no learning, no genius. Instead of these, you will have a horde of selfish and obscure mediocrities incapable of anything but mischief ... devised and regulated by the raging demagogue of the hour.

Opposing reform, 1866

For my part I do not believe that the country is in danger, I think England is safe in the care of men who inhabit her; that she is safe in something much more precious than her accumulated capital – her accumulated experience; she is safe in her national character, in her fame, in the traditions of a thousand years, and in that glorious future which I believe awaits her.

Speech to the House of Commons, third reading of the Reform Bill, 1867

I have climbed to the top of the greasy pole.

On becoming Prime Minister, 1868

... honest in the most odious sense of the word.

On Gladstone (attributed)

You know who critics are? The men who have failed in literature and art.

Lothair (1870)

I look upon Parliamentary government as the noblest government in the world.

3 April 1872

I believe that without *party* Parliamentary government is impossible.

Ibid.

In my opinion no minister in this country will do his duty who neglects any opportunity of reconstructing as much as possible our colonial empire, and of responding to those distant sympathies which may become the source of incalculable strength and happiness to this land.

1872

The principles of liberty, of order, of law and of religion ought not to be entrusted to individual opinion or to the caprice and passion of multitudes, but should be embodied in a form of permanence and power. We associate with the monarchy the ideas which it represents – the majesty of the law, the administration of justice, the fountain of mercy and of honour.

Ibid.

The issue is no mean one. It is whether you will be content to be a comfortable England, modelled and moulded upon continental principles, and meeting in due course an inevitable fate, or whether you will be a great country, an imperial country, a country where your sons when they rise, rise to paramount positions, and obtain not merely the esteem of their countrymen, but command respect in the rest of the world.

Speech at Crystal Palace, 1872

If Gladstone fell into the Thames, that would be a misfortune, and if anybody pulled him out that, I suppose, would be a calamity.

Cited in W. Meynell, *Benjamin Disraeli: An Unconventional Biography* (1903)

The world is weary of statesmen whom democracy has degraded into politicians.

Lothair (1870)

I am dead: dead, but in the Elysian fields.

On his elevation to the House of Lords, 1876

Lord Salisbury and myself have brought you back peace – but a peace I hope with honour.

On returning from the Congress of Berlin

A sophistical rhetorician, inebriated with the exuberance of his own verbosity, and gifted with an egotistical imagination, that can at all times command an interminable and inconsistent series of arguments, malign an opponent and glorify itself.

On Gladstone, speech at Knightsbridge, 1878

As I sat opposite the Treasury Bench, the ministers reminded me of one of those marine landscapes not very unusual on the coasts of South America. You behold a range of exhausted volcanoes, not a flame flickers on a single pallid crest, but the situation is still dangerous. There are occasional earthquakes, and ever and anon the dark rumbling of the sea.

Attributed

Posterity will do justice to that unprincipled maniac Gladstone, an extraordinary mixture of envy, vindictiveness, hypocrisy and superstition; and with one commanding characteristic whether Prime Minister, or Leader of the Opposition, whether preaching, praying, speechifying or scribbling, never a gentleman.

Letter to Lord Derby, 1878

What you say about Gladstone is most just. What restlessness! What vanity! And what unhappiness must be his! Easy to say he is mad. It looks it. My theory about him is unchanged; a ceaseless Tartuffe from the beginning. That sort of man does not get mad at seventy.

Letter to Lord Bradford, 1879

One of the greatest of Romans, when asked what were his policies, replied, *Imperium et Libertas.* That would not make a bad programme for a British Ministry.

Mansion House speech, 1879

The greatest opportunity that can be offered to an Englishman – a seat in the House of Commons.

Endymion (1880)

Action may not always bring happiness; but there is no happiness without action.

Attributed

Nurture your mind with great thoughts.

Ibid.

When I want to read a novel, I write one.

Ibid.

In a progressive country change is constant, and the great question is, not whether you should resist change which is inevitable, but whether that change should be carried out in deference to the manners, the customs, the laws, and the traditions of the people, or in deference to abstract principles and arbitrary and general doctrines.

Ibid.

I never offered an opinion until I was sixty, and then it was one which had been in our family for generations.

Ibid.

Robert Dole
b. 1923; US Senator

Good news is, a bus full of supply-siders went over the cliff. Bad news is, there were three empty seats.
1981

A little gridlock might be good from time to time.
c.1992

Stephen Dorrell
b. 1952; Conservative MP, 1979–, Cabinet minister 1994–97

Even if science was wrong on that subject, we've removed from the human food chain the organs that could conceivably be linked to a transmission.
On BSE, 1995

Fyodor Dostoevsky
1821–81; Russian novelist

What man wants is simply independent choice, whatever that independence may cost and wherever it may lead.
Notes from the Underground (1864)

The Socialist who is a Christian is more to be dreaded than the Socialist who is an atheist.
The Brothers Karamazov (1880)

Alec Douglas-Home
1903–95; Conservative MP, Foreign Secretary 1960–63, 1970–74,
Prime Minister 1963–64

Patriotism in the twentieth century is still a noble thing if one
thinks of our flag ... as a banner proclaiming the image of the
kind of life and the values in which British people believe.

On patriotism

I could never be Prime Minister. I do my sums with
matchsticks.

1962

When I have to read economic documents I have to have a box
of matches and start moving them into position to simplify and
illustrate the points to myself.

The Observer, 16 September 1962

As far as the Fourteenth Earl is concerned, I suppose Mr
Wilson, when you come to think of it, is the fourteenth
Mr Wilson.

Daily Telegraph, 22 October 1963

There are two problems in my life. The political ones are
insoluble and the economic ones are incomprehensible.

1964

I am a fan of television as far as sport and ceremonial are
concerned. I think it less suited to politics than to anything
else. You are dealing with the most complicated issues in a very
short time and it is bound to be superficial.

1988

Caroline Douglas-Home

b. 1937; daughter of Alec Douglas-Home

He is used to dealing with estate workers. I cannot see how anyone can say he is out of touch.

On her father becoming Prime Minister, 1963

Alan Duncan

b. 1957; Conservative MP 1992–, Cabinet minister 2010–

'Communities' do not exist. The new communitarianism shares the contradiction that which bedevils all collectivist philosophies. It is that collective activities are not practicable much above the level of the family or the team-sport.

Saturn's Children (1990)

The idea of a 'community' is either a meaningless metaphysical abstraction, a banal shorthand description of existing social realities, or a euphemism for state power. No coherent policy can be derived from it.

Ibid.

… it is pointless to persist with the conventional responses to the increase in crime. More police, more prisons and more effective judicial procedures are clearly not working, except in so far as they satisfy a patent public thirst for retribution.

Ibid.

The analysis of the economics of the drugs trade is too compelling to ignore. Logic suggests that the only completely effective way to ameliorate the problem, and especially the crime which results from it, is to bring the industry into the open by legalising the distribution and consumption of all dangerous drugs, or at the very least decriminalising their consumption.

Ibid.

There is no reason to suppose that the number of consumers would increase if dangerous drugs were legalised. A sensible legislation would retain strict official control over the distribution and quality of drugs, and perhaps include the establishment of a register of users of hard drugs. Evidence from Holland and the United States, where experiments in the decriminalisation of soft drugs are taking place, suggests consumption tends not to rise, but drug-related crime does tend to fall.

Ibid.

Although the democratic state has a constant urge, as de Tocqueville forecast, to act as an 'immense, protective power which is alone responsible for securing their enjoyment and watching over their fate', it is perfectly respectable to believe that people are a judge of their own best interests, even if they choose to consume harmful drugs.

Ibid.

At least if I'd been f**cking somebody I would have been having some fun.

After being criticised for a property deal, 1994

The outpouring of fury we've witnessed has been like a spring revolution.

On the MPs expenses scandal, 21 May 2009

Iain Duncan Smith

b. 1954; Member of Parliament 1992–, Leader of the Conservative Party 2001–03, Secretary of State of Work and Pensions 2010–

I say to everyone here today: You either want my mission … or you want Tony Blair. There is no third way. To those who doubt and to those who deliberate, I say this: Don't work for Tony Blair. Get on board. Or get out of our way. For we have got work to do. And to the Prime Minister I say this: The quiet man is here to stay and he's turning up the volume.

Conservative Party Conference, 10 October 2001

We must hold on to our respect for civil liberties – it is, after all, what marks out our open society from the tyranny of the men of violence. But in many areas of our life, we shall also have to find a new balance between human rights and human safety. The Human Rights Act passed two years ago is proving an obstacle to protecting the lives of British citizens. When we cannot deport those who threaten the life of a British Prime Minister and promote terrorism from the safety of our own country; when we cannot refuse entry to terrorist suspects on the grounds of national security; when we cannot even extradite people accused of violence against America to the United States – then it is time to change the law.

Ibid.

As a Conservative, I am proud of what our Party has done for this country. As a British citizen, I am still prouder of what this country has done for the world. As the years go by, the mission of a Party, just like the destiny of a nation, changes. But we face change, and we lead others through change, on the foundations of values and beliefs which do not change.

Ibid.

Today, this country is engaged in a ferocious conflict, a struggle for civilisation itself. We should remember why we are fighting, what we believe, and who we are. Let's keep faith with ourselves and our ideals. Let's keep faith with freedom.

Conservative Party Conference 2001

Well football teams are perhaps easier to control than political parties, I'm sure the Prime Minister would agree with me, but yeah I think every team needs discipline and a sense of self-belief and that's important, that's what leadership's all about.

Interview with Frost, 9 June 2002

I think almost every political leader is always told that the next speech they make is the most crucial one.

Ibid.

I went up to the top of the career ladder and I came down again, I am past all that.

The Guardian, 26 May 2010

A system that was originally designed to support the poorest in society is now trapping them in the very condition it was supposed to alleviate.

BBC News interview, 27 May 2010

Aspiration, it seems, is in danger of becoming the preserve of the wealthy.

Daily Telegraph, 28 May 2010

We have to challenge the whole idea that it's acceptable for a society like Britain to have such a significant number of people who do not work one day of the week and don't have any possibility of improving the quality of their lives.

Daily Mail, 28 May 2010

If you knowingly and willingly embark on criminal behaviour, the consequences of that should be that you lose some of your benefits under the current system.

6 September 2011

Restoring our economy must go hand in hand with restoring society.

Conservative Party Conference 2011

What we are engaged in is more than benefit change and more than just welfare reform. It is social reform, leading to social recovery.

Ibid.

Luck is great, but most of life is hard work.
   The Guardian, 9 December 2011

Kids are meant to believe that their stepping stone to massive money is *The X Factor*.
   Ibid.

For those who are able to work, work has to be seen as the best route out of poverty. For work is not just about more money – it is transformative. It's about taking responsibility for yourself and your family.
   Speaking at the Abbey Community Centre in London, 13 June 2012

When the news is good, the BBC view is: 'Get the government out of the picture quickly, don't allow them to say anything about it.' When the news is bad: 'Let's all dump on the government.'
   Interview with the BBC's Economics Editor Stephanie Flanders,
   18 August 2012

It's fairness to say those who work hard, get up in the morning, cut their cloth – in other words 'we can only afford to have one or two children because we don't earn enough'. They pay their taxes and they want to know that the same kind of decision-making is taking place for those on benefits.
   5 November 2012

William Durant and Ariel Durant
1885–1981 and 1888–1981; American political philosophers

A great civilisation is not conquered from without until it has destroyed itself within. The essential cause of Rome's decline lay in her people, her morals, her class struggle, her failing trade, her bureaucratic despotism, her stifling taxes, her consuming wars.
   Caesar and Christ (1944)

The experience of the past leaves very little doubt that every economic system must sooner or later rely upon some form of the profit motive to stir individuals and groups to productivity. Substitutes like slavery, police supervision, or ideological enthusiasm prove too unproductive, too expensive or too transient.

The Lessons of History (1968)

Nothing is clearer in history than the adoption by successful rebels of the methods they were accustomed to condemn in the forces they deposed.

Ibid.

Utopias of equality are biologically doomed, and the best that the amiable philosopher can hope for is an approximate equality of legal opportunity. A society in which all potential abilities are allowed to develop and function will have a survival advantage in the competition of groups.

Ibid.

E

Max Eastman

1883–1969; American intellectual and poet

I never dreamed that, however that they [the American intelligentsia] could sink to the depth of maudlin self-deception and perfectly abject treason to truth, freedom, justice, and mercy that many of them have reached in regard to the Russian debacle.

> On the failure of liberals to confront the failure of the Russian
> Socialist revolution, *Reflections on the Failure of Socialism* (1955)

Anthony Eden

1897–1977; Prime Minister 1955–57

That is a good question for you to ask, not a wise question for me to answer.

> On being asked what effect the death of Stalin would have on
> international affairs, 1953

[Nasser] is the best sort of Egyptian and a great improvement on the Pashas of the past.

> After meeting Nasser in Cairo, February 1955

We are in armed conflict; that is the phrase I have used. There has been no declaration of war.

> On the Suez Crisis, 1 November 1956

Dwight D. Eisenhower

1890–1969; US President 1953–61

You do not lead by hitting people over the head – that's assault, not leadership.
  Attributed

Humility must always be the portion of any man who receives acclaim earned in blood of his followers and sacrifices of his friends.
  Guildhall address, London, 12 June 1945

I hate war as only a soldier who has lived it can, only as one who has seen its brutality, its stupidity.
  Canadian Club, Ottawa, 10 January 1946

A people that values its privileges above its principles soon loses both.
  First Inaugural Address, 20 January 1953

There is in world affairs a steady course to be followed between an assertion of strength that is truculent and a confession of helplessness that is cowardly.
  State of the Union Address, 2 February 1953

Every gun that is made, every warship launched, every rocket fired signifies, in the final sense, a theft from those who hunger and are not fed, those who are cold and are not clothed.
  'The Chance for Peace' address, 16 April 1953

The world moves, and ideas that were good once are not always good.
  Press conference, Washington DC, 31 August 1955

The only way to win World War III is to prevent it.
  Radio and TV address, 19 September 1956

The final battle against intolerance is to be fought – not in the chambers of any legislature – but in the hearts of men.
> Campaign speech, Los Angeles, 19 October 1956

I like to believe that people in the long run are going to do more to promote peace than our governments. Indeed, I think that people want peace so much that one of these days governments had better get out of their way and let them have it.
> TV talk with Harold Macmillan, 31 August 1959

In the councils of government, we must guard against the acquisition of unwarranted influence, whether sought or unsought, by the military-industrial complex.
> Farewell address, radio and TV, 17 January 1961

T. S. Eliot
1888–1965; poet and critic

The historical sense involves a perception, not only of the pastness of the past, but of its presence.
> 'Tradition and the Individual Talent' (1920)

It is not enough to understand what we ought to be, unless we know what we are;
And we do not understand what we are,
Unless we know what we ought to be.
> 'Religion and Literature' (1935)

Envy is everywhere.
Who is without envy? And most people
Are unaware or unashamed of being envious.
> *The Elder Statesman* (1958)

The difference between being an elder statesman
And posing successfully as an elder statesman

Is practically negligible.
  Ibid.

We know too much, are convinced of too little. Our literature
is a substitute for religion, and so is our religion.
  'A dialogue on dramatic poetry' (1928)

Ebeneezer Elliott

1781–1849; poet

What is a Communist? One who has yearnings
For equal division of unequal earnings
Idler or bungler, or both, he is willing,
To fork out his copper and pocket your shilling.
  Corn-Law Rhymes (1831)

Ralph Waldo Emerson

1803–82; American essayist, lecturer and poet

The punishment which the wise suffer, who refuse to take part in
the government – is to live under the government of worse men.
  Epigrams

There is always a certain meanness in the argument of
conservatism, joined with a certain superiority in its fact.
  The Conservative (1842)

The two parties which divide the state, the party of
Conservatism and that of Innovation, are very old, and have
disputed the possession of the world ever since it was made.
  Ibid.

The democrat is a young Conservative, the Conservative is an old
democrat. The aristocrat is the democrat ripe and gone to seed.
  Representative Men (1850)

Democracy becomes a government of bullies tempered by editors.

Attributed

Euripides
480–405 BC; Greek dramatist

Moderation, the noblest gift of heaven.

Medea (c.430 BC)

Nigel Evans
b. 1957; Conservative MP 1992–

I am proud to be Welsh and I am also an unashamed, Union-Jack waving Brit.

13 June 1995

I'm used to being unpopular. I am a Conservative and I'm from Wales.

Attributed

F

Michael Fabricant

b. 1950; Conservative MP 1992–

Much as I would like the whole world to disarm and allow a free market to operate, as long as other countries support their industries, we must intervene to do the same.

May 1993

Nicholas Fairbairn

1933–95; Conservative MP, 1974–92

A little boy sucking his misogynist thumb and blubbing and carping in the corner of the front bench below the gangway is a mascot which Parliament can do without.

On Edward Heath

He has no place in the Party. He has no future in Parliament. He has no place, for Parliament is a generous place; democracy a generous thing. May I suggest he pursues his alternative career and conducts orchestras, since he does not know how to conduct himself.

Ibid.

What's a skirt but an open gateway?

Attributed

You are a silly, crude bitch and since you are a potential breeder, God help the next generation.

To a young woman heckler

The Hon. lady was once an egg and people on both sides of this House greatly regret its fertilisation.

To Edwina Currie referring to the 'salmonella in eggs affair', 1988

She is a lady short on looks, absolutely deprived of any dress sense, has a figure like a Jurassic Park monster, is very greedy when it comes to loot, no tact and wants to upstage everybody else. I cannot think of anybody else I would sooner not appoint to this post than the Duchess of York.

On the suggestion that the Duchess of York should become UN ambassador

Lucius Carey, 2nd Viscount Falkland

c.1610–43; British author and politician

When it is not necessary to change, it is necessary not to change.

Attributed

Michael Fallon

b. 1952; Conservative MP 1983–92 1997–, Business Minister 2012–, Energy Minister 2013–

Dr Cable spoke of responsible capitalism. Well, he slips his electronic tag occasionally. There is another side to responsible capitalism and that is responsible government. I believe there are limits to government.

Speech at the Institute of Directors, 22 November 2012

Life would be a lot easier if we didn't have the coalition. The process of coalition for both sides is time-consuming, bits of it can be tedious, there are an awful lot of people to be consulted, getting agreement across Whitehall is made doubly difficult by the coalition.

The House magazine, 6 June 2013

Nigel Farage

b. 1964; MEP 1999–, leader of UKIP 2006–09, 2010–

If he wants to restrict it to those parties who are likely to form the next government, he'd better not be booking studio time himself.

Hitting back at David Cameron who said only those who can govern should take part in the TV debates

You have the charisma of a damp rag, and the appearance of a low-grade bank clerk.

Speech in the European Parliament on Van Rompuy, 24 February 2010

The euro *Titanic* has now hit the iceberg – and there simply aren't enough lifeboats to go round.

Speech held in the European Parliament in Strasbourg, 13 June 2012

Once again, I challenge the Prime Minister to have an open debate with me on why he believes we must stay part of this failing, corrupt EU. The future of our nation is at stake. Mr Cameron, you have my phone number.

Daily Telegraph, 6 July 2012

No deals with the Tories; it's war.

Twitter, 26 November 2012

We wouldn't want to be like the Swiss, would we? That would be awful! We'd be rich!

On David Cameron's speech on Britain's relationship with the European Union, 23 January 2013

Herbert Fisher

1865–1940; British historian and Liberal politician

Purity of race does not exist. Europe is a continent of energetic mongrels.

A History of Europe (1934)

Howard Flight

b. 1948; Conservative MP 1997–2005

I've always been a passionate believer in capitalism; to me it is like a Bach fugue – a wonderfully complicated thing which has come about naturally and works.

Attributed

We're going to have a system where the middle classes are discouraged from breeding because it's jolly expensive. But for those on benefits, there is every incentive. Well, that's not very sensible.

Evening Standard, 25 November 2010

Malcolm 'Steve' Forbes Jr

b. 1947; American publisher

Capitalism works better than any of us can conceive. It is also the only truly moral system of exchange.

May 1993

Capitalism is the real enemy of tyranny.

Ibid.

Gerald Ford

1913–2006; US President 1974–77

Get those nigger babies off my TV set.

To White House staff after watching pictures of the war in Biafra, Nigeria

If the government is big enough to give you everything you want, it is big enough to take away everything you have.

1960

Our long national nightmare is over. Our Constitution works.
Our great Republic is a government of laws and not of men.
Following Watergate, 1974

Truth is the glue that holds governments together.
1974

There is no Soviet domination of Eastern Europe and there
never will be under a Ford administration.
1976

Hugh Fortescue, 4th Earl Fortescue
1854–1932; English Liberal politician

It has been said that children should be kept at school until
fourteen years of age; but the amount and importance of the
labour which lads between ten and fourteen can perform
should not be ignored. Since the present educational system
has come into operation, the weeds have very much multiplied
in Norfolk which was once regarded as quite the garden of
England, weeding being particularly the work of children
whose labour is cheap, whose sight is keen, bodies flexible and
fingers nimble.
1880

Eric Forth
1944–2006; Conservative MP 1983–2006

Reading, 'riting, 'rithmetic, right and 'rong.
On the 5 Rs

Liam Fox

b. 1961; Conservative MP, 1992–, Cabinet minister 2010–11

Nothing could do more to harm the opponents of the government than the shocking and sickening violence of the agitators outside the Wapping plant who feel they are justified in provoking scenes of carnage to make their point and who regard the police with malevolent contempt.

January 1987

I believe strongly in competition, the supremacy of the market, in the fact that capitalism and multi-party democracies are better than other systems and that people should be supported when they can't help themselves and not when they won't help themselves.

Attributed

We don't have the money as a country to protect ourselves against every potential future threat.

Daily Telegraph, 22 July 2010

We have to look at where we think the real risks will come from, where the real threats will come from and we need to deal with that accordingly. The Russians are not going to come over the European plain any day soon.

Ibid.

I think it is unrealistic to share an aircraft carrier but, in other areas like tactical lift we can see what we can do.

On sharing aircraft carriers, 2 September 2010

New Labour was the most short-sighted, self-serving, incompetent, useless and ineffective government that Britain has known. Make no mistake, Labour's economic policies were a national security liability.

Conservative Party Conference, 6 October 2010

We are not in Afghanistan for the sake of the education policy
in a broken thirteenth-century country. We are there so the
people of Britain and our global interests are not threatened.

The Times, 21 May 2011

I think he is a ghastly creature. People who sign up to help
protect their country's national security and then betray it, I
think that's just unspeakable. So the CIA spy on people! That's
what they are for.

On whistle-blower Edward Snowden, *Evening Standard*, 8 July 2013

If the choice for me was between 'ever closer union' and
leaving, I would choose to leave.

On the future of the European Union, *Evening Standard*, 8 July 2013

Felix Frankfurter

1882–1965; American judge

Freedom of the press is not an end in itself but a means ... to a
free society.

Attributed

The history of liberty has largely been the history of the
observance of procedural standards.

1943

It is a fair summary of history to say that the safeguards of liberty
have been forged in controversies involving not very nice people.

1950

Benjamin Franklin

1706–90; American politician

Necessity has no law; I know some attorneys of the same.

Attributed

They that can give up essential liberty to obtain a little temporary safety deserve neither liberty nor safety.
   1759

No nation was ever ruined by trade.
   1774

... in this world nothing is certain but death and taxes.
   Letter to M. Lewy, 1789

Roger Freeman
b. 1942; Conservative MP 1983–97, Cabinet minister 1995–97

There's a lot that can be done in terms of encouraging more people to enjoy a cheap and cheerful service at one moment in the day for the typists and perhaps a more luxurious service for the civil servants and businessmen who might travel at a slightly different time.
   As a public transport minister, 1994

David Friedman
b. 1945; American economist

Suppose one little old lady in ten carries a gun. Suppose that one in ten of those, if attacked by a mugger, succeeds in killing the mugger instead of being killed by him – or shooting herself in the foot. On average, the mugger is much more likely to win the encounter than the little old lady. But – also on average – every hundred muggings produces one dead mugger. At those odds, mugging is an unprofitable business – not many little old ladies carry enough money to justify one chance in a hundred of being killed getting it. The number of muggers declines drastically, not because they have all been killed but because they have, rationally, sought safer professions.
   Hidden Order: The Economics of Everyday Life (1996)

Milton Friedman

1912–2006; American economist

Thank heavens we do not get all of the government that we are made to pay for.

Attributed

History suggests that Capitalism is a necessary condition for political freedom.

Capitalism & Freedom (1962)

Nothing is so permanent as a temporary government program.
Governments never learn. Only people learn.
Inflation is taxation without legislation.
Hell hath no fury like a bureaucrat scorned.
The government solution to a problem is usually as bad as the problem.
There is an invisible hand in politics that operates in the opposite direction to the invisible hand in the market. In politics, individuals who seek to promote only the public good are led by an invisible hand to promote special interests that it was no part of their intention to promote.

1983

Why would anyone be foolish to worry about money supply? The more money the merrier, right? Wrong ... If the amount of money overwhelms the capacity to produce goods, consumers, with more money to spend, bid up prices ... [People are] no wealthier than before; more bills do not bring a higher standard of living any more than if everyone added two zeroes to his or her salary. Remember wealth is measured by the goods and services it can buy, not by numerals.

New Ideas from Dead Economics (1989)

G

Sir George Gardiner
1935–2002; Conservative MP 1974–97

Receiving support from Ted Heath in a by-election is like being measured by an undertaker.
   1975

David Garrick
1717–79; English actor, playwright, theatre manager and producer

Heart of oak are our ships
Heart of oak are our men:
We always are ready;
Steady boys, steady,
We'll fight and we'll conquer again and again.
   Heart of Oak (1770)

Charles de Gaulle
1890–1970; President of France 1945–6, 1958–69

How can you govern a nation which has 246 varieties of cheese?
   1962

Politics are too serious a matter to be left to the politicians.
   Attributed

Since a politician never believes what he says, he is quite surprised to be taken at his word.
   Ibid.

George V
1865–1936; King of Britain 1910–36

How is the Empire?
>   Last words, 12 January 1936

Henry George
1839–97; American economist

To put political power in the hands of men embittered and
degraded by poverty is to tie firebrands to foxes and turn them
loose amid the standing corn.
>   *Progress and Poverty* (1870)

What protection teaches us, is to do to ourselves in time of
peace what enemies seek to do to us in time of war.
>   *Protection or Free Trade* (1886)

Edward Gibbon
1737–94; historian

It has been calculated by the ablest politicians that no state,
without being soon exhausted, can maintain above the
hundredth part of its members in arms and idleness.
>   *Decline and Fall of the Roman Empire* (1776–88)

Corruption, the most infallible symptom of constitutional liberty.
>   Ibid.

George Gilder
b. 1939; American political philosopher and speech writer to Ronald Reagan

Capitalism begins with giving. Not from greed, avarice, or even
self-love can one expect the rewards of commerce, but from a

spirit closely akin to altruism, a regard for the needs of others, a benevolent, outgoing and courageous temper of mind.
   Wealth & Poverty (1981)

Real poverty is less a state of income than a state of mind.
   Ibid.

A successful economy depends upon the proliferation of the rich, on creating a large class of risk-taking men who are willing to shun the easy channels of a comfortable life in order to create a new enterprise, win huge profits and invest them again.
   Ibid.

The man has the gradually sinking feeling that his role as provider, the definitive male activity from the primal days of the hunt through the industrial revolution and on into modern life, has been largely seized from him; he has been cuckolded by the compassionate state.
   Ibid.

Socialism presumes that we already know most of what we need to know to accomplish our national goals. Capitalism is based on an idea that we live in a world of unfathomable complexity, ignorance and peril, and that we cannot possibly prevail over our difficulties without constant efforts of initiative, sympathy, discovery and love.
   Ibid.

Whether sorting potatoes or writing software [entrepreneurs] are movers and shakers, doers and givers, brimming with visions of creation and opportunity.
   Ibid.

[Entrepreneurs] are optimists, who see in every patch of sand a potential garden, in every man a potential worker, in every problem a possible profit. Their self-interest succumbs to

their deeper interest and engagement with the work beyond themselves, impelled by their curiosity, imagination, and faith.
Ibid.

Capitalism offers nothing but frustrations and rebuffs to those who wish – because of claimed superiority of birth, credentials, or ideals – to get without giving, to take without risking, to profit without sacrifice, to be exalted without humbling themselves to understand others and meet their needs.
Ibid.

Just as the sociologist requires books and free time and the bureaucrat needs arbitrary power, the capitalist needs capital.
Ibid.

Ian Gilmour

1926–2007; Conservative MP, Cabinet minister 1979–81

Unfortunately monetarism, like Marxism, suffered the only fact that for a theory is worse than death: it was put into practice.
Dancing with Dogma (1992)

Contemporary Conservatism as practised by the leadership is, like contemporary art, seldom much admired at the time; it only achieves acceptance and admiration in retrospect.
Inside Right (1977)

Socialists may look forward to some grim utopia. Conservatives have no such illusions about the future or the past. For them there has never been a 'golden age' and there never will be. Similarly there is no fixed or golden policy to which the Conservative Party could or should turn.
Ibid.

It is certainly neither practicable nor sensible to seek consistency in Tory policy through the ages in the shallow sense of sameness. For instance the party has had the good sense to move from protection to free trade, back to protection and then again towards free trade according to the economic circumstances of the time. Again, there can be no permanent attitude to the state, since the state is continually changing.

Ibid.

Newt Gingrich
b. 1943; US Congressman

The welfare state kills more people in a year than private business.

1989

One of the greatest intellectual failures of the welfare state is the penchant for sacrifice, so long as the only people being asked to sacrifice are working, tax-paying Americans.

USA Today, 16 January 1995

A society that focuses on creating wealth will find itself getting very, very rich and dramatically increasing the scale of achievement, whereas the society that focuses on redistributing wealth will rapidly discourage people from creating it.

Attributed

No society can survive, no civilisation can survive, with having twelve year olds having babies, with fifteen year olds killing each other, with seventeen year olds dying of AIDS, with eighteen year olds getting diplomas they can't read.

Commentary, 1994

Building the Panama Canal all of us wanted to keep? We invented a nation, built a canal, manned the canal, cured yellow fever, and had a navy to protect it.

The Heritage Foundation, April 1988

Bureaucratic rules cannot take the place of common sense.

Ibid.

Today's taxes are so high they force many mothers to work. Today's taxes are anti-child, anti-family and anti-work. Furthermore, our tax system is anti-savings, anti-investment and anti-jobs.

Ibid.

Nathan Glazer

b. 1923; American sociologist

To live with the two fraternities – the fraternity of the racial and ethnic group and the fraternity of the larger American society – means to acknowledge, and to accept, differences that are not the result of discrimination but are themselves the result of a concrete group life.

Ethnic Dilemmas 1964–1982 (1983)

Every contemporary society tries to reduce differences and inequalities, and ours should too. But what is problematic is the attempt to treat every difference as the result of discrimination and as a candidate for governmental action to reduce it. In a multi-ethnic society, such a policy can only encourage one group after another to raise its claims to special treatment for its protection.

Ibid.

[T]he rising emphasis on group differences which government is called upon to correct might mean the destruction of any hope for the larger fraternity of all Americans, in which people are tied to one another in what they feel to be a common good society, and in which the tie is close enough to allow tolerance for their range of differences.

Ibid.

Lord Glenarthur

b. 1944; British peer, pilot and businessman

To go round the world in a week, which I did the other day, is very exhausting.

1988

Viscount Goderich

1782–1859; Prime Minister 1827–28

I cannot forget that the principle of our constitution is jealousy. It is jealous of the Crown, jealous of the aristocracy, jealous of the democracy, and the Roman Catholics have no right to complain, if it is jealous of them.

Speech in the House of Commons during the debate on Catholic emancipation, 1 March 1813

The science of government, whether legislative or executive, was, in fact, neither more nor less than a perpetually recurring struggle with difficulties.

Speech in the House of Lords

William Godwin

1756–1836; philosopher and novelist

Government can have no more than two legitimate purposes – the suppression of injustice within the community, and the common defence against external invasion.

An Enquiry Concerning Political Justice (1793)

Johann Wolfgang von Goethe

1749–1832; German writer and politician

Legislators and revolutionaries who promise liberty and equality at the same time are either utopian dreamers or charlatans.

Maxims and Reflections (1833), No. 953

What is the best government? That which teaches us to govern ourselves.

Ibid.

Freedom! A fine word when rightly understood. What freedom would you have? What is the freedom of the most free? To act rightly!

Egmont (1788)

Man tue was man will. (One does what one wishes.)

Ibid.

There is nothing more frightful than ignorance in action.

1826

He only earns his freedom and existence who daily conquers them anew.

Prologue in Heaven (1909–14)

The world is so empty if one thinks only of mountains, rivers and cities; but to know someone here and there who thinks and feels with us, and though distant, is close to us in spirit – this makes the earth for us an inhabited garden.

Attributed

Zac Goldsmith

b. 1975; Conservative MP 2010–

How many people in this country genuinely believe that when they cast their vote in a European election it will have any impact on how Europe is structured, on what decisions will be made within the EU, or even on the quality of those decisions? Decisions are being taken by people who are not elected, and are therefore insulated from any kind of democratic pressure.

Maiden speech, 27 May 2010

Barry Goldwater

1909–98; US Senator

The inescapable and harmful by-product of such operations as Social Security ... has been the weakening of the individual personality and of self-reliance.

1956

The conscience of the Conservative is pricked by anyone who would debase the dignity of the individual human being. Today, therefore, he is at odds with dictators who rule by terror, and equally with those gentler collectivists who ask our permission to play God with the human race.

Conscience of a Conservative (1960)

If the Conservative is less likely anxious than his liberal brethren to increase Social Security benefits, it is because he is more anxious than his Liberal brethren that people be free throughout their lives to spend their earnings when and as they see fit.

Ibid.

The effect of Welfarism on freedom will be felt later on – after its beneficiaries have become its victims, after dependence on government has turned into bondage and it is too late to unlock the jail.

> Ibid.

Let us, then, not blunt the noble impulses of mankind by reducing charity to a mechanical operation of the federal government ... Let welfare be a private concern.

> Ibid.

Extremism in the defence of liberty is no vice. Moderation in the pursuit of justice is no virtue.

> 16 July 1964

A government that is big enough to give you all you want is big enough to take it all away.

> 1964

The Conservative movement is founded on the simple tenet that people have the right to live as they please, as long as they don't hurt anyone else in the process. No one has ever shown me how being gay or lesbian harms anyone else.

> *Atlanta Journal*, 19 July 1994

Hubert Humphrey talks so fast that listening to him is like trying to read *Playboy* magazine with your wife turning over the pages.

> Attributed

Teresa Gorman

b. 1931; Conservative MP 1987–2001

Perhaps we should do something more drastic, like cutting their goolies off.

> On appropriate punishments for rapists

The enemy is the old, wet Tories who think they were born to rule.

    Attributed

I am Florence Nightingale to the middle aged woman – St Teresa of the menopause.

    On her promotion of hormone replacement therapy

I think most of the wrinkles have been ironed out.

    On HRT for older women, 1988

They tried to demoralise me, but as far as I am concerned they were just abusing me.

    On the whips' pressure to vote for Maastricht, 1992

The Prime Minister has got the Parliamentary Party by the goolies.

    On John Major

Compassion is a disease for which Conservatism is the only cure.

    February 1998

I deplore smoking, but I'm against banning smoking; it's not the substances that are at fault, but inadequate people.

    The Independent, 19 October 1993

America changed my life. It was the first time I'd lived in a capitalist society; it was like coming out from behind the iron curtain.

    Cited in BBC online, 1 March 2000

I haven't taken the course of Cecil Parkinson and Peter Walker and everyone else who talks posh; I dare say some of the Tory old guard think I am quite frightful – a common, vulgar little woman and an upstart from nowhere.

    Attributed

Michael Gove

b. 1967; Conservative MP 2005–, Education Secretary 2010–

I'm a decentraliser. I believe in trusting professionals.
   Interview with Andrew Marr, 28 March 2010

I was a union member in my youth as well and I went on strike, and I don't think it solved anything. It only made the situation worse for everyone involved.
   Ibid.

Nations succeed when they put talent first: those societies which have guaranteed the highest standards for all their citizens, throughout the ages, have been those which have been the purest meritocracies.
   Daily Mail, 21 September 2011

Those who don't promote on merit, whether crony-ridden sheikhdoms or creaking Euro institutions, find they quickly decline, whatever riches they start out with.
   Ibid.

The children in our poorest schools are, overwhelmingly, from our poorest homes. Many of them will have the talent to rise to the very top. To become business leaders, academics, surgeons and head teachers. But they will achieve their full potential only if we ditch, once and for all, the dismally defeatist mindset which believes that, in education, second-best is good enough.
   Ibid.

You wouldn't tolerate an underperforming surgeon in an operating theatre, or an underperforming midwife at your child's birth. Why is it that we tolerate underperforming teachers in the classroom?
   Daily Mail, 13 January 2012

I refuse to surrender to the Marxist teachers hell-bent on destroying our schools.
Daily Mail, 23 March 2012

It's often the case that successful people invite criticism.
Referring to Rupert Murdoch at the Leveson Inquiry, 29 May 2012

Richard Wagner is an artist of sublime genius and his work is incomparably more rewarding – intellectually, sensually and emotionally – than, say, the Arctic Monkeys.
Speech at Cambridge University, 24 November 2012

It's wrong to say to gay men and women that their love is less legitimate. It's wrong to say that because of how you love and who you love, you are not entitled to the same rights as others. It's wrong because inequality is wrong.
Daily Mail, 2 February 2013

Everything I do in office is intended to clear away the obstacles to children having every possible opportunity.
Ibid.

I'm a Conservative because I believe in making opportunity more equal.
Ibid.

The accumulation of cultural capital – the acquisition of knowledge – is the key to social mobility.
Speech to Social Market Foundation, 5 February 2013

The current leadership of the Labour Party react to the idea that working-class students might study the subjects they studied with the same horror that the Earl of Grantham showed when a chauffeur wanted to marry his daughter.
Referencing *Downton Abbey*, 5 February 2013

One set of history teaching resources targeted at Year 11s – fifteen- and sixteen-year-olds – suggests spending classroom time depicting the rise of Hitler as a *Mr Men* story ... I may be unfamiliar with all of Roger Hargreaves's work but I am not sure he ever got round to producing Mr Anti-Semitic Dictator, Mr Junker General or Mr Dutch Communist Scapegoat.

On history teaching, 9 May 2013

Proper history teaching is being crushed under the weight of play-based pedagogy which infantilises children, teachers and our culture.

Speech at Brighton College, 9 May 2013

You come home to find your seventeen-year-old daughter engrossed in a book. Which would delight you more – if it were *Twilight* or *Middlemarch*?

Ibid.

Ed Miliband complaining about school spending is about as credible as Kim Kardashian complaining about invasion of privacy.

On Ed's efforts at Prime Minister's Questions, 3 July 2013

Ian Gow
1937–90; Conservative MP 1974–90

If paternity leave was granted, it would result in a direct incitement to a population explosion.

1979

Phil Gramm
b. 1942; US Senator

Balancing the Budget is like going to heaven. Everybody wants to do it, but nobody wants to do what you have to do to get there.

16 September 1990

No great cause has ever been won under the banner of Moderation.

Attributed

The answer is not more government – it's more opportunity. And the path to greater opportunity for all our people will be found by controlling public spending and letting the people who do the work pay the taxes and pull the wagon keep more of what they earn.

Republican Convention, 1992

All over the world people are rejecting government as a decision-maker. All over the world people are rejecting government as a source of wisdom, a source of prosperity or a source of efficiency. All over the world people are turning to individual freedom and free enterprise and individual initiative.

31 January 1993

Chris Grayling
b. 1962; Conservative MP 2001–, Employment Minister 2010–12, Justice Secretary 2012–

Gone are the days of a top-down, Whitehall knows best approach. We will give the best of the private and voluntary sector the freedom to do what works to help people.

Daily Mail, 1 April 2011

Horace Greeley
1811–72; journalist

Go West, young man, and grow up with the country.

Attributed

Damian Green

b. 1956; Conservative MP 1997–; Immigration Minister 2010–12,
Police and Justice Minister 2012–

Whether you come here to work, study, or get married, we as
a country are entitled to check that you will add to the quality
of life in Britain. What we need is a national consensus on how
we can make immigration work for Britain. We are evidently a
long way from such a consensus but I want to start to build it.
The legitimate question in today's world is how we can benefit
from immigration ... Importing economic dependency on the
state is unacceptable. Bringing people to this country who can
play no role in the life of this country is equally unacceptable.
Everyone who comes here must be selected to make a positive
contribution.

Speech at Policy Exchange, 2 February 2012

George Grenville

1712–70; Prime Minister 1763–65

A wise government knows how to enforce with temper or to
conciliate with dignity.

Speech against the expulsion of John Wilkes from Parliament, 1769

John Gummer

b. 1939; Conservative MP 1970–74, 1979–2010

Poverty is considered quaint in rural areas because it comes
thatched.

Attributed

Nobody need be worried about BSE in this country or
anywhere else.

As Agriculture Minister, 1990

H

William Hague
b. 1961; Conservative MP 1989–, Cabinet minister 1995–97,
Conservative Party leader 1997–2001

I can think of no single act by any government that I would
welcome more than the return of capital punishment.
  1978

I shall give high priority to learning the Welsh national anthem.
  On becoming Welsh Secretary, July 1995

Never again will we have a divided organisation; never again
will the voice of our members go unheard; and never again will
we allow the good name of our party to be blackened by the
greed and selfishness of a few.
  First speech as Leader of the Conservative Party, Conservative Party
  Conference, 10 October 1997

It is time for a change.
  Ibid.

New Labour are for everything but nothing: tough, tender; hot,
cold; soft, hard; fast, slow; for you, for me; to give, to take; to
stop, to start.
  Ibid.

Labour have lost their moral compass. They care most of all
about what sounds good; what trips off the tongue; what plays
well on the television bulletins; and what gets a headline in
tomorrow's papers.
  Ibid.

Imagine if the Second World War had been fought this way. You can just hear them in 1940: 'We shall review them on the beaches; we shall review them in the fields and the streets; we shall review them in the hills; we shall never publish the results.'

Ibid., parodying New Labour's penchant for policy reviews

We have no intention of stooping to a new politics without conscience. Let them stoop. We will conquer.

Ibid.

We are the only party in Britain which believes in freedom as a birth right to be protected rather than a concession to be handed down.

Ibid.

Yet again, we have the nauseating spectacle of Labour politicians who took every advantage and opportunity for themselves and then use their power to deny the same opportunity to the generation that comes after them.

Ibid.

Compassion is not a bolt-on extra to Conservatism. It is at its very core.

Ibid.

For Conservatives ... compassion does not end when you send your cheque to the Inland Revenue.

Ibid.

It is an abdication of leadership to lead the people in to the casual destruction of our constitution.

Ibid.

Europe itself is not a nation and should not aspire to be a nation.

Ibid.

... we say no to abolishing the pound for the foreseeable future.
    Ibid.

It did enormous damage to the credibility of our party and we
paid the price.
    Ibid., on the decision to join the ERM

I believe in freedom, enterprise, education, self-reliance,
obligation to others and the nation.
    Ibid.

I cannot think of a better guide to Conservatives than those
famous words of Rabbi Hillel: 'If I am not for myself, who
should be for me? ... But if I am only for myself, who am I?'
    Speech to Conservative Friends of Israel, 1997

It was inevitable that the *Titanic* would set sail, but that does not
mean it was a good idea to be on it.
    On the single European currency, *Daily Telegraph*, 7 January 1998

One of the reasons we lost in 1997 was that we appeared to
have become the economics party, as we were shining an
intense searchlight on a particular set of economic issues.
    Speech on freedom and the family, Social Market Foundation,
    January 1998

... the institutions which Conservatives value flourish in the
space created by limited government and a market economy.
Strong families, good schools, proud cities – all need to be able
to shape their own characters free from the heavy burden of
intrusive and expensive government. David Willetts calls that
civic Conservatism; I would call it popular Conservatism.
    Ibid.

We are not just atomised individuals pursuing our own narrow
economic self-interest.
    Ibid.

I do not mind Conservatives learning from Maureen Lipman and showing a little bit more respect for those -ologies. There is evidence of the right way forward buried in the latest sociological research.

Ibid.

It is the political, democratic sovereignty of the people – exercised at the ballot box, expressed through the legal sovereignty of Parliament and held in stewardship by the government – which is the key to accountable government today.

Speech to the Centre for Policy Studies, February 1998

Labour has embarked on a journey of constitutional upheaval without a route map. They have no clear idea of where the journey will take them or what the final destination will look like.

Ibid.

The government is now embarking on what is potentially the most damaging step of all: removing the main independent element in the House of Lords by excluding the hereditary peers.

Ibid.

Labour is playing Jenga.

Ibid., on Labour's plans for constitutional change

Tony Blair would call them Uncool Britannia.

Ibid., on the people he grew up with

I have no interest in leading a bunch of Blue Trotskyites trotting into the Wilderness.

Ibid., on the importance of 'One Nation' ideas

If political integration is pushed too far, it becomes impossible to sustain accountability and democracy.

Speech to INSEAD, France, May 1998

Perhaps the best definition of a nation is this: it is a group of people who feel enough in common with one another to accept government from each other's hands. That is why democracy functions best within nations.

Ibid.

We're having a Common Sense Revolution, so let's have some common sense language about Labour: it's high time this bunch of hypocrites stopped preaching to others what they don't practice themselves.

Conservative Party Conference, 7 October 1999

When can you be absolutely, 100 per cent, cast-iron sure that a Labour promise is going to be broken? The moment Tony Blair puts it in his own handwriting. If he was Pinocchio, he'd have a nose bigger than Concorde.

Ibid.

It is the forces of Conservatism which, in a dangerous century beset by Socialism, Communism and national Socialism, have left our country at the end of that century free and proud and strong.

Ibid.

God save us from the spineless crawling to the government of Liberal politicians.

Ibid.

A battle of ideas has commenced over the value of nation in the modern world. This Party will not be found wanting. This country has such great strengths. Our traditions. Our institutions. Our values. The instincts of our people. The Conservative Party trusts in these things and we will protect these things. We always have and we always will.

Ibid.

I say to the people of Britain: if you believe that our country is unique in the world but is in danger of losing its identity; if you believe that Britain is a place where you should be rewarded for doing the right thing, but now you are penalised for it; if you believe in Britain as a healthy democracy, but that the standards of democracy are now being tarnished and diminished; if you believe in Britain as a country where the law is enforced and respected, but that now it is not respected enough; if you believe in Britain as a country that will work with its neighbours but never submit to being governed by anyone else; if you believe in an independent Britain, then come with me, and I will give you back your country.

Ibid.

Labour's looked like a Conference from the past. After all the years of trying to control the trade unions, it was back to beer and sandwiches in Brighton last week. Tony Blair likes beer and sandwiches without the beer. I like it without the sandwiches. Come to think of it, I like it without the unions.

Conservative Party Conference, 5 October 2000

What a bunch they are – this soap opera of a government. In last week's episode of the Neighbours from Hell: Robin has fallen out with Peter. Peter won't talk to Geoffrey any more. Geoffrey won't lend his holiday home to Tony. Mo has been sent to Coventry. Clare doesn't like the tent run by Tony's crony. Tony's crony blames Chris and Peter. Tony rows with Gordon. Peter won't speak to Gordon. And Gordon won't speak to anyone at all.

Ibid.

The only person in the country still stuck in the fascination stage with New Labour is the leader of the Liberals. But of course we've witnessed the four stages of the Liberal Party too. Irrelevance, irrelevance, irrelevance, and irrelevance.

Ibid.

Making the most of being British means that if taxes are lower in Britain than elsewhere in Europe, we should be making them lower still to ensure that we keep our competitive advantages.

Ibid.

I was the driver's mate, delivering the bottles and beer around South Yorkshire. We used to have a pint at every stop – well the driver's mate did, not the driver, thankfully – and we used to have about ten stops in a day. You worked so hard you didn't feel you'd drunk ten pints by four o'clock, you used to sweat so much. But then you had to lift all the empties off the lorry. It's probably horrifying but we used to do that then go home for tea and then go out in the evening to the pub.

Interview, *GQ* magazine, August 2000

Nothing is more absurd than a Prime Minister who has committed us in principle to joining the Euro saying last week that he was against it. He talks about his five tests; we know what they are: Does Peter want it? Will Gordon let me? Will the French like it? Will Robin notice? Can I get away with it?

To the House of Commons, Prime Minister's Questions, 25 October 2000

In the Prime Minister, we have a man who has forfeited the right to be believed or to be trusted. In more than twenty years in politics, he has betrayed every cause he believed in, contradicted every statement he has made, broken every promise he has given and breached every agreement that he has entered into ... There is a lifetime of U-turns, errors and sell-outs.

To the House of Commons, Prime Minister's Questions, 6 December 2000

Talk about Europe and they call you extreme. Talk about tax and they call you greedy. Talk about crime and they call you reactionary. Talk about immigration and they call you racist; talk about your nation and they call you Little Englanders ... This government thinks Britain would be all right if we had a different people. I think Britain would be all right, if only we had a different government.

Spring Conference speech, March 2001

We have not been able to persuade a majority, or anything approaching a majority, that we are yet the alternative government that they need.

On losing the 2001 general election

I am told that in my time at the Dispatch Box I have asked the Prime Minister 1,118 direct questions, but no one has counted the direct answers – it may not take long.

To the House of Commons, Prime Minister's Questions, 18 July 2001

Listen, just because I tell jokes, it doesn't mean you're allowed to have political opinions.

Hague's famous outwitting of long-serving captain, Paul Merton on *Have I Got News For You*, 5 February 2003

In this country the language of human rights has sometimes been cheapened by laws that are out of touch with the people.

Conservative Party Conference, 3 October 2006

The British people believe that political integration has gone far enough, and so do we. So we renew this pledge: that under a Conservative government there would be no Treaty changes that transfer more competences to the EU without a referendum of the British people.

Ibid.

To see how the post of a permanent President of the European Council could evolve is not difficult even for the humblest student of politics, and it is, of course, rumoured that one Tony Blair may be interested in the job. If that prospect makes us uncomfortable on the Conservative benches, just imagine how it will be viewed in Downing Street! I must warn ministers that having tangled with Tony Blair across the Dispatch Box on hundreds of occasions, I know his mind almost as well as they do. I can tell them that when he goes off to a major political conference of a centre-right party and refers to himself as a Socialist, he is on

181

manoeuvres, and is busily building coalitions as only he can. We can all picture the scene at a European Council sometime next year. Picture the face of our poor Prime Minister as the name Blair is nominated by one President and Prime Minister after another: the look of utter gloom on his face at the nauseating, glutinous praise oozing from every Head of government, the rapid revelation of a majority view, agreed behind closed doors when he, as usual, was excluded. Never would he more regret no longer being in possession of a veto: the famous dropped jaw almost hitting the table, as he realises there is no option but to join in. Then the awful moment when the motorcade of the President of Europe sweeps into Downing Street. The gritted teeth and bitten nails: the Prime Minister emerges from his door with a smile of intolerable anguish; the choking sensation as the words, Mr President, are forced from his mouth. And then, once in the Cabinet room, the melodrama of, When will you hand over to me? all over again.

House of Commons, 21 January 2008

Before turning to domestic issues, I was going to be nice to the Rt Hon. and learned lady. She has had a difficult week. She had to explain yesterday that she dresses in accordance with wherever she is going: she wears a helmet on a building site, she wears Indian clothes in the parts of her constituency with a large representation of Indian people, so when she goes to a Cabinet meeting, she presumably dresses as a clown. As I said, I was going to be nice to her before her previous response.

To Harriet Harman in the House of Commons, Prime Minister's Questions, 2 April 2008

Tony Blair exploited to the full the transformation of British fortunes achieved by Conservatives in the '80s and '90s, while he and Gordon Brown will leave behind them a nation diminished by their catastrophic stewardship of the British finances.

Conservative Party Conference, 2009

We should never be ashamed of saying we will promote our own national interest, for the British national interest is no narrow agenda.

Ibid.

We cannot have a foreign policy without a conscience. Foreign policy is domestic policy written large. The values we live by at home do not stop at our shores.

Hague talks of his values based on foreign policy, August 2010

Governments that use violence to stop democratic development will not earn themselves respite forever. They will pay an increasingly high price for actions which they can no longer hide from the world with ease, and will find themselves on the wrong side of history.

Hague's attitude towards the 2011 Libyan Civil War, as told to Sky News's *Murnaghan Show*

On the question of taking credit for what goes right and blame for what goes wrong – having led the Conservative party for four years, I have never heard of this notion before.

8 March 2011

A burning building with no exits. I might take the analogy too far but the euro wasn't built with exits so it is very difficult to leave it.

On the European currency, September 2011

Lord Hailsham

1907–2001; Conservative MP 1963–70, Cabinet minister 1956–64, Lord Chancellor 1970–74, 1979–87

Conservatives do not believe that the political struggle is the most important thing in life. The simplest of them prefer fox hunting – the wisest religion.

The Case for Conservatism (1946)

The responsibility of a political party is in inverse proportion to its chances of getting into office.

House of Lords, 13 February 1961

A great party is not to be brought down because of a squalid affair between a woman of easy virtue and a proved liar.

On the Profumo affair, 13 June 1963

The moment politics becomes dull, democracy is in danger.

1966

Since the War, Parliament seems to me to have gone legislation-mad; we are passing too many laws, too ill-thought out, too little intelligible and too little related to the moral understanding of the people. Let us have a little respite from new law making and spend our time in consolidating, codifying, improving and I hope so – replacing.

1975

Once human beings abandon the basic structure of morality in their commerce with one another, once they abandon the object standards of right and wrong, once they cease to control their own passions, their desire for wealth or sex or even their mere dislike of their fellow men and once they begin to rationalise and sublimate these instincts by relating them to some real or imaginary political or moral cause, once it is believed that men do evil that good might come. That end justifies the means, there really is no depth to which human nature cannot fall.

1975

By far too many publicists has political crime been defended as something honourable, the perpetrators lauded as national heroes or freedom fighters, invited to international conferences, heard with respect at international gatherings and all the time the morality of the political criminal has degenerated.

1975

Like the Bible, the law should be written in a language understood by the people and not wrapped up in a learned tongue acceptable only to a cast of priestly intimates.
    1975

In a confrontation with the politics of power, the soft centre has always melted away.
    Attributed

A practical old bruiser with a first-class mind and very bad manners.
    On Denis Healey, 2 June 1987

The English, and more latterly, the British, have the habit of acquiring their institutions by chance or inadvertence, and shedding them in a fit of absentmindedness.
    Guildhall Lecture, 10 November 1987

Nations begin by forming their institutions, but in the end, are continuously formed by them or under their influence.
    Ibid.

Lord Halifax
1881–1959; Conservative politician, Foreign Secretary 1938–40

I often think how much easier the world would have been to manage if Herr Hitler and Signor Mussolini had been at Oxford.
    As Foreign Secretary 1938–41

Alexander Hamilton
1755–1804; American constitutionalist

Why has government been instituted at all? Because the passions of men will not conform to the dictates of reason and justice without constraint.
    The Federalist Papers (1788)

Christine Hamilton

b. 1949; media personality and wife of Neil Hamilton

I would fight the world on Neil's behalf. We have set about rebuilding our lives. We have done it before. We can do it again. We've hit a rock but we will go on.

Attributed

Get those greasy reptiles off the church daffodils.

To reporters stalking her home, 1997

Why don't you get a proper job instead of shovelling shit?

Ibid.

Neil Hamilton

b. 1949; Conservative MP 1983–97

Joining the ERM is no soft option. We have a choice. Either we can use interest rates to stabilise the currency, in which case the economy will go up and down; or we can stabilise the economy, in which case the currency goes up and down. There is no way of wishing away that distinction and that choice.

Speech to the House of Commons, 1 May 1990

I am a humble lawyer, and my only connection with the world of nuts and bolts has been the occasional throwing of a spanner into the works over the years.

Speech to the House of Commons, 14 December 1992

Isn't it fantastic that just at the moment when we are getting rid of passports for people in Europe we are introducing them for cows and sheep?

Speech to the House of Commons, 4 October 1993

I have always believed that a government had a limited capacity to do good and a virtually infinite capacity to do harm.

Speech to the House of Commons, 4 February 1994

I must remember to declare it in the Register of Interests.

Referring to a biscuit received during a factory visit, 1994

The Norwegians recently voted in a referendum not to join the European Communit*j*. That preserves the option for Britain to have a referendum to decide whether we wish to join Norway.

Speech to North West Young Conservatives Conference,
2 February 1995

J. H. Hammond

1807–64; American politician

In all social systems there must be a class to do the mean duties … It constitutes the very mudsills of society … Fortunately for the South, she found a race adapted for that purpose … We use them for that purpose and call them slaves.

American Senator (1858)

Philip Hammond

b. 1955; Conservative MP 1997–, Transport Secretary 2010–11, Defence Secretary 2011–

The military never uses a full word if they can create an abbreviation.

The Independent, 14 August 2012

While I believe firmly in open markets and free trade, I also believe an open market needs a level playing field.

Conservative Party Conference, 3 October 2012

It is a significant gamble to assume that troops in our UK armed forces would volunteer for a Scottish defence force.

Speech in Edinburgh on Scottish independence, 14 March 2013

I remember the day after the general election when Harold Wilson had lost, I remember quite clearly cycling from my house in Hutton along Long Ridings and feeling what a relief to live in a country with a Tory government again.

New Statesman, 29 May 2013

Daniel Hannan

b. 1971; Conservative MEP 1999–

An absolute majority is not the same as the rule of law. I accept that there is a minority in this house in favour of a referendum. That there is a minority in this house against the ratification of the Lisbon Treaty. But this house must nonetheless follow its own rulebooks. And by popular acclamation, to discard the rules under which we operate is indeed an act of arbitrary and despotic rule. It is only my regard for you Mr Chairman and my personal affection for you that prevents me from likening it to the *Ermächtigungsgesetz* of 1933 which was also voted through by a parliamentary majority.

Speech in the European Parliament, 12 December 2007

You cannot spend your way out of recession or borrow your way out of debt. And when you repeat, in that wooden and perfunctory way, that our situation is better than others', that we are well placed to weather the storm, I have to tell you, you sound like a Brezhnev-era apparatchik giving the party line. You know, and we know, and you know that we know that it's nonsense! Everyone knows that Britain is worse off than any other country as we go into these hard times. The IMF has said so. The European Commission has said so. The markets have said so, which is why our currency has devalued by 30 per cent. And soon, the voters too will get their chance to say so. They can see what the markets have already seen: that you are the devalued Prime Minister of a devalued government.

Attacking Gordon Brown to his face in the European Parliament, 24 March 2009

Any American reader who wants to know where Obamification will lead should spend a week with me in the European Parliament. I'm working in your future and, believe me, you won't like it.

Daily Telegraph, 14 June 2010

There comes a point when our presence is doing more harm than good, serving to destabilise Pakistan rather than to stabilise Afghanistan. We are reaching that point now.

Daily Telegraph, 26 June 2010

Sir William Harcourt

1827–1904; Liberal MP, Chancellor of the Exchequer 1892–95

The Conservatives, mark my word, never yet took up a cause without betraying it in the end.

The Times, 1885

Warren Harding

1865–1923; US President 1921–23

Government, after all, is a very simple thing.

Attributed

Jeffrey Peter Hart
b. 1930; American academic

Within their own environment, however, we do not seem to encounter much criticism or independence – merely a lot of people who tend to sound the same.
>   On liberal academics, *Acts of Recovery* (1989)

The traditional attitudes and ideas of Western Culture form, so to speak, the thesis, while liberalism constitutes the antithesis, the negative image. Thus, from the liberal perspective, most traditional virtues become negative qualities.
>   Ibid.

In this melodrama the result is always predictable and therefore boring.
>   Ibid., on liberal pieties

The liberal converts pity into a kind of nervous tic, the habitual response to everything.
>   Ibid.

Mere beauty happens to be extremely important to me.
>   Ibid., responding to liberal criticism of the Carnival Queen being chosen for her mere beauty

Communism has been the dominant fact of the 20th century, fascism a mere blip by comparison. Perhaps a 100 million have been killed…
>   *Communism, It's All Over*, June 1989

During his first term as President, Ronald Reagan said two things that aroused fury on the left. He said that the Soviet Union is an evil empire and that Communism is a vast historical mistake. He was correct on both accounts.
>   Ibid.

Friedrich von Hayek
1899–1992; Austrian economist

The system of private property is the most important guarantee
of freedom, not only for those who own property, but scarcely
less for those who do not.
Road to Serfdom (1944)

The more the state plans the more difficult planning becomes
for the individual.
Ibid.

We have progressively abandoned that freedom in economic
affairs without which personal and political freedom has never
existed in the past.
Ibid.

It is now often said that democracy will not tolerate capitalism.
If capitalism means here a competitive system based on free
disposal over private property, it is far more important to
realise that only within this system is democracy possible.
When it becomes dominated by a collectivist creed, democracy
will inevitably destroy itself.
Ibid.

In any society freedom of thought will probably be of direct
significance only for a small minority. But this does not mean
that anyone is competent, or ought to have power, to select
those to whom this freedom is to be reserved.
Ibid.

Our freedom of choice in a competitive society rests on the fact
that if one person refuses to satisfy our wishes, we can turn to
another. But if we face a monopolist we are at his mercy.
Ibid.

I am certain that nothing has done so much to destroy the juridical safeguards of individual freedom as the striving after this miracle of social justice.

Economic Freedom & Representative Government (1973)

One cannot help a country to maintain its standard of life by assisting people to consume more than they produce.

Daily Telegraph, 26 August 1976

Liberty not only means that the individual has both the opportunity and the burden of choice; it also means that he must bear the consequences of his actions ... Liberty and responsibility are inseparable.

Constitution of Liberty (1960)

The greatest danger to liberty today comes from the men who are most needed and most powerful in modern government, namely, the efficient expert administrators exclusively concerned with what they regard as the public good.

Ibid.

It is of the essence of the demand for equality before the law that people should be treated alike in spite of the fact that they are different.

Ibid.

The great aim of the struggle for liberty has been equality before the law.

Ibid.

... responsibility ... often evokes the outright hostility of men who have been taught that it is nothing but circumstances over which they have no control that has determined their position in life or even their actions. This denial of responsibility is, however, commonly due to a fear of responsibility, a fear that necessarily becomes a fear of freedom.

Ibid.

[The] impersonal process of the market ... can be neither just or unjust, because the results are not intended or foreseen.

'Social or Redistributive Justice', in *The Essence of Hayek* (1984)

Jerry Hayes

b. 1953; Conservative MP 1983–97

UKIP, the sort of party one instinctively feels watches *Roots* backwards so that there is a happy ending.

The Guardian, 21 May 2013

If you want a friend in politics, buy a dog.

Jerry Hayes's blog, 22 June 2013

Henry Hazlitt

1894–1993; author

[The] private sector of the economy is, in fact, the voluntary sector; and ... the public sector is, in fact, the coercive sector. The voluntary sector is made up of the goods and services for which people voluntarily spend the money they have earned. The coercive sector is made up of the goods and services that are provided, regardless of the wishes of the individual, out of taxes that are seized from him.

From *The Wisdom of Henry Hazlitt* (1993)

Edward Heath

1916–2005; Conservative MP 1950–2001, Prime Minister 1970–74

I owe everything to my mother.

1950

We may be a small island but we are not a small people.

1970

This would at a stroke reduce the rise in prices, increase production and reduce unemployment.

On proposals to reduce taxation, 16 June 1970

We will have to embark on a change so radical, a revolution so quiet and yet so total, that it will go far beyond the programme for a parliament.

Conservative Party Conference, October 1970

We are going to build on the past but we are not going to be strangled by it.

1972

The unpleasant and unacceptable face of capitalism.

On the Lonrho affair, 15 May 1973

Our problem at the moment is a problem of success.

Six weeks before the three-day week, November 1973

I am not a product of privilege. I am a product of opportunity.

February 1975

Let nobody think that cuts in government expenditure can be made easily or painlessly because they cannot ... Civil servants too have wives and families, and civil servants too have to have consideration.

1976

Britain has now come to the end of the present road. The rest of the world knows it. The rest of the world is very sorry, but the rest of the world regrets that it is unable to oblige any longer.

Ibid.

Please don't applaud – it may irritate your neighbour.

Conservative Party Conference, October 1981

I think Churchill would be appalled at the Thatcher government.

On Thatcher

Whatever the lady does is wrong. I do not know of a single right decision taken by her.

Ibid.

There's a lot of people I've encouraged and helped to get into the House of Commons. Looking at them now, I'm not so sure it was a wise thing to do.

1989

My mission is humanitarian. Therefore it in no way represents the British government.

Former Prime Minister on his mission to release Western hostages in Baghdad, 1990

You don't have to leave No. 10 in tears.

Independent on Sunday, 23 January 1990

Out go the estate-owners, in come the estate agents.

September 1990

Rejoice, Rejoice!

Upon hearing the news of Margaret Thatcher's resignation, November 1990

Do you know what Margaret Thatcher did in her first Budget? Introduced VAT on yachts! It somewhat ruined my retirement.

28 November 1992

I saw him [Norman Tebbit] in the members' lobby trying to persuade new members to vote against the government.

1993

A tragedy for the party. He's got no ideas, no experience and no hope.

On William Hague's election to the leadership of the Conservative Party, 1997

It is most appropriate that I make the final points of my statement and my final remarks in the House about Europe. I have been a committed European since my Oxford days. My pro-European outlook was reinforced by my wartime experiences. In 1945, as both the victors and the vanquished surveyed the devastation wrought upon the continent, it became obvious that Europe could not afford another war ... In the modern world it is only right that we should share our sovereignty with our European neighbours, for the greater benefit of all ... I have no doubt whatever that a united Europe is here to stay. I believe that it is in British interests, and I believe that we should do everything that we can to help it and to help its people. We shall then be helping ourselves as a people and as a country, and we shall be supporting our own continent. That will be for the good not only of Europe as a whole, but of the world.

House of Commons Farewell Speech, 9 May 2001

Robert Heinlein

1907–88; American science-fiction writer

An armed society is a polite society.

Beyond This Horizon (1942)

Peter Hennessy

b. 1947; political historian

He seemed like a benign and decent beached whale washed up on the harder shores of modern Conservatism.

On R. A. Butler, 1987

Patrick Henry
1736–99; American revolutionary leader

Is life so dear, or peace so sweet, as to be purchased at the price of chains and slavery? Forbid it, Almighty God! I know not what course others may take; but as for me, give me liberty or give me death.
> Speech, 23 March 1775

The constitution is not an instrument for government to restrain the people, it is an instrument for the people to restrain the government – lest it come to dominate our lives and interest.
> Attributed

We are not weak, if we make proper use of those means which the God of nature hath placed in our power ... The battle, sir, is not to the strong alone; it is to the vigilant, the active, the brave.
> Attributed

I have disposed of all my property to my family. There is one thing more I wish I could give to them, and that is the Christian religion. If they had that and I had not given them one cent, they would be rich. If they have not that, and I had given them the world, they would be poor.
> Last Will and Testament (20 November 1798), as quoted in *Patrick Henry: Life, Correspondences and Speeches* (1891) by William Wirt Henry, Vol. H

Auberon Herbert
1838–1906; British philosopher

If government half a century ago had provided us with all our dinners and breakfasts, it would be the practice of our orators today to assume the impossibility of our providing for ourselves.
> Attributed

Nick Herbert

b. 1963; Conservative MP 2005–, Justice Minister 2010–12

Whether it was Magna Carta in 1215, the Bill of Rights in 1689, the Great Reform Act of 1832 or the Representation of the People Acts in the nineteenth and twentieth century, it is Parliament which has by popular will secured liberty and equality. It was Parliament which defended the right to trial by jury. It was Parliament which abolished the slave trade and the death penalty. It was Parliament which gave equal voting rights to women, and legalised homosexuality. In more recent times it was Parliament which blocked the government's plans for 90- and then 42-days' pre-charge detention. I do not profess that Parliament has been on the right side of every argument, or that legislators always get it right – far from it. But when Parliament falls short, it is accountable to the people whose rights and responsibilities are affected, in a way that the courts are not.

'Rights without responsibilities – a decade of the Human Rights Act', London 2008

Joseph Hergesheimer

1880–1954; American writer

No one can walk backwards into the future.

The Three Black Pennies (1917)

Michael Heseltine

b. 1933; Conservative MP 1970–2001, Cabinet minister 1979–86, 1990–97

The Red Flag was never flown throughout these islands yet, nor for a thousand years has the flag of any other alien creed.

1976

Our way depends on exhortation, incentive, encouragement and reward in a free society. Labour's way depends on control, constraint, compulsion in a command economy. In our society you persuade people to give of their best. In their society a sulky, resentful, bitter people comply, as their choice to do otherwise dies with the crushing of their hopes. Our way throughout history has powered a great and free society. Their way has powered the tyrannies. The Labour way gives power to the state, trusts no one, offers no faith. Our way puts faith in people, leaves power with the people, and therefore, trusts the people.

Ibid.

You cannot restore our cities while running down our countryside.

1977

When Michael Foot decries the judges, does he wonder that the young criminal gets the message? Are Labour Cabinet ministers who stand shoulder to shoulder in the picket lines really free from all guilt when violence later erupts around the heads of our long suffering police?

Ibid.

Throughout history under every system those who exercised power and responsibility enjoyed privileges beyond the means of the people at large. The only distinction that I would draw is that in a free enterprise system those who enjoy the privileges expect to pay for them themselves, whilst under a Socialist system those who enjoy the privileges are expert at finding someone else to pay for them.

Ibid.

I knew that 'He who wields the knife never wears the crown'.

1986

The market has no morality.

27 June 1988

Polluted rivers, filthy streets, bodies bedded down in doorways are no advertisement for a prosperous or caring society.
Conservative Party Conference, 10 October 1989

The Tory recognises the contrast between laissez-faire and noblesse oblige.
The Observer, 18 March 1990

I am persuaded that I now have a better prospect than Mrs Thatcher of leading the Conservatives to a fourth electoral victory and preventing the calamity of a Labour government. 14 November 1990 She has made a remarkable contribution to Britain's history and has led this country with great distinction in the 1980s.
BBC TV news, 22 November 1990

The essence of being a Prime Minister is to have large ears.
Interview on Radio 4, 1990

I went up the greasy pole of politics step by step.
After his challenge for leadership of the Conservative Party, 1990

If I have to intervene to help British companies, I'll intervene before breakfast, before lunch, before tea and before dinner. And I'll get up the next morning and I'll start all over again.
Conservative Party Conference, 7 October 1992

The self-appointed king of the gutter.
On Neil Kinnock

A one-man band who has transformed a party without a leader into a leader without a party ... And he was a leader with more answers than there were questions, and more news conferences than there were newspapers.
On Paddy Ashdown, 1992

Karl Hess

1923–94; American libertarian, editor, speechwriter and philosopher

Libertarianism is the view that each man is the absolute owner of his own life, to use and dispose of it as he sees fit; that all man's social actions should be voluntary and that respect for every other man's similar and equal ownership of life and, by extension, the property and fruits of that life, is the ethical basis of a humane and open society. In this view, the only function of law or government is to provide the sort of self-defence against violence that an individual, if he were powerful enough, would provide for himself.

Quoted by J. Tuccille in *Radical Libertarianism* (1970)

Gertrude Himmelfarb

b. 1922; political philosopher

Liberals have always known that power tends to corrupt and absolute power tends to corrupt absolutely ... [We] are now discovering that absolute liberty also tends to corrupt absolutely.

On Looking into the Abyss (1994)

A liberty that is divorced from tradition and convention, from morality and religion, that makes the individual the sole repository and arbiter of all values and puts him in an adversarial relationship to society and the state – such a liberty is a grave peril to liberalism itself. For when that liberty is found wanting, when it violates the moral sense of the community or is incompatible with the legitimate demands of society, there is no moderating principle to take its place, no resting place between the wild gyrations of libertarianism and paternalism.

Ibid.

Thomas Hobbes
1588–1679; philosopher

How could a state be governed ... if every individual remained free to obey or not to obey the law according to his private opinions?
Leviathan (1651)

Liberties depend on the silence of the law.
Ibid.

Intemperance is naturally punished with diseases; rashness, with mischance; injustice, with violence of enemies; pride, with ruin; cowardice, with oppression; and rebellion, with slaughter.
Ibid.

For the laws of nature (as justice, equity, modesty, mercy, and, in sum, doing unto others as we would be done to) of themselves, without the terror of some power, to cause them to be observed, are contrary to our natural passions, that carry us to partiality, pride, revenge and the like.
Ibid.

[in a state of nature] No arts; no letters; no society; and which is worst of all, continual fear and danger of violent death; and the life of man, solitary, poor, nasty brutish and short.
Ibid.

Eric Hoffer
1902–83; American author

I doubt if the oppressed ever fight for freedom. They fight for pride and power: the power to oppress others. The oppressed want above all to imitate their oppressors; they want to retaliate.
The True Believer (1951)

It is to escape the responsibility for failure that the weak so eagerly throw themselves into grandiose undertakings.

Ibid.

We clamour for equality chiefly in matters in which we cannot ourselves hope to obtain excellence.

The Passionate State of Mind (1955)

No matter how noble the objectives of a government, if it blurs decency and kindness, cheapens human life, and breeds ill will and suspicion – it is an evil government,

Ibid.

We cannot win the weak by sharing our wealth with them. They feel our generosity as oppression.

The Ordeal of Change (1963)

There can be no freedom without freedom to fail.

Ibid.

Douglas Hogg

b. 1945; Conservative MP 1979–2010, Cabinet minister 1995–97

Beef is a perfectly safe and a good product.

As Agriculture Minister, 1995

Oliver Wendell Holmes Jr

1841–1945; American jurist

The life of the law has not been logic; it has been experience. The law embodies the story of a nation's development through many centuries, and it cannot be dealt with as if it contained the axioms and corollaries of a book of mathematics.

The Common Law (1881)

Homer

c.8th century BC; Greek poet

Without a sign, his sword the brave man draws
And asks no omen but his country's cause.
The Iliad

For a better and higher gift than this there cannot be, when
with accordant aims man and wife have a home. Great grief
is it to foes and joy to friends; but they themselves know its
meaning.
The Odyssey

Sidney Hook

1902–89; American social philosopher

To silence criticism is to silence freedom.
New York Times, 30 September 1951

Sir John Hoskyns

b. 1927; businessman, Head of Margaret Thatcher's Policy Unit 1979–82

The Tory Party never panics, except in a crisis.
Sunday Times, 19 February 1989

Michael Howard

b. 1941; Member of Parliament 1983–2010, Home Secretary 1993–97,
Leader of the Conservative Party 2003–05, Member of the House of
Lords 2010–

To spend many years in prison for a crime you did not commit
is both a terrible thing and one for which release from prison
and financial recompense can make amends. Even this injustice
cannot be compared to the icy comfort of a posthumous

pardon. We cannot but be relieved that the death penalty was not available when we consider the irreparable damage which would have been inflicted on the criminal justice system in this country had innocent people been executed.

1994

'I've got my rights' is the verbal equivalent of two-fingers to authority. There is now a palpable sense of outrage that 'so-called' human rights have tipped the balance of justice in favour of the criminal and the wrong-doer – rather than the victim and the law abider.

On human rights, 10 January 2003

An increase in the number of criminals in prison leads to a large fall in crime.

Lecture in London, 2003

I wasn't born into the Conservative Party. I chose it. I chose it because I thought, as I still do, that it offers Britain its brightest future.

Michael Howard's campaign launch, 30 October 2003

Political correctness is, in essence, about power. It is someone telling someone else what to do, how to behave, how to speak, how to think ... sometimes there comes a limit to seeing the other person's point of view.

Speech in Stafford on 'political correctness', 26 August 2004

West Side Story may have been written by an American at the tail end of the 1950s, but these attitudes are all too prevalent in British society today.

On personal responsibility over socio-economic factors in criminal behaviour, 10 August 2004

I was born and grew up in South Wales. As you may have heard, we've just been left off the new EU map. I know people in Brussels feel strongly about Neil Kinnock, but I really do think that is going too far.

Conservative Party Conference, 5 October 2004

Tony Blair has been all talk. He gets swept away with his rhetoric and his dreams. He's told us about the Euro being our 'destiny.' Well, you know, most people don't actually want a date with destiny. They just want a date with a dentist.

Ibid.

The first problem I'll get a grip on is crime. The gloves will come off. What Giuliani did in New York, what Ray Mallon did in Middlesbrough, we'll do for the whole of Britain. A war on crime.

Ibid.

Too many people now believe that they are no longer responsible for their actions. It's always someone else's fault. And while we've let responsibility decline, we've allowed 'rights' to proliferate. You hear it all the time: 'I've got my rights.' The verbal equivalent of two fingers to authority.

Ibid.

It's time to bring powers back to Britain. There's a word for it – accountability. That's what most people want.

Ibid.

No Conservative Home Secretary will ever say 'there is no obvious limit to legal immigration'.

Ibid.

I am a Conservative because I believe that if people are given a choice, they will make the right decision for themselves and their families.

Ibid.

My father told me Britain was the best country in the world. I think it was. And I think it still is. But I know we could be doing so much better. And it's because I think I can help make things better that I am standing before you today. Put simply, I'm here so I can give back to Britain a tiny fraction of what Britain has given to me.

Ibid.

No one should be over-powerful: not ministers; not trade unions; not corporations; not the European Union. Wherever we see bullying by the over-mighty, we must stand up to it. Wherever we see one group flicking two fingers to the law, we must fight back. We must never forget that our duty is to stand up for those who do the right thing. It is our responsibility to protect their freedoms – whoever they are, wherever they live, whatever their background.

Conservative Party Conference, 6 October 2005

This is a great party – the longest standing, most successful party in the history of democracy. There has been no other party that has done so much or achieved so much as ours. We are its trustees.

Ibid.

At its best, we have a party broad and generous, broad in appeal and generous in outlook – a party capable of representing all Britain and all Britons.

Ibid.

I think the Lib Dems have tended to campaign in Labour areas by suggesting that they're quite like the Labour party only a bit nicer, and tended to campaign in Conservative areas by suggesting they're quite like the Conservatives but a bit nicer.

11 May 2011

Sir Gerald Howarth

b. 1947; Conservative MP 1983–92, 1997–, International Security
Strategy Minister 2010–12

I fear the playing field is not being levelled I believe the
pendulum is swinging so far the other way, and there are plenty
in the aggressive homosexual community who see this as but a
stepping stone to something even further.

Equal marriage debate, House of Commons, 20 May 2013

Geoffrey Howe

b. 1926; Conservative MP 1964–66, 1970–92, Chancellor of the
Exchequer 1979–83, Foreign Secretary 1983–89, Leader of the House
of Commons 1989–90

Britain is poised today on the brink of hyper-inflation. It could
destroy our society, as it did in Germany in the 1920s. There
is only a wafer-thin majority of error between our present
condition and British inflation of 50 and 100 per cent a year …
that is why it is of such paramount importance for us to come to
grips with this present inflation.

1975

Phrases like 'catching up' and 'cost of living increase' which trip
off the tongue of many negotiators should be on the way out. In
the not too distant future, the notion of automatic pay increase
must become as exceptional as it was novel a generation ago.

As Chancellor of the Exchequer, 1982

Inflation is a great moral evil. Nations which lose confidence in
their currency lose confidence in themselves.

The Times, July 1982

The British disease is considering others more responsible than
ourselves.

As Chancellor of the Exchequer, 1986

The future, where most of us are destined to spend the rest of our lives.

Interview for *A Week in Politics*, Channel 4, 1986

I believe both the Chancellor and the Governor are cricketing enthusiasts so I hope there will be no monopoly of cricketing metaphors. It's rather like sending your opening batsmen to the crease only for them to find that before the first ball is bowled, their bats have been broken by the team captain. The time has come for others to consider their own response to the tragic conflict of loyalties with which I have myself wrestled for perhaps too long.

Resignation speech to the House of Commons, 13 November 1990

Margaret Thatcher was beyond argument a great Prime Minister. Her tragedy is that she may be remembered less for the brilliance of her many achievements than for the recklessness with which she later sought to impose her own increasingly uncompromising views.

1994

If the Conservative party is losing its head, a heavy responsibility now rests with Labour and the Liberal Democrats to hold their nerve. In the complex and interdependent world we inhabit today, to walk away from the European Union into the unknown would be a very dangerous choice indeed.

On an in–out EU referendum, *The Observer*, 18 May 2013

David Howell

b. 1936; Conservative MP 1966–97, Cabinet minister 1979–83

That speech must have affected every thinking Conservative MP and many others as well.

On Geoffrey Howe's resignation speech, precipitating Margaret Thatcher's downfall, 1990

Elbert Hubbard

1856–1915; American writer, publisher, artist and philosopher

Every tyrant who has lived has believed in freedom – for himself.

Attributed

David Hume

1711–76; philosopher

Nothing appears more surprising to those who consider human affairs with a philosophical eye, than the ease with which the many are governed by the few.

Essays: Of the First Principles of Government (1742)

Douglas Hurd

b. 1930; Conservative MP 1974–97, Cabinet minister 1985–95

The United Nations should not be called on to deal with every situation regardless of the circumstances or the prospects of success … The way to build up its reputation is to encourage it to take on those activities it can do, and refuse those things which are at present beyond its power.

The UN, A Conservative Analysis, CPC (1967)

There is a market for medical services as far as for any other commodity. We must let the demand find its own level by the free play of the market.

Character in *The Smile on the Face of the Tiger* (1969)

It will be a long road back.

After the February 1974 general election

There's so much more to nick.

As Home Secretary, giving his explanation for increases in crime

The low price and high purity of the drugs being peddled on London streets are grim indications of the amount of drugs still reaching this country and there are no signs of crack being widely used in London yet.

1986

There's a lot of overcrowded prisons in the south, and we're planning a new one.

As Home Secretary, 1988

The family is our first defence against crime. For too long in this country we have pushed parental responsibility to the sidelines.

Ibid., 1989

This is the last speech in the last debate on the Maastricht treaty.

As Foreign Secretary closing the debate on Maastricht, 1992

The survival of the Conservative government is not at stake, what is at stake is the survival of a credible foreign policy.

As Foreign Secretary on the Maastricht Treaty, 1992

To expect the Liberals to control Labour would be like asking Dad's Army to restrain the Mongol hordes.

1992

Because you can't help everybody, it doesn't mean you can't help somebody.

On the decision to bring a wounded five-year-old girl from Sarajevo to London for treatment

There is I think a real danger that, egged on by the media, all parties in this House, all of us, may play out the old play, not realising that beyond the footlights half the audience has crept away and the other half is sitting there in mounting irritation.

15 November 1995

Henry Hyde

1924–2007; US Republican Congressman

Abortion is the killing of an innocently inconvenient human life.

US News & World Report, 4 May 1981

Balancing the Budget is a fundamental condition of governing. For most of the nation's history, balancing budgets in peacetime was assumed as a normal operating procedure.

USA Today, 26 January 1995

I

Michael Ivens
1924–2001; business leader

I believe that Conservatism suffers great damage if it identified
with an illiterate pseudo-Darwinism of competitive nature, red
in tooth and claw.
   1988

J

Andrew Jackson
1767–1845; US President 1829–37

Peace, above all things, is to be desired, but blood must
sometimes be spilled to obtain it on equable and lasting terms.
    Attributed

Robert H. Jackson
1892–1954; US Attorney General 1940–41

It is not the function of the government to keep the citizen
from falling into error; it is the function of the citizen to keep
the government from falling into error.
    Attributed

James VI & I
1566–1625; King of Scotland 1567 and England and Wales 1603

I will govern according to the commonweal but not according
to the common will.
    Address to the House of Commons, 1621

Anthony de Jasay
b. 1925; Hungarian-born philosopher and journalist

People who live in states have as a rule never experienced the
state of nature and vice-versa, and have no practical possibility
of moving from the one to the other ... On what grounds,
then, do people form hypotheses about the relative merits

of state and state of nature? … My contention here is that preferences for political arrangements of society are to a large extent produced by these very arrangements, so that political institutions are either addictive like some drugs, or allergy-inducing like some others, or both, for they may be one thing for some people and the other for others.

The State (1985)

Thomas Jefferson
1743–1826; US President 1801–09

Experience hath shewn, that even under the best forms [of government] those entrusted with power have, in time, and by slow operations, perverted it into tyranny.

Preamble to a Bill for the more general diffusion of knowledge, 1778

The legitimate powers of government extend to such acts only as they are injurious to others.

Notes on the State of Virginia (1781–93)

I am not a friend to a very energetic government. It is always oppressive.

Letter to James Madison, 1787

A little rebellion now and then … is a medicine necessary for the sound health of government.

Ibid.

The tree of liberty must from time to time be refreshed with the blood of tyrants and patriots. It is its natural manure.

To William Stephens Smith, 1787

I have no ambition to govern men. It is a painful and thankless office.

To John Adams, 1796

Delay is preferable to error.
>   Letter to George Washington, 1792

Whenever a man has cast a longing eye on offices, a rottenness begins in his conduct.
>   To T. Coxe, 1799

I swear upon the altar of God, eternal hostility to every form of tyranny over the mind of man.
>   To Dr Benjamin Rush, 23 September 1800

It is error alone which needs the support of government. Truth can stand by itself.
>   1804

The man who never looks into a newspaper is better informed than he who reads them, inasmuch as he who knows nothing is nearer to truth than he whose mind is filled with falsehoods and errors.
>   1807

The freedom and happiness of man ... are the sole objects of all legitimate government.
>   To Thaddeus Kosciusko, 1810

Never spend your money before you have it.
>   Letter to his granddaughter Cornelia, c.1811

I would rather be exposed to the inconveniences attending too much liberty than to those attending too small a degree of it.
>   To Archibald Stuart, 1811

I place economy among the first and most important virtues, and public debt as the greatest of dangers ... We must make our choice between economy and liberty, or profusion and servitude. If we can prevent the government from wasting the

labours of the people under the pretence of caring for them, they will be happy.
> To William Plumer, 21 July 1816

We must make our election between economy and liberty, or profusion and servitude.
> Letter to Samuel Kercheval, 1816

All authority belongs to the people.
> To Spencer Roane, 1821

… lawyers, whose trade it is to question everything, yield to nothing and to talk by the hour.
> *Autobiography* (1821)

The constitutions of most of our States assert that all power is inherent in the people; that … it is their right and duty to be at all times armed.
> Letter to John Cartwright, 1824

Nothing … is unchangeable but the inherent and unalienable rights of man.
> Ibid.

To compel a man to subsidise with his taxes the propagation of ideas which he disbelieves and abhors is sinful and tyrannical.
> On 'Big Government'

The price of liberty is eternal vigilance.
> Attributed

Douglas Jerrold
1803–57; English dramatist and writer

Dogmatism is puppyism come to its full growth.
> *Wit & Opinions* (1858)

Boris Johnson

b. 1964; Member of Parliament 2001–8, Mayor of London 2008–

[I am] a wise guy playing the fool to win.
Sunday Times, 16 July 2000

Maybe the Tories would do better, and be in a position to act Right, if they began by talking Left, by explaining the minimal Tory view of the state and society. Because no one looking at the Thatcherites' spending record could be in any doubt: those people thought there was such a thing as society.
Daily Telegraph, 30 November 2000

This is the government that promised to build a 'New Britain', that told us that 'things could only get better', and what was their salient commitment to the nation yesterday, apart from some hoary old bilge about drunken yobbery? It was to pick on a small group of a few thousand eccentrics who like to potter around the countryside on their horses, endlessly breaking their collarbones, and to tell them that whatever they're doing, they mustn't. This is government of the fox, for the fox, by the fox.
Ibid., 7 December 2000

I was at this party in Islington the other day and we were all glugging back the champagne, and suddenly I could resist it no longer. The urge rose within me, as though some genie had seized the diaphragm. 'Hague,' I roared. 'Haguey! Don't you think he's absolutely right to say this stuff about crime? Isn't he spot on?' And their eyes bulged like the very crustaceans on the canapés.
Ibid., 20 December 2000

Among the many reasons for mourning the passing of Auberon Waugh is that he will not be here to witness the final obliteration of hunting by the Labour Party … If I were not a Tory, I think I would become one on this issue alone.
Ibid., 18 January 2001

Hunting is crucial to Labour, because it gives some contour to the semolina-like blob of Tony Blair's ideology. For the millions of Labour voters who have been depressed by the government's failures in the public services, it is one of the few overt chances they will get for class warfare; and conversely the quarrel over hunting enables Labour ministers to caricature their opponents as tweed-wearing Waugh-reading defenders of atavism.

Ibid.

Devolution is causing all the strains that its opponents predicted, and in allowing the Scots to make their own laws, while free-riding on English taxpayers, it is simply unjust. The time will come when the Scots will discover that their personal care for the elderly is too expensive, and they will come, cap in hand to Uncle Sugar in London. And when they do, I propose that we tell them to hop it.

Ibid., 1 February 2001

There is one measurement I hesitate to mention, since the last time I did, I am told, the wife of the editor of *The Economist* cancelled her subscription to the *Daily Telegraph* in protest at my crass sexism. It is what is called the Tottometer, the Geiger counter that detects good-looking women. In 1997, I reported these were to be found in numbers at the Labour conference. Now – and this is not merely my own opinion – the Tories are fighting back in a big way.

The Spectator, 10 February 2001

No one obeys the speed limit except a motorised rickshaw.

Daily Telegraph, 12 July 2001

Yes, cannabis is dangerous, but no more than other perfectly legal drugs. It's time for a rethink, and the Tory party – the funkiest, most jiving party on Earth – is where it's happening.

Ibid.

If this is war, let's win it. Let's fly with whatever it takes to the mountain eyrie of Bin Laden, winkle him out, and put him on trial. If we can find good evidence that he is guilty, and he puts up any resistance, then let's not even bother with the judicial process. Let's find the scum who did this and wipe them off the face of the Earth.

Ibid., 20 September 2001

I don't see why people are so snooty about Channel 5. It has some respectable documentaries about the Second World War. It also devotes considerable airtime to investigations into lap dancing, and other related and vital subjects.

Ibid., 14 March 2002

The royal family are living memorials, the history of the country written in their DNA, a bit like the inscriptions on the Menin Gate. Unlike the Menin Gate, thanks to human reproduction, those genes can go on forever.

Ibid., 4 April 2002

We are still the second most important country on Earth. The trick of maintaining such influence, of course, is to go around pretending to be very bumbling and hopeless and self-deprecating, a skill at which we excel.

Ibid., 11 April 2002

Nor do I propose to defend the right to talk on a mobile while driving a car, though I don't believe that is necessarily any more dangerous than the many other risky things that people do with their free hands while driving – nose-picking, reading the paper, studying the A–Z, beating the children, and so on.

1 August 2002

I forgot that to rely on a train, in Blair's Britain, is to engage in a crapshoot with the devil.

Daily Telegraph, 3 July 2003

A horse is a safer bet than the trains.
    Ibid.

I have as much chance of becoming Prime Minister as of being decapitated by a Frisbee or of finding Elvis.
    Daily Mail, 22 July 2003

The dreadful truth is that when people come to see their MP, they have run out of better ideas.
    Daily Telegraph, 18 September 2003

Give that man a handbag! And while you're at it, tell him to wear a powder blue suit and a pineapple coloured wig next time he wants to impersonate this century's greatest peace time Prime Minister.
    Lend Me Your Ears (2003)

There seems no reason to behave respectfully towards that little old woman coming out of the Post Office if you feel that she belongs to a culture that is alien from your own … Why not piss against the wall if you feel that it is not really your wall, but part of a foreign country.
    Ibid.

Mrs Thatcher pioneered a revolution that was imitated in one way or another, around the world.
    Ibid.

There is no need here to rehearse the steps of matricide. Howe pounced, Heseltine did his stuff. After it was all over, my wife, Marina, claimed she came upon me, stumbling down a street in Brussels, tears in my eyes, and claiming that it was as if someone had shot Nanny.
    Ibid.

We seem to have forgotten that societies need rich people, even sickeningly rich people, and not just to provide jobs for those who clean swimming pools and resurface tennis courts.

Ibid.

You know, whenever George Dubya Bush appears on television, with his buzzard squint and his Ronald Reagan side-nod, I find a cheer rising irresistibly in my throat. Yo, Bush baby, I find myself saying, squashing my beer can like some crazed red-neck. You tell 'em boy. Just you tell all those pointy-headed liberals where to get off.

Ibid.

As snow-jobs go, this beats the Himalayas... It is just flipping unbelievable. He is a mixture of Harry Houdini and a greased piglet. He is barely human in his elusiveness. Nailing Blair is like trying to pin jelly to a wall.

Reaction to the Hutton Report, *Daily Telegraph*, 29 January 2004

That is the best case for Bush; that, among other things, he liberated Iraq. It is good enough for me.

Daily Telegraph, 26 February 2004

Some readers will no doubt say that a devil is inside me; and though my faith is a bit like Magic FM in the Chilterns, in that the signal comes and goes, I can only hope that isn't so.

Ibid., 4 March 2004

If Amsterdam or Leningrad vie for the title of Venice of the North, then Venice – what compliment is high enough? Venice, with all her civilisation and ancient beauty, Venice with her addiction to curious aquatic means of transport, yes, my friends, Venice is the Henley of the South.

Ibid., 11 March 2004

Look the point is … er, what is the point? It is a tough job but somebody has got to do it.

On being appointed shadow Arts Minister, 7 May 2004

There is absolutely no one, apart from yourself, who can prevent you, in the middle of the night, from sneaking down to tidy up the edges of that hunk of cheese at the back of the fridge.

On the dangers of obesity, *Daily Telegraph*, 27 May 2004

My chances of being PM are about as good as the chances of finding Elvis on Mars, or my being reincarnated as an olive.

'You ask the questions', *The Independent*, 17 June 2004

I didn't see it, but it sounds barbaric. It's become like cock-fighting: poor dumb brutes being set upon each other by conniving television producers.

On *Big Brother*, *The Observer*, 20 June 2004

I will never vote to ban hunting. It is a piece of spite that has nothing to do with animal welfare, and everything to do with Blair's manipulation of rank-and-file Labour chippiness and class hatred.

Friends, Voters, Countrymen (2004)

On being sacked Ok, I said to myself as I sighted the bird down the end of the gun. This time, my fine feathered friend, there is no escape.

Ibid.

Voting Tory will cause your wife to have bigger breasts and increase your chances of owning a BMW M3.

During the Tory campaign trail, 2004

What's my view on drugs? I've forgotten my view on drugs.

Ibid.

I've got my fingers in several dykes.
> Conservative Party Conference, 6 October 2004

I advise you all very strongly – go for a run, get some exercise and have a beautiful day.
> Cornered by reporters asking about his affair after a morning run, 15 November 2004

I have not had an affair with Petronella. It is complete balderdash. It is an inverted pyramid of piffle. It is all completely untrue and ludicrous conjecture. I am amazed people can write this drivel.
> Denying accusations of his having an affair with Petronella Wyatt, *Mail on Sunday*, 7 November 2004

Nothing excites compassion, in friend and foe alike, as much as the sight of you ker-splonked on the tarmac with your propeller buried six feet under.
> On being sacked from the Tory frontbench, *Daily Telegraph*, 2 December 2004

My friends, as I have discovered myself, there are no disasters, only opportunities. And, indeed, opportunities for fresh disasters.
> On being sacked by Michael Howard, 2004

Vote Johnson, vote often – there is a ready supply of Johnsons waiting to step into whatever breaches are left in whatever constituencies.
> While out visiting his dad's Teignbridge constituency, 2005

Ken [Livingstone] doesn't think he's got anything to say sorry for and if that's really his feeling, then I think that he should stick to his guns.
> Opposing Ken Livingstone's apology for a 'Nazi' comment, February 2005

But here's old Ken – he's been crass, he's been insensitive and thuggish and brutal in his language – but I don't think actually, if you read what he said, although it was extraordinary and rude, I don't think he was actually anti-Semitic.

The Times, 17 February 2005

I love tennis with a passion. I challenged Boris Becker to a match once and he said he was up for it but he never called back. I bet I could make him run around.

Daily Express, 21 March 2005

I'm having Sunday lunch with my family. I'm vigorously campaigning, inculcating my children in the benefits of a Tory government.

Asked whether he was canvassing at Sunday lunchtime, *The Guardian*, 11 April 2005

Howard is a dynamic performer on many levels. There you are. He sent me to Liverpool. Marvellous place. Howard was the most effective Home Secretary since Peel. Hang on, was Peel Home Secretary?

On Michael Howard, *The Times*, 19 April 2005

Hello, I'm your MP. Actually I'm not. I'm your candidate. Gosh.

Canvassing in Henley, 2005

Terrible outbreak of afternoon kipping in Henley. Always in their dressing gowns, hard at it.

Ibid.

What we hate, what we fear, is being ignored.

On the fears of MPs, 21 April 2005

The trouble with campaigning in the wilds of Oxfordshire is that you lose touch with the main battle. I feel lost in the jungle, way up the Nong River, seventy-five clicks beyond the Do Long bridge.

The Guardian, 2 May 2005

Life isn't like coursework, baby. It's one damn essay crisis after another.

In an article titled 'Exams work because they're scary', *Daily Telegraph*, 12 May 2005

I'm kicking off my diet with a cheeseburger – whatever Jamie Oliver says, McDonald's are incredibly nutritious and, as far as I can tell, crammed full of vital nutrients and rigid with goodness.

While campaigning at McDonald's in Botley, Oxford, May 2005

If there is one thing wrong with us all these days, it is that we are so mollycoddled, airbagged and swaddled with regulations and protections that we have lost any proper understanding of risk. As long as tobacco is legal, people should be free to balance the pleasures and dangers themselves.

Daily Telegraph, 23 June 2005

I want now to reassure all smokers that in one way I am on their side. It is precisely my continued failure to take up smoking that leads me to oppose a ban on smoking in public places... Above all, a ban on smoking in public places substitutes the discretion of the state for the individual will, in a way that is morally sapping.

Ibid.

It is no use the Muslim Council of Great Britain endlessly saying that 'the problem is not Islam', when it is blindingly obvious that in far too many mosques you can find sermons of hate, and literature glorifying 9/11 and vilifying Jews.

Daily Telegraph, 14 July 2005

The proposed ban on incitement to 'religious hatred' makes no sense unless it involves a ban on the Koran itself.

Ibid., 21 July 2005

When is Little Britain going to do a sketch, starring Matt Lucas as one of the virgins? Islam will only be truly acculturated to our way of life when you could expect a Bradford audience to roll in the aisles at Monty Python's Life of Mohammed.

Ibid.

I got to page 1264 of *War and Peace*. It was really hotting up, but unfortunately I lost my copy.

September 2005

I'm backing David Cameron's campaign out of pure, cynical self-interest.

On the 2005 Conservative leadership contest, *The Independent*, 5 October 2005

I think I was once given cocaine but I sneezed so it didn't go up my nose. In fact, it may have been icing sugar.

Evening Standard, 17 October 2005

All politicians in the end are like crazed wasps in a jam jar, each individually convinced that they are going to make it.

On his political ambitions, November 2005

My ambition silicon chip has been programmed to try to scramble up this ladder, so I do feel a kind of sense that I have got to.

Ibid.

I have successfully ridden two horses for quite a long time. But I have to admit there have been moments when the distance between the two horses has grown terrifyingly wide, and I did momentarily come off.

Reflecting on his very public 2004 downfall, November 2005

[I have been propelled] as a fat German tourist may be transported by superior alpinists to the summit of Everest.
    Praising colleagues at *The Spectator* in his leaving speech,
    December 2005

We can be as nice as pie, we can take our ties off and break-dance down the esplanade and all wear earrings and all the rest of it. It won't make any difference to the electorate if they don't think we're going to offer a new and improved, basically Conservative approach to government.
    Conservative Party Conference, 2005

Celebrating. I do think there's every chance. There's a swing on.
    When asked what he will be doing the day after the election, 2005

There is no finer subject. I say that without prejudice to other subjects, which you can basically read in your bath.
    On the subject of classics, 2005

It's time they were ejected into outer space.
    On the Labour Party, 2005

I think they get a fair squeeze of the sauce bottle.
    Questioned by Michael Crick on his dedication to his political career
    and the Conservative Party, 2005

We will demonstrate that we are the party that cares about the older generation by propelling a man who is so full of vim he will give me a thrashing on the squash court and has nine-and-a-half grandchildren.
    Trying to get his dad elected in Teignbridge, 2005

For ten years we in the Tory party have become used to Papua New Guinea-style orgies of cannibalism and chief-killing, and so it is with a happy amazement that we watch as the madness engulfs the Labour Party.
    Daily Telegraph, 2006

I am far too terrified to dissent from the growing world creed of global warming.

Daily Telegraph, 2 March 2006

I'm like a greased panther, a coiled spring, all that suppressed kinetic energy.

Commenting on England v. Germany Legends match, 3 May 2006

What I would advise fans is to expect little and possibly they'll receive even less.

Ibid.

I'm a rugby player, really, and I knew I was going to get to him, and when he was about two yards away I just put my head down. There was no malice. I was going for the ball with my head, which I understand is a legitimate move in soccer.

On his tackle on German midfielder Maurizio Gaudino in a charity football match, May 2006

She [Polly Toynbee] incarnates all the nannying, high-taxing, high-spending, schoolmarminess of Blair's Britain. She is the defender and friend of everyone whose non-job has ever been advertised in the *Guardian* appointments page, every gay and lesbian outreach worker, every clipboard-toter and pen-pusher and form-filler whose function has been generated by mindless regulation. Polly is the high priestess of our paranoid, mollycoddled, risk-averse, airbagged, booster-seated culture of political correctness and 'elf 'n' safety fascism.

Daily Telegraph, 23 November 2006

There are not many Lib Dems in Parliament, but even in that tiny group they incarnate dozens of diametrically opposing positions. You want to know what the Lib Dem policy is on taxation, for instance, and you want to know whether you are for or against a 50 per cent tax rate. One half of your cerebrum thinks it quite right that the rich should pay more; the other lobe thinks tax is quite high enough already. You are a perfect

Lib Dem, a mass of contradictions, and your party supplies exactly what you are looking for.
Have I Got Views For You (2006)

It is utterly absurd that Labour should be calling on us all to remember the value of that inclusive word 'British', when it is the government's own devolution programme which has fomented the rising sense of Scottishness and Englishness.
Ibid.

We need an alternative, and one that doesn't just involve crucifying our landscape with wind farms which, even when they are in motion, would barely pull the skin off a rice pudding.
Ibid.

We should never forget that in asking people to vote for us we are essentially asking to take charge of taxation and spending, and that our prime duty is to bring a new and more sensible – and more Conservative – style of economic management … the public sector is continuing to expand, and Brown is taking ever more money from the private sector to fund this expansion, and therefore preventing its use in wealth creation or the generation of new jobs.
Ibid.

It is time for concerted cultural imperialism. They are wrong about women. We are right. We can't have them blowing us up. The deluded fanatics must be helped to a more generous understanding of the world. Female education is the answer to the global population problem. It is the ultimate answer to the problem of Islamic fundamentalist terrorism.
Ibid.

If we Tories wished to reverse just one year's growth in Whitehall, we would have to sack the equivalent of the entire population of Ilfracombe, the seaside town in Devon!
Ibid.

I have founded the Pie Liberation Front. Our campaign to smuggle traditional British food to schoolchildren begins next week. Will you be our honorary patron?

The Independent, 1 January 2007

We have all connived in the fiction that our kids are getting brighter, because that conceals the growing gulf in attainment between much of the maintained sector and the grammar schools/independent schools. The result is that the market has, inevitably, asserted itself, and in a way that is socially regressive.

Ibid.

The other day I was giving a pretty feeble speech when it went off the cliff and became truly abysmal. It was at some kind of founder's dinner for a university, and I had badly miscalculated my audience. I thought it was going to be a bunch of students, and when I saw the elite group of retired generals, former Telegraph editors and Nobel Prize-winning economists, all in black tie, with their wives, I desperately tried to extemporise something profound. There were some musty sepulchres set into the wall of the ancient hall, so I started burbling about social mobility in the eighteenth century and widening participation in universities today. Frankly, I thought my sermon was more or less ideal. I began some guff-filled sentence with the words, 'I am sure we all agree...' It seemed to go well, so I did it again. 'I am sure we all agree we need world-class skills...', I said, or something equally banal, at which point a man down the table shot to his feet and shouted, 'Well, I don't! I don't agree with what you are saying at all. It seems to me to be quite wrong for you to claim that we all agree when I don't agree.' And blow me down, he appeared to be wearing long purple vestments. It was, of course, Britain's most turbulent priest, the Bishop of Southwark. I realised I was being heckled by a blooming bishop, and from that moment on my speech was irretrievable. I told a long and rambling story about sheep, in the hope that the man of God would be appeased, and sat down. I did sniff him later on, and though there was an aroma of hot cassock he didn't seem notably drunk.

The Spectator, 27 January 2007

Here we are in one of the most depressed downs in southern England, a place that is arguably too full of drugs, obesity, underachievement and Labour MPs.

GQ, 2007

'Tee hee,' I said to myself as I took in the ludicrously arrogant Darth Vader-style snout. What was it saying, with the plutocratic sneer of that gleaming grille?
It was saying 'out of my way, small car driven by ordinary person on modest income. Make way for Murano!'

On test driving a Nissan Murano, *Life in the Fast Lane* (2007)

My hair has yet to induce epilepsy and cost considerably less than £400,000 to design.

When Boris's hair was compared to the new London 2012 Olympic logo, 9 June 2007

Statistically, I am due to be fired again.

When asked if he was due to be included in the latest Tory reshuffle, June 2007

It may be that the psychological effort needed to haul myself around into a more gaffe-free zone proves too difficult.

Ibid.

When I look at the streets of London I see a future for the planet, a model of cooperation and harmony between races and religions, in which barriers are broken down by tolerance, humour and respect – without giving way either to bigotry, or the petty balkanisation of the Race Relations industry.

July 2007

If you ask me my vision for London, let me say that one of the most important things I want is a city where Jacqui Smith feels safe enough to pop out and buy a kebab – at any time of day or night.

17 February 2008

Look, I wouldn't trust Harriet Harman's political judgement.

When told that Harriet Harman thought he had won the election for London Mayor, BBC News, 2 May 2008

I've always known my life would be turned into a farce. I'm just glad it's been entrusted to two such distinguished men of letters.

Postcard to Toby Young, in *The Spectator*, 3 May 2008

We either unleash a full-hearted attack on the nannying, mollycoddling, Harriet Harperson hopelessness of our times, or else too many of our children will grow up fat, unhappy, or violent; we will never win Wimbledon, and football will remain a game in which, in Gary Lineker's immortal words, twenty-two men run around for ninety minutes and then the Germans win.

Daily Telegraph, 1 July 2008

Hypocrisy is at the heart of our national character – without the oil of hypocrisy, the machinery of convention would simply explode.

Ibid.

I rubbed my eyes and emitted a sigh as tragic as Prince Charles on beholding the blueprints for the gherkin.

Daily Telegraph, 15 July 2008

Tesco, the destroyer of the old-fashioned high street, Tesco the slayer of small shops, Tesco through whose air-conditioned portals we are all sucked like chaff, as though hypnotised by some Moonie spell.

Ibid.

Had it been us staging the Games, I don't think we would necessarily have done the switcheroo with the girl with the braces.

> When asked whether he had any criticisms of the Beijing Olympic Games, *The Guardian*, 21 August 2008

Unlike the current occupant of the White House, he has no difficulty in orally extemporising a series of grammatical English sentences, each containing a main verb.

> Endorsing Barack Obama, *Telegraph* column, 21 October 2008

We're not Hobbits. I am not about building homes for Hobbits.

> On the average floor space in London homes, November 2008

Virtually every single one of our international sports were invented or codified by the British. And I say this respectfully to our Chinese hosts, who have excelled so magnificently at ping-pong. Ping-pong was invented on the dining tables of England in the nineteenth century and it was called wiff-waff!

> At the ceremonial passing of the Olympic flag from China to the UK, 2008

You great big quivering gelatinous invertebrate jelly of indecision, you marched your troops up to the top of the hill in October of [2007]. Show us that you've got enough guts to have an election 4 June. Gordon: Man or Mouse?!

> Enticing Gordon Brown to call an election for June 2009, *Wall Street Journal*, 3 January 2009

What is a gaffe? A gaffe is in the eye of the beholder.

> *Wall Street Journal*, 3 January 2009

We have the right kind of snow, just the wrong quantity.

> BBC Radio 2, 2 February 2009

You should not underestimate my militant determination to increase cycling.

> *New Statesman*, 26 February 2010

If Gordon Brown is on course to win the election, then Elvis Presley is on course to win *The X Factor* and Shergar to win the Grand National.

On Brown's chances of winning the general election, 1 March 2010

They are a bunch of euro-loving road-hump fetishists who are attempting like some defective vacuum cleaner to suck and blow at the same time.

On the Lib Dems, *Daily Telegraph*, 19 April 2010

Whatever type of Wall's sausage is contrived by this great experiment, the dominant ingredient has got to be conservatism. The meat in the sausage has got to be Conservative, I would say. With plenty of bread and other bits and pieces.

On the possibility of a coalition after the UK general election, BBC News, 7 May 2010

All those snooty Europhile politicians and journalists who sneered at us for our doubts should be forced to crawl in penitence to Dublin Castle, scourging themselves with copies of the Maastricht Treaty. We have been vindicated, and the least they can do is admit it.

Daily Telegraph, 13 December 2010

It is not just that I love skiing, and am more or less addicted to the joy of hurling myself down the slopes.

Ibid., 20 February 2011

I object furiously to the element of compulsion, not just because it offends the principles of liberty, but because the whole problem of politics over the past thirty years is that we have proceeded by central legislation rather than leaving decisions to individuals and to communities.

Ibid.

I will greatly miss Alan Johnson, not just because he is a nice guy but also for the satisfaction I used to get when I saw a headline saying 'Johnson in new gaffe' and realised it wasn't me.

Ibid., 23 January 2011

The two men look vaguely similar; they both appear to believe in the efficacy of Grecian 2000; they both favour long and rambling speeches on Socialist economic and political theory, with Col Gaddafi's efforts perhaps having a slight edge in logic and coherence.

Comparing Gordon Brown to Colonel Gaddafi, 28 February 2011

By all means let us have a referendum – the one we were promised, on the Lisbon EU Treaty.

28 February 2011

Whatever happens in the world, whatever the catastrophe, we approach it like some vast BBC reporter with an addiction to the first person singular. We just have to put ourselves at the centre of the story.

Remarks after the Japanese tsunami, 14 March 2011

Rugby is a fantastic way of letting off steam. At the end of a game of rugby, you sit in the changing room with the relief of one who has just survived being beaten up by the secret police.

29 March 2011

One of the great things about journalism is that if you are in doubt about what to write there is always space for knocking copy – and the more popular and well-loved the topic of your piece, the more acute the demand for someone who is willing to step up and put the boot in.

18 April 2011

We need to remember that we can't compete endlessly with other nations that set their income taxes substantially lower than ours. They will attract jobs, and investment. They may generate more tax – and they may even persuade their tennis champs to run that extra half yard.

4 July 2011

It would be an utter travesty to blame these events on the police. The police did not riot. The police did not loot or recklessly set fire to property. The police did not attack innocent bystanders.

Evening Standard, 9 August 2011

Spending an hour with the FT is like being trapped in a room with assorted members of a millennialist suicide cult. If their pundits are to be believed, the skies of the City will shortly be dark with falling bankers, and then for the rest of us it's back to the 1930s, with barrels for trousers, soup kitchens and buddy can you spare a dime.

Daily Telegraph, 14 October 2011

I have been asked to have a go in it myself but I think it would be electorally inadvisable.

On the new Olympic pool, 2012

Can I say anything good about Ken Livingstone? A long time ago he did some good things, but I can't now remember what any of them were.

4 May 2012

Today Lord Justice Leveson will be under huge pressure to propose some form of statutory control of the press. I hope and pray that the government will not take that backward step.

The Sun, 28 November 2012

Possibly the most deluded measure to come from Europe since Diocletian tried to fix the price of groceries across the Roman Empire.

On EU bonuses, 27 March 2013

I'm very attracted to it. I may be diverting from Tory party policy here, but I don't care.

On 24-hour drinking legislation

Will I throw my hat into the ring? It depends on what kind of ring it is and what kind of hat I have in my hand.

When asked by the *Oxford Mail* if he will stand for Leader of the Conservative Party

Some time before the end of August, I will grab a week's leave, like a half-starved sea lion snatching an airborne mackerel, and whatever happens that leave will not be taken in some boarding house in Eastbourne. It will not take place in Cornwall or Scotland or the Norfolk Broads. I say stuff Skegness. I say bugger Bognor. I am going to take a holiday abroad.

Refusing to take a holiday in Britain

It was not only a joy to take the hospitality of the royal box. It was a civic duty.

On his decision to watch the Wimbledon final from the royal box

We need to end the appalling tendency of the present Livingstone regime in City Hall to treat fare-dodging as a kind of glorious Che Guevara two-fingers to the capitalist conspiracy.

On fare-dodging under Ken Livingstone

Their policy on cake is pro-having it and pro-eating it.

Discussing Liberal Democrat policies

The President is a cross-eyed Texan warmonger, unelected, inarticulate, who epitomises the arrogance of American foreign policy.

On George W. Bush

The Lib Dems are not just empty. They are a void within a vacuum surrounded by a vast inanition.

On the Liberal Democrats

Dr Samuel Johnson

1709–84; lexicographer

Most of the misery which the defamation of blameless actions
or the obstruction of honest endeavours brings upon the world
is inflicted by men that propose no advantage to themselves
but the satisfaction of poisoning the banquet which they cannot
taste, and blasting the harvest which they have no right to reap.

The Rambler (1751)

That man is little to be envied whose patriotism would not gain
force upon the plain of Marathon, or whose piety would not
grow warmer among the mists of Iona.

Journey to the Western Isles of Scotland (1775)

A man is never more innocently involved than in the making of
money.

Attributed

It is better that some should be unhappy than that none should
be happy, which would be the case in a general state of equality.

Life of Samuel Johnson (1791)

Your levellers wish to level down as far as themselves; but they
cannot bear levelling up to themselves.

Ibid.

Robert Jones

1950–2007; Conservative MP 1983–97

Margaret Thatcher and Ted Heath both have a great vision. The
difference is that Margaret Thatcher has a vision that Britain
will one day be great again, and Ted Heath has a vision that one
day Ted Heath will be great again.

On Thatcher and Heath

Keith Joseph
1918–94; Conservative MP 1956–87, Cabinet minister 1970–74, 1979–86

Problems reproduce themselves from generation to generation. I refer to this as a cycle of deprivation.
1972

Incomes policy alone as a way to abate inflation caused by excessive money supply is like trying to stop water coming out of a leaky hose without turning off the tap.
Speech in Preston, 5 September 1974

People who could not tell a lathe from a lawnmower and have never carried the responsibilities of management never tire of telling British management off for its alleged inefficiency.
The Times, 9 August 1974

The balance of our population, our human stock, is threatened. A high and rising proportion of children are being born to mothers least fitted to bring children into the world and bring them up.
Speech in Birmingham, 19 October 1974

We need more inequality in order to eliminate poverty.
1975

Our human stock is threatened … These mothers … single parents from classes four and five are now producing a third of all births. If we do nothing, the nation moves towards degeneration.
Ibid.

Conservatism, like selfishness, is inherent in the human condition.
New Statesman, 1975

Our opponents are driven by their vision, a messianic vision
of the perfectibility of man. It may have been conceived
with fine intentions; it may have been born of a passion, but
it has become an engine of tyranny, impoverishment and
unemployment.

1976

Socialist short-cuts to Utopia only turn into blind alleys. Slum
and slump and siege.

Ibid.

The idea that all the ills of mankind – greed, violence,
corruption, cruelty, poverty – all stemmed from the institution
of private property and would disappear if the state owned
all, or nearly all, is against history, common sense and human
nature. These ills are as old as mankind. They are at their worst
where the state is strongest.

Ibid.

Oil will not save us, because by over manning we are blunting
our competitiveness faster than oil will make good. Unless
over manning is halted and corrected, no subsidies, no forced
investment, no sector linking parties, nothing will rescue
us from a stagnant and declining standard of living and
unemployment.

1977

Without competition the pursuit of profit is immoral and mere
exploitation.

1978

If we are going to be prosperous we need more millionaires and
more bankrupts.

House of Lords, 19 February 1988

There are no illegitimate children – only illegitimate parents.

1991

How on earth do the birds know it's a sanctuary?
Attributed

Bertrand de Jouvenel

1903–87; French philosopher, political economist and futurist

The more one considers the matter, the clearer it becomes that redistribution is in effect far less a redistribution of free income from the richer to the poorer, as we imagined, than a redistribution of power from the individual to the state.

The Ethics of Redistribution (1949)

K

Elie Kedourie

1926–92; British historian

If, making use of William James's distinction, we were to divide
Conservatives into those who are tender-minded and those who
are tough-minded, it is the latter whom Salisbury may be said
to represent and exemplify. And if, today, he seems to us a very
remote figure, this is not only because the assumptions and
conditions of British politics have changed utterly since his day,
but also because, during Baldwin's ascendancy and afterwards,
it is largely a tender-minded Conservatism which has set the
tone and dominated the Party's rhetoric.

Encounter (1972)

Conservatism follows and does not precede the existence of
a Conservative party. It is a natural attempt by a body with a
long continuous existence to articulate and make intelligible to
itself its own character.

1984

Jack Kemp

1935–2009; US Congressman

There are no limits on our future if we don't put limits on our
people.

6 April 1987

We don't believe children are just mouths to feed. They are
hearts, minds, and souls for our future. And they deserve our
protection not only after their birth, but before they are born.

Republican Convention 1992

John Fitzgerald Kennedy
1917–63; US President 1961–63

Those who make peaceful revolution impossible will make violent revolution inevitable.
> Attributed

If a free society cannot help the many who are poor, it cannot save the few who are rich.
> Inaugural speech, 20 January 1961

Let us never negotiate out of fear. But let us never fear to negotiate.
> Ibid.

Ask not what your country can do for you. Ask what you can do for your country.
> Ibid.

Liberty without learning is always in peril and learning without liberty is always in vain.
> 18 March 1963

Alan Keyes
b. 1950; American conservative political activist

Affirmative action is a betrayal of the principles of the civil rights movement.
> Attributed

Martin Luther King Jr
1929–68; American civil rights leader

The time is always right to do what is right.
> Attributed

Nothing in all the world is more dangerous than sincere ignorance and conscientious stupidity.

Strength to Love (1963)

Injustice anywhere is a threat to justice everywhere.

Ibid.

The ultimate measure of a man is not where he stands in moments of comfort and convenience, but where he stands at times of challenge and controversy.

Ibid.

I have a dream that one day on the red hills of Georgia the sons of former slaves and the sons of former slave-owners will sit down together at the table of brotherhood.

Washington DC, 1963

Rudyard Kipling

1856–1936; poet and writer

Take up the White Man's Burden.

1899

Politicians. Little tin gods on wheels.

On politicians

Russell Kirk

1918–94; American political theorist

Privilege, in any society, is the reward of duties performed.

Enlivening the Conservative Mind (1953)

Equality in the sight of God, equality before the law, security in what is one's own, participation in the common activities and consolations of society – these are the true natural rights.

Ibid.

The twentieth-century Conservative is concerned, first of all, for the regeneration of spirit and character – with the perennial problem of the inner order of the soul, the restoration of the ethical understanding, and the religious sanction upon which any life worth living is founding. This is conservatism at its highest.

Ibid.

The intelligent Conservative combines a disposition to preserve with an ability to reform.

Intelligent Woman's Guide to Conservatism (1957)

The better natures among us, surely, will be hard put ... to love America if it becomes a nation wholly mannerless, an uncivil society, in which generosity and charity are scorned as weakness, in which all great literature, and the whole stock of the moral imagination, is rejected out of a lust for the gratification of carnal appetites and a taste for second-hand violence and concupiscence.

Prospects for Conservatives (1989)

The Conservative of reflection will not be afraid to defend the manners and tastes of a gentle and generous nature ... in this industrial age.

Ibid.

Henry Kissinger

b. 1923; American Secretary of State 1973–77

Of all the men running, Richard Nixon is the most dangerous to have as President. I would never work for that man. That man is a disaster.

During Presidential election campaign, 1968

There cannot be a crisis next week. My schedule is already full.

1969

Power is the great aphrodisiac.

1971

You can't win through negotiations what you can't win on the battlefield.

1973

No foreign policy, no matter how ingenious, has any chance of success if it is borne on the minds of a few and carried in the hearts of none.

August 1973

We must learn to distinguish morality from moralising.

1976

The illegal we do immediately. The unconstitutional takes a little longer.

1977 (attributed)

History knows no resting places and no plateaux.

White House Years (1979)

The management of a balance of power is a permanent undertaking, not an exertion that has a foreseeable end.

Attributed

The statesman's duty is to bridge the gap between his nation's experience and his vision.

Years of Upheaval (1982)

In crises the most daring course is often the safest.

Ibid.

An Iranian moderate is one who has run out of ammunition.

1987

History has so far shown us only two roads to international stability: domination and equilibrium.

1991

Statesmen who base their policy on the expectation of recurrent miracles usually suffer shipwreck.

Newsweek, 27 September 1993

The main advantage of being famous is that when you bore people at dinner parties they think it is their fault.

1995 (attributed)

Dame Jill Knight

b. 1924; Conservative MP 1966–97

Anyone in his position needs to be whiter than white.

On Nelson Mandela, Radio Ulster, 1990

William Knudsen

1879–1948; leading American automotive industry executive

Germany has been transformed since my last visit several years ago … the Reich is the miracle of the twentieth century.

As President of General Motors, 1938

Helmut Kohl

b. 1930; German Chancellor 1982–98

I have been underestimated for decades. I have done very well that way.
1987

We Germans now have the historic chance to realise the unity of the Fatherland.
1990

Irving Kristol

1920–2009; American journalist

A welfare state, properly conceived, can be an integral part of a Conservative society.
The American Spectator (1977)

People need religion. It's a vehicle for a moral tradition. A crucial role. Nothing can take its place.
Two Cheers for Capitalism (1979)

New conservatism is anti-romantic in substance and temperament. Indeed, it regards political romanticism – and its twin, political utopianism – of any kind as one of the plagues of our age. This is but another way of saying it is a philosophical – political impulse rather than a literary – political impulse. Or, to put it still another way: its approach to the world is more 'rabbinic' than 'prophetic'.
Reflections of a Neoconservative (1983)

Neo-conservatives are unlike old Conservatives because they are utilitarians, not moralists, and because their aim is the prosperity of post-industrial society, not the recovery of a golden age.
Times Higher Educational Supplement, 1987

L

Norman Lamont

b. 1942; Conservative MP 1972–97, Cabinet minister 1989–93,
Chancellor of the Exchequer 1990–93

There is plenty of scope for the House of Commons to fulfil its
traditional functions of scrutinising and amending legislation.
Defending entry to the EEC, 1973

A price worth paying.
Answering criticism on the level of unemployment, 16 May 1991

The turn of the tide is sometimes difficult to discern. What we
are seeing is the return of that vital ingredient, confidence. The
green shoots of economic spring are appearing once again.
Conservative Party Conference, 9 October 1991

Je ne regrette rien.
Following UK withdrawal from the ERM, 1992

The Exchange Rate Mechanism is not an optional extra, an
add-on to be jettisoned at the first hint of trouble. It has been
and will remain at the heart of our macro-economic policy.
1992

All I want to say, particularly to our partners … is don't
push it, don't push it, because that isn't going to help us get it
through.
On the Maastricht Treaty, 1992

We give the impression of being in office but not in power.
House of Commons, 9 June 1993

Our ability to make our own laws without outside interference has gone.
　　1996

Ian Lang
b. 1940; Conservative MP 1979–97, Cabinet minister 1990–97

Karaoke Kinnock, the man who'll sing any song you want him to.
　　1992

Too many people have forgotten that it was he who led us to an election victory last year that many thought impossible.
　　On John Major, 1993

Job insecurity is a state of mind.
　　As President of the Board of Trade, 1995

Andrew Lansley
b. 1956; Conservative MP 1997–, Health Secretary 2010–12, Leader of the House of Commons 2012–

Look back to 1948 when the British Medical Association denounced Aneurin Bevan as 'a would-be Führer' for wanting them to join a National Health Service. And Bevan himself described the BMA as 'politically poisoned people'. A survey at the time showed only 10 per cent of doctors backed the plans ... But where would we be today if my predecessors had caved in?
　　Daily Telegraph, 27 January 2012

Ivan Lawrence
b. 1936; Conservative MP 1974–97

This is a man who will stop at nothing.
　　On Saddam Hussein during the Gulf Crisis, 1990

Nigel Lawson

b. 1932; Conservative MP 1974–92, Chancellor of the Exchequer 1983–89

The Conservative Party has never believed that the business of government is the government of business.

> 10 November 1981

I shall resist the temptation to dwell on the golden age of the '50s and '60s when I was a financial journalist. But I must say I am struck by the modern obsession with inevitably speculative forecasts of the short-term future, at the expense of informing the reader about what is actually happening in the present.

> As Chancellor of the Exchequer, 1984

One of the important things this government has tried to do is rehabilitate the idea of profit in political discourse. I don't think the man in the street ever thought that profit was a dirty word, but it had almost become a dirty word among the intelligentsia.

> As Chancellor of the Exchequer, 1986

In the next parliament, we aim to eliminate inflation altogether.

> Ibid.

I would not take too much notice of teenage scribblers in the City who jump up and down in an effort to get press attention.

> As Chancellor of the Exchequer, responding to economists' gloomy economic predictions

You don't make the poor rich by making the rich poor.

> As Chancellor of the Exchequer (quoting Barin Bauer, economist), 1987

The sharp deterioration has now come to an end.

> As Chancellor of the Exchequer, 1989

Inflation is a disease of money.
> 1989

He has an infallible knack for getting the wrong end of every stick.
> On Neil Kinnock

I think we've been treated to a dose of the sort of sanctimonious humbug which is characteristic of sections of the British press. It is the politics of envy and an awful lot of humbug. Everybody knows that people get paid all different salaries, that newspaper editors don't do all that badly, but it's a sort of nauseating form of demagoguery.
> Responding to criticisms of the directorships he accepted immediately after leaving office

I was a very convenient scapegoat for many people in the party because I had resigned and was expendable.
> Television interview, 1992

The heart of the matter is that the very nature of the European Union, and of this country's relationship with it, has fundamentally changed after the coming into being of the European monetary union and the creation of the eurozone, of which – quite rightly – we are not a part. That is why, while I voted 'in' in 1975, I shall be voting 'out' in 2017.
> On an EU referendum, *The Times*, 7 May 2013

Peter Lilley
b. 1943; Conservative MP 1983–

Of course nobody likes the Conservatives. They only vote for us because they think we are right.
> Attributed

Rush Limbaugh

b. 1951; US political commentator

Poverty and suffering are not due to the unequal distribution of goods and resources, but to the unequal distribution of capitalism.

The Way Things Ought to Be (1992)

I prefer to call the most obnoxious feminists what they really are: feminazis.

Ibid.

Abraham Lincoln

1809–65; US President 1861–65

The probability that we may fail in the struggle ought not to deter us from the support of a cause we believe to be just.

December 1839

Discourage litigation. Persuade your neighbour to compromise whenever you can. As a peacemaker the lawyer had a superior opportunity of being a good man. There will still be business enough.

c.1850

No man is good enough to govern another man without that other's consent.

16 October 1854

In all that the people can individually do well for themselves, the government ought not to interfere.

On government, c.1854

Those who deny freedom to others, deserve it not for themselves.

1856

Any people anywhere being inclined and having the power have the right to rise up and shake off the existing government, and force a new one that suits them better.

In support of Texas's secession from Mexico

Property is the fruit of labour; property is desirable; it is a positive good in the world. That some should be rich shows that others may become rich, and, hence, is just another encouragement to industry and enterprise.

On labour and industry

I will say then that I am not, nor have ever been in favour of bringing about in any way the social and political equality of the white and black races.

Campaigning for President, 1958

What is conservatism? Is it not adherence to the old and tried, against the new and untried?

27 February 1860

Even when you cease to be slaves, you are yet far removed from being placed on an equality with the white race. You are cut off from many of the advantages which the other race enjoys. It is better for us both to be separated.

As President, in a meeting with free Negro leaders, 1862

The central act of my administration, and the great event of the nineteenth century ... It is a momentous thing to be the instrument ... of the liberation of a race.

Referring to the Emancipation Proclamation, 1862

If my name ever goes into history, it will be for this act, and my whole soul is in it.

Signing the Emancipation Proclamation, 1863

Walter Lippmann

1889–1974; American intellectual and political commentator

Where all men think alike, no one thinks very much.
  Attributed

No a priori reasoning can anticipate the precise formulae
which will reconcile the varied interests of men ... Thus in
Plato's great scheme each man was assigned his station and
his duties; any architectural plan is necessarily based on the
same presumption. But Plato's scheme only worked in Plato's
imagination; never in the real world ... For the scheme implies
that men will remain content in the station which the visionary
has assigned to them. To formulate such plans is not to design a
society for real men. It is to re-create men to fit the design.
  The Good Society (1937)

Lord Liverpool

1770–1828; Prime Minister 1812–27

On peace our greatness as a nation completely and almost
wholly depends.
  29 February 1792

Not to protect the agricultural interest would be in reality to
discourage it.
  15 March 1815

Selwyn Lloyd

1904–78; Conservative MP 1945–76, Cabinet minister 1955–63,
Speaker of the House of Commons 1971–76

I do not speak any foreign language. Except in war, I have never
visited any foreign country. I do not like foreigners.
  1978

John Locke
1632–1704; philosopher

I have always thought the actions of men the best interpreters of their thoughts.
Attributed

The Care therefore of every man's Soul belongs unto himself, and is to be left unto himself. But what if he neglect the Care of his Soul? I answer, What if he neglects the Care of his Health, or of his Estate, which things are nearly related to the government of the Magistrate than the other? Will the magistrate provide by an express Law, That such a one shall not become poor or sick? Laws provide, as much as is possible, that the Goods and Health of Subjects be not injured by the Fraud and Violence of others; they do not guard them from the Negligence or Ill-husbandry of the Possessors themselves.
A Letter Concerning Toleration (1689)

Wherever law ends, tyranny begins.
Two Treatises of Government (1690)

Whenever the Legislators endeavour to take away, and destroy the Property of the People, or to reduce them to Slavery under Arbitrary Power, they put themselves into a state of War with the People, who are thereupon absolved from any farther Obedience ... [Power then] devolves to the People, who have a Right to resume their original Liberty, and, by the Establishment of a new Legislative (such as they shall think fit) provide for their own Safety and Security, which is the end for which they are in Society.
Second Treatise of Civil Government (1690)

The freedom of men under government is to have a standing rule to live by, common to every one of that society, and made by the legislative vested in it; a liberty to follow my own will in all things, when the rule prescribes not, and not to be subject to the inconsistent, uncertain, unknown arbitrary will of another man.

On government

M

Douglas MacArthur
1880–1964; American general

No man is entitled to the blessings of freedom unless he be vigilant in its preservation.
  Speech in Japan, 3 May 1948

It is fatal to enter any war without the will to win it.
  Republican National Convention, 1952

Thomas Babington Macaulay
1800–59; historian, critic and politician

An acre in Middlesex is better than a principality in Utopia.
  Lord Bacon (1837)

Free trade, one of the greatest blessings which a government can confer on a people, is almost in every country unpopular.
  On Mitford's *History of Greece*

The science of government is an experimental science and like all other experimental sciences it is generally working itself clearer and clearer and depositing impurity after impurity.
  On government

I have long been convinced that institutions purely democratic must, sooner or later, destroy liberty or civilisation or both.
  Letter to H. S. Randall, 1857

Those who compare the age in which their lot has fallen with a golden age which exists only in imagination, may talk of degeneration and decay; but no man who is correctly informed as to the past will be disposed to take a morose or desponding view of the present.

History of England 1841–61 (1848–59)

Joseph McCarthy
1908–57; US Senator

I have here in my hand a list of 205 ... members of the Communist Party and whom nevertheless are still working and shaping policy in the state department.

1950

It's the most unheard-of thing I've ever heard of.

1950s

McCarthyism is Americanism with its sleeves rolled.

1952

I think it is a shoddy, unusual thing to do to use the floor of the Senate to attack your opponent without any proof whatever.

Responding to criticism, 1956

David Maclean
b. 1953; Conservative MP 1983–2010

Most [street beggars] are Scottish and I've never met one yet who politely and gently asked for money ... There are no genuine beggars. Those who are in need have got all the social benefits they require ... Beggars are doing so out of choice because they find it more pleasant ... I always give them something – I give them a piece of my mind.

As a Home Office minister, 1997

Iain Macleod

1913–70; Conservative MP 1950–70, Cabinet minister 1952–63, 1970

The Conservative Party always in time forgives those who were wrong. Indeed, often, in time, they forgive those who were right.

The Spectator, 21 February 1964

Revolutions in this country, and especially within the Tory Party, are rarely plotted. They just happen.

Ibid., 30 July 1965

He is a waste paper basket, filled with lightly given promises and pledges.

On Harold Wilson

John F. Kennedy has described himself as an idealist without illusions. Harold Wilson is an illusionist without ideals.

Ibid.

Harold Macmillan

1894–1986; Conservative MP 1924–29, 1931–45, 1945–64, Prime Minister 1957–63

Housing is not a question of conservatism or socialism. It is a question of humanity.

September 1925

He enjoys prophesying the imminent fall of the capitalist system, and is prepared to play a part, any part, in its burial, except that of mute.

On Aneurin Bevan, speech in the House of Commons, 1934

Toryism has always been a form of paternal socialism.

1936

He is forever poised between a cliché and an indiscretion.
  On Anthony Eden

Indeed, let's be frank about it, some of our people have never
had it so good.
  Speech at Bedford, 20 July 1957

I thought the best thing to do was settle up these little
local difficulties, and then turn to the wider vision of the
Commonwealth.
  The Times, 8 January 1958, following the resignation of three Cabinet
  ministers

The wind of change is blowing through this continent whether
we like it or not, this growth of political consciousness is a
political fact.
  Speech to South African Parliament in Cape Town, 3 February 1960

As usual the Liberals offer a mixture of sound and original
ideas. Unfortunately, none of the sound ideas is original and
none of the original ideas is sound.
  1961

Events, dear boy, events.
  When asked what he most feared

First of all the Georgian silver goes, and then all that nice
furniture that used to be in the saloon. Then the Canalettos go.
  Speech to the Tory Reform Group mocking privatisation,
  8 November 1985

Selling the family silver.
  Referring to the privatisation of profitable nationalised industries,
  1986

Robert McNamara
1916–2009; American Secretary of Defense 1961–68

The major part of the US military task [in Vietnam] can be completed by the end of 1965.

As US Defense Secretary, 1962

James Madison
1751–1836; US President 1809–17

I believe there are more instances of the abridgement of the freedom of the people by gradual and silent encroachments of those in power than by violent and sudden usurpations.

Speech at the Virginia Convention to ratify the federal constitution, 1788

Magna Carta
1215

No freeman shall be taken, or imprisoned, or outlawed, or exiled, or in any way harmed, nor will we go upon him, nor will we send upon him, except by the legal judgement of his peers or by the laws of the land.
To none will we sell, no none deny or delay, right or justice.

Henry Sumner Maine
1822–88; British legal scholar

[A] formidable conception bequeathed to us by Rousseau is that of the omnipotent democratic state rooted in natural right; the state which has at its disposal everything which individual men value, their property, their persons, and their independence; the state which is bound to respect neither precedent nor prescription; the state which may make laws for its subjects ordaining what they shall drink or eat, and in what way they shall spend their earnings; the state which can confiscate all the land of the community, and which, if the effect on human motives is what may be expected to be, may force us to labour on it when the older incentives to toil have disappeared. Nevertheless this political speculation, of which the remote and indirect consequences press us on all sides, is of all speculations the most baseless. The natural condition from which it starts is a simple figment of the imagination.

Popular Government (1886)

Comte Joseph Marie de Maistre
1753–1851; French philosopher, writer, lawyer and diplomat

The more you examine the part human action plays in the formation of political constitutions, the clearer it becomes that it is effective only in an extremely subordinate role or as a simple instrument...

Attributed

The fundamentals of political constitutions exist before all written law.

Attributed

Lady Olga Maitland
b. 1944; Conservative MP 1992–97

Of course we are not patronising women. We are just going to explain to them in words of one syllable what it is all about.

Attributed

John Major

b. 1943; Conservative MP 1979–2001, Cabinet minister 1987–90,
Prime Minister 1990–97

Conservatives should welcome controls on prices and incomes,
even as a permanent feature of the economy.
> 1973

His idea of policy is to spend, spend, spend. He is the Viv
Nicholson of politics.
> Comparing Michael Foot to the 1960s pools winner

If the policy isn't hurting, it isn't working.
> 27 October 1989

It will take some time, it always does, to change the economy.
It's like turning the *Titanic* round, as you know.
> As Chancellor of the Exchequer, 1990

'If' is a very large preposition.
> 1990

Sustainable growth that is sustainable.
> Ibid.

I believe in the next ten years we will have to continue to make
changes that will genuinely produce across the whole of this
country a genuinely classless society.
> 23 November 1990

I'm not running as Son of Margaret Thatcher, I'm running as
myself on my own priorities and my own programme.
> Interview on *Walden*, 25 November 1990

I'm my own man.
> On becoming Prime Minister, 1990

You can't influence Europe's future from the terraces. You have
to be on the pitch and playing hard.
    Altrincham, 29 November 1990

Gentlemen, I think we had better start again somewhere else.
    Following the IRA attack on Downing Street, 7 February 1991

My aim for Britain in the Community can be simply stated. I
want us to be where we belong. At the very heart of Europe.
    Speech in Bonn, 11 March 1991

I've got it, I like it and with your help, I'm going to keep it.
    On the premiership, Conservative Party Conference, 11 October
    1991

We are not wholly an island, except geographically.
    1992

The chameleon of politics consistent only in his inconsistency.
    On Neil Kinnock, 1992

The matter of the timing of the Maastricht treaty is now
and will remain a matter for the British parliament and for
no one else.
    Edinburgh summit, 1992

Not tonight Josephine, we'll debate it at some other time.
    To John Smith, Leader of the Labour Party, during the Maastricht
    debate, 1992

This is becoming more fun than I had imagined.
    During the Maastricht debate, 1992

That part of it is behind us now ... I'm drawing a line under
the sand.
    Seeking to heal party divisions after the ratification of the Maastricht
    Treaty, 1992

I was under no illusions when I took Britain into the ERM. I said at the time that membership was no soft option. The soft option, the devaluer's option, the inflationary option, would be a betrayal of our future … there is going to be no devaluation, no realignment.

10 September, 1992, six days before Britain pulled out of the ERM

We secured stable exchange rates in the ERM – and we'll keep our position there.

1992

I respect and accept your decision not to stay on.

In his letter to the resigning Chancellor, Norman Lamont

One week before the election, the Labour Party start cuddling up to the Liberal Democrats for support. It is like leaning on candy floss.

1992

The Liberal Democrats are a Trojan horse to the Labour Party.

Ibid.

Society needs to condemn a little more and understand a little less.

Mail on Sunday, 21 February 1993

Fifty years from now, Britain will still be the country of long shadows on county cricket grounds, warm beer, invincible green suburbs, dog lovers, and – as George Orwell said – old maids bicycling to Holy Communion through the morning mist.

22 April 1993

I was in short trousers; we had ration cards; Hitler had been dead for only seven years. They were, I remember, happy days.

On the year *The Mousetrap* opened, 1993

I'm fit, I'm well, I'm here and I'm staying.
> Speech to the Conservative Women's Conference, 4 June 1993

It is time to get back to basics: to self-discipline and respect for the law, to consideration for others, to accepting responsibility for yourself and your family, and not shuffling it off on to the state.
> Conservative Party Conference, 8 October 1993

We don't want three more of the bastards out there spreading poison.
> On why he chose not to sack the Eurosceptic ministers in his party, 1994

I see public service as a duty and if you can serve, I believe you have an obligation to do so.
> Resignation statement, July 1995

In short, it is time to put up or shut up.
> Ibid.

Do I look nervous?
> Attributed

With the retirement of 'Dickie' Bird, something sad will have gone out of English cricket.
> 1996

He made a great contribution to public life, especially in France.
> At the funeral of President Mitterrand, 1996

Something that I was not aware had happened turned out to have happened.
> On the arms to Iraq scandal, 1996

Events made a monkey of us.
> Referring to the decision to join the ERM

A sound bite never buttered a parsnip.
>April 1997

He behaves like an agitated parrot with constipation. He is more funny than wise.
>On Frank Dobson

Like me or loathe me – please don't bind my hands.
>Appealing for unity in the Conservative Party, April 1997

Well, it's over, we lost.
>2 May 1997

When the curtain falls it is time to get off the stage.
>Resignation statement, 2 May 1997

I hope to get to the Oval in time for lunch.
>Last words as Prime Minister, 2 May 1997

In retrospect I think her behaviour was intolerable.
>On Margaret Thatcher's behaviour during his premiership, 10 August 1999

James Harris, 3rd Earl of Malmesbury
1807–89; British statesman

I very much doubt whether many persons will be found to seek for the honour of a life peerage, for it seems to me that it would amount I will not say to an insult but to a very humiliating slight to offer a gentleman a peerage and at the same time to tell him that the title and dignity conferred upon him shall not descend to his son.
>On the first plan to introduce life peers, 1869

Lord Mancroft
1914–87; British Conservative politician

All men are born equal but quite a few eventually get over it.
　1967

José Martí
1853–95; Cuban revolutionary and poet

The spirit of a government must be that of the country. The
form of the government must come from the make-up of the
country. Government is nothing but the balance of the natural
elements of a country.
　Our America (1891)

Allan Massie
b. 1938; British journalist and author

Mrs Thatcher gained power at a time when it seemed that the
collective was depriving the individual of responsibility for his
own life. Even crime was no longer an individual act: it was a
response to social conditions (a view which insulted all decent
people living in the same conditions but abstaining from criminal
activity). She disagreed … To dramatise this, she insisted
'society did not exist', though it was against an exaggerated view
of society that she was reacting. Nothing she said would have
been denied by Protestant churchmen before this century.
　Sunday Times, 1989

Michael Mates
b. 1934; Conservative MP, 1974–2010

If one cannot come to the House of Commons and tell them
what is wrong with the system, if one cannot speak in this

place, not about innocence or guilt, not about trials, not about
sub judice, but what is wrong with the system, then what is the
point of being here?

> On alleged attempts by the Serious Fraud Office to pervert the
> course of justice

Reginald Maudling

1917–79; Conservative MP 1950–79, Cabinet minister 1955–64

There comes a time in every man's life when he must make way
for older men.

> On being replaced by John Davies as Shadow Foreign Secretary,
> November 1976

The broad stream of British foreign policy should not be
sharply diverted with every change of government, for the
national interest does not change much as it needs to adapt to
external circumstances. In these circumstances the primary
function of opposition is to exercise vigilance, to keep a critical
eye on the performance of the government, to chide when it
displays tardiness or lack of vision, to suggest when new ideas
are needed and openly support where support is justified and
necessary.

> *The Times*, 1976

Brian Mawhinney

b. 1940; Conservative MP 1979–2005, Cabinet minister 1994–97

And in Frank Dobson's Camden, would you believe, they gave a
grant to the Camden Hopscotch Asian Women's Group.

> As Conservative Party Chairman, condemning a Home Office-
> funded community project, 1995

David Maxwell-Fyfe
1900–67; Conservative MP

Gratitude is not a normal feature of political life.
    Attributed

Loyalty is the Tory's secret weapon.
    Attributed

Theresa May
b. 1956; Conservative MP 1997–, Home Secretary 2010–

I was looking at a photograph of the 1997 election campaign yesterday, and I thought: 'My God. Did I really have that hairstyle? And that Tory blue suit?'
    Daily Telegraph, 2 June 2002

Like Indiana Jones, I don't like snakes – though that might lead some to ask why I'm in politics.
    The Guardian, 12 March 2005

Targets don't fight crime.
    Speech to the National Policing Conference, 29 June 2010

There is nothing inevitable about crime and there is nothing inevitable about anti-social behaviour.
    Speech at Coin Street Community Centre, 28 July 2010

You can't solve a problem as complex as inequality in one legal clause.
    Speech on equality, 17 November 2010

I was in the Commons recently and saw a young lady wearing a nice pair of shoes. I said I liked them and she said my shoes were the reason she became involved in politics.
    Interview in Chelmsford, 18 November 2010

We all know the stories about the Human Rights Act … about the illegal immigrant who cannot be deported because, and I am not making this up, he had a pet cat.

Conservative Party Conference speech, 4 October 2011

A lot of men in politics suddenly woke up to the issue of women in politics when they realised: hey, there are votes in this!

Daily Telegraph, 21 December 2012

I will not allow a Delia Smith cookbook in my house! It's all so precise with Delia, and it makes cooking seem so inaccessible.

Ibid.

The deportation of Abu Qatada has taken twelve years and cost over £1.7 million in legal fees for both sides. That is not acceptable to the public and it is not acceptable to me. We must make sure that it never happens again.

House of Commons, 8 July 2013

Patrick Mayhew

b. 1929; Conservative MP 1974–97, Cabinet minister 1992–97

Well, nobody is dead. At the end of this opera, everybody's dead.

On being told that nearly thirty people had been injured in a Belfast explosion, while at the opera

Michael Medved

b. 1948; film critic

The days when Hollywood captured the imagination of the entire world with stirring accounts of our heroic history have given way to an era of self-flagellation and irresponsible revisionism – with a series of preachy, politically correct, propagandistic presentations of our country's many crimes and misdemeanours.

Hollywood vs. America (1992)

Edwin Meese

b. 1931; US Attorney General 1985–88

The protests in Beijing should be taken as a stinging rebuke to the notion of cultural relativism, and specifically of the idea that political freedom is a Western idea not universally acceptable.

Communist Nations are Thirsty For Freedom (June 1989)

What is happening in Beijing gives lie to the notion that freedom is divisible; that one can have economic freedom without political freedom, or vice-versa. After all, it was Deng's free market economic reforms, established out of necessity, that created the political climate which led to the democratic process.

Attributed

David Mellor

b. 1949; Conservative MP 1979–97

Nick Ross (interviewer): It does boil down to a barrel of oil at the end of the day.
David Mellor: Well, I think that's a crude way of putting it.

Exchange on the Iran–Iraq war, 1987

In the National Health Service, for years there has been a sterile political debate.

As Junior Health Minister, 1989

To the man in the street, a number of people he has barely heard of are replaced by a number of people he has never heard of.

On the Cabinet reshuffle, 1993

When I should like to have been seen as a tower of strength, I am perceived by some as a point of weakness.

In his resignation letter to John Major

I don't know why he keeps on at it. Perhaps it's the influence of his Rasputin mini-me, Steve Hilton.

On the Big Society, 14 February 2011

Henry Louis Mencken

1880–1956; American satirist and newspaper editor

When a new source of taxation is found it never means in practice, that an old source is abandoned. It merely means that the politicians have two ways of milking the taxpayer whereas previously they had one.

1925

I do not have [Thomas Jefferson's] confidence in the wisdom and rectitude of the common man, but I go with him in his belief that the very commonest of common men have certain inalienable rights.

1927

Frank Meyer

1909–72; American philosopher and political activist

Unless men are free to be vicious they cannot be virtuous.

In Defense of Freedom: A Conservative Credo (1962)

The state must be limited to its proper function in order of preserving order. But this will only be possible when the person is considered as the central moral entity, and society as but a set of relations between persons, not as an organism superior to persons.

Ibid.

If ultimate moral righteousness rests in society, it is justified in enforcing its righteousness, and the state which is its arm cannot be limited by any rights inherent in individual persons.

Ibid.

John Stuart Mill

1806–73; philosopher

The only freedom which deserves the name is that of pursuing our own good in our own way, so long as we do not attempt to deprive others of theirs or impede their efforts to obtain it.

On Liberty (1859)

The liberty of the individual must be this far limited; he must not make himself a nuisance to other people.

Ibid.

The sole end for which mankind are warranted, individually or collectively in interfering with the liberty of action of any of their number, is self-protection.

Ibid.

If all mankind minus one were of one opinion, and only one person were of the contrary opinion, mankind would be no more justified in silencing that one person, than he, if he had the power, would be justified in silencing mankind.

Ibid.

Over himself, over his own body and mind, the individual is sovereign.

Ibid.

The Conservatives, being by the law of their existence the stupidest party.

Considerations of Representative Government (1861)

Lord Milner

1854–1925; Imperialist

You have been born an Englishman and as such have come first in the lottery of life.

House of Commons

John Milton

1608–74; poet

As good almost kill a man as kill a good book; who kills a man kills a reasonable creature, God's image; but he who kills a good book, kills reason itself.

Areopagitica (1644)

Give me the liberty to know, to utter, and to argue freely according to conscience, above all liberties.

Ibid.

…though all the winds of doctrine were let loose to play upon the earth, so Truth be in the field, we do injuriously by licensing and prohibiting to misdoubt her strength. Let her and Falsehood grapple; who ever knew Truth put to the worse in a free and open encounter?

Ibid.

Ludwig von Mises

1881–1973; Austrian economist

A nation is the more prosperous today the less it has tried to put obstacles in the way of the spirit of free enterprise and private initiative.

The Anti-Capitalist Mentality (1956)

Nobody is needy in the market economy because of the fact that some people are rich. The riches of the rich are not the cause of the poverty of anybody. The process that makes some people rich is, on the contrary, the corollary of the process that makes many people's satisfaction.

Ibid.

What is wrong with our age is precisely the widespread ignorance of the role which ... policies of economic freedom played in the technological evolution of the last two hundred years.

Human Action (1949)

It is always the individual who thinks. Society does not think any more than it eats or drinks.

Ibid.

It is ... wrong to assume that there prevails within a market economy, not hampered and sabotaged by government interference, a general tendency towards the formation of monopoly. It is a grotesque distortion of the true state of affairs to speak of monopoly capitalism instead of monopoly interventionism and of private cartels instead of government cartels.

Ibid.

Molière

1622–73; French dramatist

Of all human follies there's none could be greater than trying to render our fellow men better.

The Misanthrope (1666)

Thomas Molnar
1921–2010; Hungarian-born author

Passion for equality blinds the utopian to the fact that society, as a whole, is based on inequality of men in two respects: the inventor, the innovator, the exceptional man creates something new and insures continuous progress; the others emulate his work or merely improve their own lot by benefiting from his creativity.

Utopia: The Perennial Heresy (1967)

No more eloquent funeral oration could be pronounced over the tomb of an ideology that has failed its believers because they despised the true nature of man.

Ibid., on the failed utopia of the Soviet Union

Lord Robert Montagu
1825–1902; British Conservative politician

To give education gratuitously will only degrade the education so given in the estimation of the parents.

Opposing free education, 1870

Montesquieu
1689–1755; French jurist and philosopher

It is true that in democracies the people seem to act as they please. But political liberty does not consist simply in doing whatever one wishes. In governments, that is, in societies directed by laws, liberty can consist only in the power of doing what we ought to do, without being constrained from doing what we ought not to do. We must distinguish freedom from liberty. Again, liberty is the right to do everything the law permits. If a citizen does what the law prohibits, he sacrifices his liberty.

The Spirit of the Laws (1748)

But constant experience shows us that every man invested with power is apt to abuse it, and to carry his authority as far as it will go.
Ibid.

Commerce is a cure for the most destructive prejudices.
Ibid.

Peace is the natural effect of trade.
Ibid.

Useless laws weaken the necessary laws.
Ibid.

David Montgomery, 2nd Viscount Montgomery of Alamein
b. 1928; British Conservative politician

There was universal support for it and very little opposition.
Describing the reform of the drink licensing laws, 1987

Thomas Moore
1886–1971; British Conservative politician

If I may judge from my personal knowledge of Herr Hitler, peace and justice are the key-words of his policy.
1933

Penny Mordaunt
b. 1973; Conservative MP 2010–

These reforms are going to lead to a constitutional crisis.
On Lords reform, 26 June 2012

Oswald Mosley

1896–1980; Member of Parliament 1918–31

I am not and have never been a man of the right. My position was on the left and is now in the centre of politics.

1968

Lord Mountbatten

1900–79; British statesman and naval officer, last Viceroy of India 1947

Actually, I vote Labour, but my butler's a Tory.

1945

Malcolm Muggeridge

1903–90; social commentator

Searching in my mind for an appropriate name for the seventies, I settle for the Decade of the Great Liberal Death Wish. It seems to me that this process of death wishing, in the guise of liberalism, has been eroding the civilisation of the west for a century and more, and is now about to reach its apogee.

Things Past (1978)

Previous civilisations have been overthrown without by the incursion of barbarian hordes; ours has dreamed up its own dissolution in the minds of its own intellectual elite.

Ibid.

Liberalism will be seen historically as the great destructive force of our time; much more so than Communism, Fascism, Nazism, or any of the other lunatic creeds which make such immediate havoc...

Ibid.

There is no snobbishness like that of professional egalitarians.
Chronicles of Wasted Time (1978)

Charles Murray
b. 1943; American libertarian political scientist and writer

We believe that human happiness requires freedom and that freedom requires limited government.
What It Means to Be a Libertarian: A Personal Interpretation (1997)

N

Richard Needham
b. 1942; Conservative MP 1979–97, Cabinet minister 1992–95

I wish that old cow would resign.
> Caught out on a mobile phone talking about Margaret Thatcher, 1990
> – he later said sorry

Godfrey Nicholson
1901–91; British Conservative politician

A platitude is a truth we are tired of hearing.
> House of Commons, 10 July 1933

Harold Nicolson
1886–1968; British diplomat, author, diarist and politician

… the mind and manners of a clothes brush.
> On Austen Chamberlain, *Diary*, 6 June 1936

I think it is a combination of real religious fanaticism with spiritual trickiness which makes one dislike Mr Chamberlain so much. He has all the hardness of a self-righteous man, with none of the generosity of those who are guided by durable moral standards.
> On Neville Chamberlain, *Diary*, 26 April 1939

Attlee is a charming and intelligent man, but as a public speaker he is, compared to Winston [Churchill], like a village fiddler after Paganini.
> *Diary*, 10 November 1947

Friedrich Nietzsche

1844–1900; philosopher

Every tradition grows ever more venerable – the more remote its origin, the more confused that origin is. The reverence due to it increases from generation to generation. The tradition finally becomes holy and inspires awe.

Human, all too Human (1878)

Robert A. Nisbet

1913–96; American sociologist

I cannot help thinking that what we need above all else in this age is a new philosophy of laissez-faire. The old laissez-faire failed because it was based on erroneous premises regarding human behaviour ... because it mistook for ineradicable characteristics of individuals characteristics that were in fact inseparable from social groups ... Far from proving a check upon the growth of the omnicompetent state, the old laissez-faire actually accelerated its growth. Its indifference to every form of community and association left the state as the sole area of reform and security ... To create conditions in which the autonomous individuals could prosper, could be emancipated from the binding ties of kinship, class and community, was the objective of the older laissez-faire. To create conditions within which autonomous groups may prosper must be, I believe, the prime objective of the new laissez-faire.

The Quest for Community (1953)

Richard Nixon

1913–94; US President 1969–74

I also believe that academic freedom should protect the right of a professor or student to advocate Marxism, Socialism,

Communism or any other minority viewpoint – no matter how distasteful to the majority.

On free speech

What are our schools for if not indoctrination against Communism?

1962

This is the greatest week in the history of the world since the creation.

On the first landing on the moon, 1969

By taking this action, I hope that I will have hastened the start of the healing.

Resignation speech, 8 August 1974

I've analysed the best I can ... and I have not found an impeachable offence, and therefore resignation is not an acceptable course.

Ibid.

I have impeached myself by resigning.

Interview with David Frost, 15 April 1977

While technically I did not commit a crime, an impeachable offence ... these are legalisms, as far as the handling of this matter is concerned; it was so botched up, I made so many bad judgements. The worst ones, mistakes of the heart, rather than the head. But let me say, a man in that top job – he's got to have a heart, but his head must always rule his heart.

Ibid.

When the President does it, that means it is not illegal.

Ibid.

You must pursue this investigation of Watergate even if it leads to the President. I'm innocent. You've got to believe I'm innocent. If you don't, take my job.

> On the 1972–74 Watergate scandal

I can see clearly now ... that I was wrong in not acting more decisively and more forthrightly in dealing with Watergate...

> Ibid.

I was under medication when I made the decision to burn the tapes.

> Explaining his interpretation of executive privilege

I gave 'em a sword. And they stuck it in, and they twisted it with relish. And I guess if I had been in their position, I'd have done the same thing.

> 1977

A man is not finished when he is defeated. He is finished when he quits.

> 10 December 1978

The successful leader does not talk down to people. He lifts them up.

> Attributed

Once you get into this great stream of history, you can't get out.

> Attributed

If you want to make beautiful music, you must play the black and the white notes together.

> Attributed

We are all in it together. This is a war. We take a few shots and it will be over. We will give them a few shots and it will be over.

> Attributed

I can take it ... The tougher it gets, the cooler I get...
    Attributed

Steven Norris
b. 1945; Conservative MP 1983–97

It's like a vasectomy – you can have all of the fun without any of
the responsibility.
    On the benefits of a peerage

You have your own company, your own temperature control,
your own music and you don't have to put up with dreadful
human beings sitting alongside you.
    On the benefits of commuting by car rather than public transport, as
    Minister of Transport, 1995

Lord North
1732–92; Prime Minister 1770–82

Men may be popular without being ambitious, but there is
hardly an ambitious man who does not try to be popular.
    Attributed

The American disputes are settled and there is nothing to
interrupt the peace and prosperity of the nation.
    1771

I never should be so presumptuous as to think myself capable
of directing the departments of others ... I do not think our
constitution authorises such a character as that animal called a
Prime Minister.
    1778

[Affairs of state] can hardly be well conducted unless there is a
person in the Cabinet capable of leading, of discerning between

opinions, of deciding quickly and confidently, and connecting all the operations of government...

To King George III, 1778

Oliver North

b. 1943; American national security staff and author

I remember watching on television as the Berlin Wall came down. I had tears in my eyes ... I felt that way again in 1990, when, for the second time in eleven years, the people of Nicaragua rejected a brutal and corrupt regime. And yet again in 1991, watching Boris Yeltsin stop a Soviet tank during the second Russian Revolution.

Under Fire (1991)

Michael Novak

b. 1933; American philosopher

It is an analytical mistake to hold that Socialism respects the social nature of humans, while democratic societies are characterised by 'progressive individualism'. In actual history, exactly the reverse happens. One may test this proposition empirically. In which actual nations do voluntary associations and cooperative habits actually thrive, and in which do they wither?

Confessions of a Catholic (1983)

O

Patrick James 'P. J.' O'Rourke
b. 1947; American political satirist

You can't get rid of poverty by giving people money.
  Attributed

Giving money and power to government is like giving whiskey
and car keys to teenage boys.
  Attributed

There is only one basic human right, the right to do as you
damn well please.
  Speech to the Cato Institute, 1993

There are just two rules of governance in a free society: Mind
your own business. Keep your hands to yourself.
  Ibid.

When buying and selling are controlled by legislation, the first
things to be bought and sold are legislators.
  Attributed

The American political system is like fast food – mushy,
insipid, made out of disgusting parts of things and everybody
wants some.
  Attributed

Matthew Oakeshott

1901–90; philosopher

To be a Conservative is to prefer the tried to the untried, the fact to the mystery, the actual to the possible, the limited to the unbounded, the near to the distant, the sufficient to the super-abundant, the convenient to the perfect present, laughter to utopian bliss.

Rationalism in Politics (1962)

To be Conservative is not merely to be averse from change, which may be an idiosyncrasy: it is also a manner of accommodating ourselves to changes, an activity imposed upon all men. For a change is a threat to identity and any change is an emblem of extinction.

Ibid.

George Osborne

b. 1971; Member of Parliament 2001–, Chancellor of the Exchequer 2010–

It's normally the kiss of death to be identified as a rising star, or someone to watch.

BBC, 10 May 2005

I reject absolutely the idea that people should know their place, and know their class.

The Guardian, 16 July 2005

I think the British people are very, very attached to the idea that the health service is free at the point of use. But there is no reason why every doctor, nurse and teacher in this country has to be employed by the state.

Ibid.

The foundations of a strong economy don't rest alone on the decisions of Chancellors or the spending programmes of government.

Daily Telegraph, 22 July 2005

Some things never change, suck up to the government and you get an honour.

Ibid., on his own family's baronetcy

The Conservative Party mustn't sound like the old man on the park bench who says things were better in 1985, or 1955, or 1855.

Attributed

Most successful politicians don't let the job swamp their lives.

Daily Mail, 21 September 2008

They all said I was a very young guy. Well there is nothing I can do about that but with each day that passes the problem solves itself.

Ibid.

Believe me, I understand that most higher rate taxpayers are not the super-rich.

Conservative Party Conference, 4 October 2010

Britain has no divine right to be one of the richest countries in the world.

Ibid.

Cutting Budget deficits can never be just an exercise in economics.

Ibid.

I've learned to be true to yourself, stick to the big arguments, don't get distracted by the everyday kerfuffle that is in the nature of any democratic system.

Daily Telegraph, 16 March 2010

If someone believes that living on benefits is a lifestyle choice, then we need to make them think again.

> Conservative Party Conference, 4 October 2010

If we don't get a grip on government spending, there will be no growth.

> Ibid.

In opposition, you move to the centre. In government, you move the centre.

> His supposed mantra that he and his team live by, *The Spectator*, 26 March 2011

We want the words: 'Made in Britain, 'Created in Britain', 'Designed in Britain', 'Invented in Britain', to drive our nation forward. A Britain carried aloft by the march of the makers. That is how we will create jobs and support families. We have put fuel into the tank of the British economy.

> Ibid.

I did meet Mickey Mouse in California, and he seems to be writing the Labour party's economic policy at the moment.

> 10 August 2011

Tax cuts should be for life, not just for Christmas.

> *Daily Telegraph*, 30 September 2011

I'm a Conservative who believes in lower taxes. They lead to a more enterprising economy. But I'm not somebody who believes you can fund lower taxes by borrowing more money.

> Ibid.

I was shocked to see that some of the very wealthiest people in the country have organised their tax affairs, and to be fair it's within the tax laws, so that they were regularly paying virtually no income tax. And I don't think that's right.

> 10 April 2012

Tax avoidance is morally repugnant.
Budget speech, 2012

This country borrowed its way into trouble, now we're going to work our way out.
Ibid.

We simply cannot justify those earning £15,000 paying for those earning £80,000.
Ibid.

The Conservative party, the modern Conservative party, is on the side of people who want to work hard and get on.
On the *Today* programme, 8 October 2012

Just as we should never balance the Budget on the backs of the poor, so it is an economic delusion to think you can balance it only on the wallets of the rich.
Conservative Party Conference, 9 October 2012

It's not easy cutting welfare bills. It's not easy cutting the deficit.
The Guardian, 25 October 2012

P

Reginald Paget

1908–90; Conservative MP 1945–74

From Lord Hailsham we have had a virtuoso performance in the
art of kicking a fallen friend in the guts. When self-indulgence
has reduced a man to the shape of Lord Hailsham, sexual
continence requires no more than a sense of the ridiculous.

    Defending Harold Macmillan over Profumo, 1963

Lord Palmerston

1784–1865; Prime Minister 1855–65

I object to it because I think it at variance with the national
character ... I think a true Englishman hates doing a thing
in secret or in the dark. I do not believe that a majority of
Englishmen would consent to give their votes in secret even if
the law permitted them to do so ... I say that for men who are
charged with the high and important duty of choosing the best
men to represent the country in Parliament to go sneaking to
the ballot-box and poking in a piece of paper, looking round see
that no one could read it, is a course which is unconstitutional
and unworthy of the character of straightforward and honest
Englishmen.

    At the general election of 1852

An ancient sage said there were two things over which the gods
themselves had no power – past events and arithmetic.

    Attributed

Your Lordship is like a favourite footman on easy terms with
his mistress. Your dexterity seems a happy compound of the

smartness of an attorney clerk and the intrigue of a Greek lower empire.

On Peel

His life has been one great appropriation clause. A burglar of others' intellect – there is no statesman who has committed political larceny on so grand a scale.

Ibid.

The Right Honourable Gentleman is reminiscent of a poker. The only difference is that a poker gives off occasional signs of warmth.

Ibid.

Cecil Parkinson

b. 1931; Conservative MP 1970–92, Cabinet minister 1981–83, 1987–90

I have my own Parkinson's Law: in politics people give you what they think you deserve and deny you what they think you want.

Attributed

The cost of the Eurotunnel project has risen, but it is usual in these projects and the Anglo-French consortium is looking into ways to bridge the gap.

As Transport Secretary, 1989

I'm a great believer in leaving politics when you've reached your ceiling. *(Pause)* Though I did lower the ceiling somewhat…

On leaving the Commons, 1992

I'm very pleased we've won another seat … I was actually thinking John Major was going to remain leader of the party and the only Conservative Member of Parliament.

On hearing of a second Tory victory, 1 May 1997

Christopher Patten

b. 1944; Conservative MP 1979–92, Governor of Hong Kong 1993–97

A kind of walking obituary for the Labour Party.
  On Michael Foot

John Stuart Mill, rewritten by Ernest Hemingway.
  On David Owen

I've always had a great respect and been very candid with her,
and I hope the reverse is the case.
  On Margaret Thatcher, 1989

The argument about Labour destroying any prospects of
recovery may be déjà vu here ... It's certainly not déjà vu in the
country. It's very much vu. It's very much what, er ... It's very
much, er ... shows what sort of an education I had.
  1992

The Liberal Democrats couldn't survive a moment's scrutiny
of their policies. At local level they back four routes for a
bypass – North, South, East and West. At national level they
are just as bad.
  Ibid.

John Patten

b. 1945; Conservative MP 1979–97, Cabinet minister 1992–94

There are three prongs to our anti-crime drive: stronger
sentences, more police on the beat and prevention.
  1987

Robert Peel
1788–1850; Prime Minister 1834–35, 1841–46

I may be a Tory – I may be an illiberal – but the fact is undeniable, that when I first entered upon the duties of the Home Department, there were laws in existence which imposed upon the subjects of this realm unusual and extraordinary restrictions.

Following his resignation as Home Secretary, 1 May 1827

I am very far from being prepared to admit that the improvement of the situation of a common police constable by giving him more money would increase the efficiency of the establishment.

1829

The longer I live, the more clearly do I see the folly of yielding a rash and precipitate assent to any political measure.

1830

We are here to consult the interests and not to obey the will of the people if we honestly believe that they will conflict with those interests.

Third Reading of the Reform Bill, 1831

But it may be that I shall leave a name sometimes remembered with expressions of good will in the abodes of those whose lot it is to labour, and to earn their daily bread by the sweat of their brow, when they shall recruit their exhausted strength with abundant and untaxed food, the sweeter because it is no longer leavened by a sense of injustice.

On his resignation as Prime Minister, 29 June 1846

Constitutional liberty will be best worked out by those who aspire to freedom by their own efforts.

Last speech on foreign policy in the House of Commons, 28 June 1850

It was impossible for me to reconcile the repeal of the Corn Laws by me with the keeping together of the Conservative Party, and I had no hesitation in sacrificing the subordinate object and with it my own political interests.

Memoirs (1856)

Spencer Perceval

1762–1812; Prime Minister 1809–12

I have nothing to say to the nothing that has been said.

During a debate on corrupt electoral practices

Inadvertence is certainly never felt by me as an excuse.

Letter to Wilberforce

Ross Perot

b. 1930; independent US Presidential candidate

An empty suit that goes to funerals and plays golf.

On Dan Quayle, 1992

John Peyton

1919–2006; Conservative MP 1951–83, Cabinet minister 1970–74

We are a Party which can never forget its historic links with the land and its deep commitment to those who live and work in the countryside.

On the Conservative Party, 1977

William Pitt (the Elder)
1708–78; Secretary of State 1757–61, Prime Minister 1766–68

The atrocious crime of being a young man, which the honourable gentleman had with such spirit and decency charged upon me, I shall attempt neither to palliate nor to deny, but content myself with wishing that I shall be one of those whose follies shall cease with their youth, and not of that number who are ignorant in spite of experience.

Answering the criticism of Robert Walpole, 1741

Unlimited power is apt to corrupt the minds of those who possess it.

1770

There is something behind the throne greater than the king himself.

Ibid.

If I were an American, as I am an Englishman, while a foreign troop was landed in my country, I never would lay down my arms, never-never-never!

1777

William Pitt (the Younger)
1759–1806; Prime Minister 1783–1801, 1804–06

Necessity is the plea for every infringement of human freedom. It is the argument of tyrants; it is the creed of slaves.

House of Commons, 18 November 1783

There is no principle of the law of nations clearer than this, that, when in the cause of war any nation acquires new possessions, such nation has only temporary right to them, and they do not become property till the end of the war.

House of Commons, 30 December 1796

We must recollect ... what it is we have at stake, what it is we have to contend for. It is for our property, it is for our liberty, it is for our independence, nay, for our existence as a nation; it is for our character, it is for our very name as Englishmen, it is for everything dear and valuable to man on this side of the grave.
    22 July 1803

England has saved herself by her exertions, and will, I trust, save Europe by her example.
    Guildhall, London, 9 November 1805

Plutarch
c.46–120; Roman historian

Men, stirred by popular applause, though they bear the name of governors, are in reality the mere underlings of the multitude. The man who is completely wise and virtuous has no need at all of glory, except so far as it disposes and eases his way of action by the greater trust that it procures him.
    Lives

Polybius
c.2nd century BC; Roman historian

For peace, with justice and honour, is the fairest and most profitable of possessions, but with disgrace and shameful cowardice it is the most infamous and harmful of all.
    Histories

Karl Popper
1902–94; philosopher

Individualism was part of the old intuitive idea of justice. That justice is not, as Plato would have it, the health and harmony of the state, but rather a certain way of treating individuals, is emphasised by Aristotle … when he says justice is something that pertains to persons.

Individualism versus Collectivism (1945)

Michael Portillo

1953; Conservative MP 1984–97, 1999–2005; Cabinet minister 1992–97

Three letters send a chill down the spine of the enemy-SAS. Those letters spell out one clear message. Don't mess with Britain!

Conservative Party Conference, 1995

The European Commission might want to harmonise uniforms and cap badges, or even to metricate them. The European Court would probably want to stop our men fighting for more than forty hours a week. They would send half of them home on paternity leave.

Explaining why a common European defence policy would never work

If any of you have got an A level, it is because you have worked for it. Go to any other country, and when you have got an A level, you have bought it.
Speech to Southampton students Anyone, they say, is entitled to change his mind. Not about the defence of Britain, you're not. You either feel it in your heart, in your bones, in your gut, or you don't!

1995

Returning Officer: Everyone happy?
Portillo: Ecstatic.

2 May 1998

I regard the leadership thing as closed forever. I got quite close to it, but the moment passed … I think it would be interesting to go back as a backbencher … People thought I was too ambitious, maybe I brought some of it on myself … I think I'm a more humble person, yes. I think I was always more humble than I was made out to be.

The Guardian, 16 August 1998

The party would cheerfully engage in fighting one another over Europe, as though we were a college debating society rather than a government a week from polling day. We displayed the disciplinary qualities of a rave party rather than a political one.

The Spectator, 9 August 1998

For those that wanted the Conservatives out, my defeat was a highlight.

Attributed

I am better at politics than I am at anything else.

17 November 1998

They didn't win the last one and it is extremely rare for governing parties to improve their share of the vote, even when their opponents are as weakly led as Labour and the Liberal Democrats are now.

On the 2015 election

The euro is a disaster. It has created hardship, unemployment and division on a dangerous scale. It is the result of an ideology; and the ideologues who pursue the goal of union do not count the cost in human misery.

The Times, 9 May 2013

Enoch Powell

1912–96; Conservative MP 1950–74, Ulster Unionist MP 1974

In politics it is more blessed not to take than to give.

Daily Telegraph, 31 January 1964

History is littered with the wars which everybody knew would never happen.

Conservative Party Conference, 19 October 1967

We must be mad, literally mad, as a nation to be permitting the annual inflow of some 50,000 dependents of immigrants ...
As I look ahead, I am filled with foreboding. Like the Roman, I seem to see the River Tiber foaming with much blood.

20 April 1968

Helping industry is the elephant's pit of Socialism, a deep hole with sharp spikes at the bottom, covered over with twigs and fresh grass.

24 September 1969

Inflation is no mere monetary inconvenience. It is a social evil, an injustice between man and man and a moral evil, a dishonesty between government and people, between class and class ... The highest national interest, overtopping all others in the economic sphere is honest money – money that holds its value. Growth, full employment, expanding public services – all these are worth nothing unless that first and great condition is fulfilled.

1973

All political lives, unless they are cut off in midstream at a happy juncture, end in failure, because that is the nature of politics and of human affairs.

1977

I do not keep a diary. Never have. To write a diary every day is like returning to one's own vomit.

Ibid.

Take Parliament out of the history of England and that history itself becomes meaningless.

4 February 1979

The Prime Minister, shortly after she came into office, received a sobriquet as the 'Iron Lady'. It arose in the context of remarks which she made about defence against the Soviet Union and its allies; but there was no reason to suppose that the Right Honourable Lady did not welcome and, indeed, take pride in that description. In the next week or two this House, the nation and the Right Honourable Lady herself, will learn of what metal she is made.

House of Commons, 3 April 1982

I don't really think I have ever made a mistake.

Any Questions?, BBC Radio 4, 1982

Politicians who complain about the press are like ship's captains who complain about the sea.

Attributed

It shows that the substance under test consists of ferrous metal of the highest quality. It is of exceptional tensile strength, resistant to wear and tear, and may be used with advantage for all national purposes.

Explaining how Margaret Thatcher had stood up to the tests of the Falklands crisis

A Tory is someone who thinks institutions are wiser than those who operate them.

Daily Telegraph, 31 March 1986

Above any other position of eminence, that of Prime Minister is filled by fluke.

1987

To pretend that you cannot exchange goods and services freely with a Frenchman or an Italian, unless there is an identical standard of bathing beaches or tap water in the different countries is not logic. It is naked aggression.

The Guardian, 22 May 1990

If Toryism includes stealing from dukes, it is a Tory measure.
> On leasehold land reform plans, 1990

James Prior

b. 1927; Conservative MP 1959–87, Cabinet minister 1970–74, 1979–84

Why does he always talk about the working people as if they were a section of society apart from the rest? Perhaps the second Lord Stansgate still believes that the only way to rally the faithful is to use the class slogans of the aristocracy. Mr Benn, I have news for you. Most of us are working people.
> 1976

When Mrs Thatcher said 'We are a grandmother,' she was including Denis in her remarks.
> 1989

Francis Pym

1922–2008; Conservative MP 1961–87, Cabinet minister 1970–74, 1979–83

Stale claret in new bottles – it is a confidence trick not to be mistaken for the elixir of life.
> Attributed

We've got a corporal at the top, not a cavalry officer.
> On Margaret Thatcher 1982

Landslides, on the whole, don't produce successful governments.
> 1983

Q

Dan Quayle
b. 1947; US Vice-President 1988–92

We're going to have the best educated American people in the world.
1988

One word sums up probably the responsibility of any Vice-President. And that one word is, 'to be prepared'.
Attributed

[Republicans] understand the importance of bondage between parent and child.
He meant to say 'bonding', 1988

The Nazi holocaust was an obscene period in our country's history ... well, not our country's history, this century's history ... we all lived in this century; I didn't live in this century...
1988

There's a lot of uncharted waters in space.
1989

What a waste it is to lose one's mind – or not to have a mind.
Ibid.

The only regret I have was that I didn't study Latin harder in school so I could converse with those people.
On a visit to Latin America, 1989 (attributed)

There is an irreversible trend to freedom and democracy in
Eastern Europe. But this may change.
1990

If we do not succeed, then we run the risk of failure.
Ibid.

If you elect Bill Clinton and Al Gore you can say goodbye to
water, goodbye to food and goodbye to your jobs.
1992

The intergenerational poverty that troubles us so much today
is predominantly a poverty of values. Our inner cities are
filled with children having children having children, with
people who have not been able to take advantage of educational
opportunities, with people who are dependent on drugs or the
narcotic of welfare.
Speech, Commonwealth Club, 19 May 1992

Ultimately ... marriage is a moral issue that requires cultural
consensus, and the use of social sanctions. Bearing babies
irresponsibly is, simply, wrong. Failing to support children one
has fathered is wrong.
Ibid.

R

Ayn Rand
1905–82; novelist and political philosopher

The secret dread of modern intellectuals, liberals and Conservatives alike, the unadmitted terror at the root of their anxiety, which all their current irrationalities are intended to slave off and disguise, is the unstated knowledge that Soviet Russia is the full, actual, literal, consistent embodiment of the morality of altruism, that Stalin did not corrupt a noble ideal, that this is the only way altruism has had to be or can ever be practised.

Faith and Force: The Destroyers of the Modern World (1960)

Nancy Reagan
b. 1921; wife of Ronald Reagan

He doesn't make snap decisions, but he doesn't overthink either.

On Ronald Reagan

I believe that people would be alive today if there were a death penalty.

On capital punishment

Ronald Reagan
1911–2004; US President 1980–88

Are you willing to spend time studying the issues, making yourself aware, and then conveying that information to family and friends? Will you resist the temptation to get a government handout for your community? Realise that the doctor's fight against Socialised medicine is your fight? We can't Socialise the doctors without Socialising the patients. Recognise that government invasion of public power is eventually an assault upon your own business. If some among you fear taking a stand because you are afraid of reprisals from customers, clients, or even government, recognise that you are just feeding the crocodile hoping he'll eat you last.

27 October 1964

Have we the courage and the will to face up to the immorality and discrimination of the progressive tax, and demand a return to traditional proportionate taxation? ... Today in our country the tax collector's share is 37 cents of every dollar earned. Freedom has never been so fragile, so close to slipping from our grasp.

Ibid.

If all of this seems like a great deal of trouble, think what's at stake. We are faced with the most evil enemy mankind has known in his long climb from the swamp to the stars. There can be no security anywhere in the free world if there is no fiscal and economic stability within the United States. Those who ask us to trade our freedom for the soup kitchen of the welfare state are architects of a policy of accommodation.

Ibid.

Public servants say, always with the best of intentions, What greater service we could render if only we had a little more money and a little more power. But the truth is that outside of its legitimate function, government does nothing as well or as economically as the private sector.

Ibid.

It's time we asked ourselves if we still know the freedoms intended for us by the Founding Fathers. James Madison said, 'We base all our experiments on the capacity of mankind for self-government.' This idea that government was beholden

to the people, that it had no other source of power, is still
the newest, most unique idea in all the long history of man's
relation to man. This is the issue of this election: Whether we
believe in our capacity for self-government or whether we
abandon the American Revolution and confess that a little
intellectual elite in a far-distant capital can plan our lives for us
better than we can plan them ourselves.

    Ibid.

The Founding Fathers knew a government can't control the
economy without controlling people. And they knew when a
government sets out to do that, it must use force and coercion
to achieve its purpose. So we have come to a time for choosing.

    Ibid.

They say the world has become too complex for simple
answers. They are wrong. There are no easy answers, but there
are simple answers. We must have the courage to do what we
know is morally right. Winston Churchill said that the destiny
of man is not measured by material computation. When great
forces are on the move in the world, we learn we are spirits –
not animals. And he said, There is something going on in time
and space, and beyond time and space, which, whether we like
it or not, spells duty.

    Ibid.

We are for aiding our allies by sharing our material blessings
with nations which share our fundamental beliefs, but we are
against doling out money government to government, creating
bureaucracy, if not Socialism, all over the world.

    Ibid.

We need true tax reform that will at least make a start toward
restoring for our children the American Dream that wealth
is denied to no one, that each individual has the right to fly as
high as his strength and ability will take him ... But we cannot
have such reform while our tax policy is engineered by people

who view the tax as a means of achieving changes in our social structure.

Ibid.

Yet any time you and I question the schemes of the do-gooders, we're denounced as being opposed to their humanitarian goals. It seems impossible to legitimately debate their solutions with the assumption that all of us share the desire to help the less fortunate. They tell us we're always against, never for anything.

Ibid.

You and I are told we must choose between a left or right, but I suggest there is no such thing as a left or right. There is only an up or down. Up to man's age-old dream – the maximum of individual freedom consistent with order – or down to the ant heap of totalitarianism. Regardless of their sincerity, their humanitarian motives, those who would sacrifice freedom for security have embarked on this downward path. Plutarch warned, The real destroyer of the liberties of the people is he who spreads among them bounties, donations and benefits.

Ibid.

You and I have a rendezvous with destiny. We will preserve for our children this, the last best hope of man on earth, or we will sentence them to take the first step into a thousand years of darkness. If we fail, at least let our children and our children's children say of us we justified our brief moment here. We did all that could be done.

Ibid.

Government is just like a big baby – an alimentary canal with a big appetite at one end and no responsibility at the other.

1965

Welfare's purpose should be to eliminate, as far as possible, the need for its own existence.

Los Angeles Times, 7 January 1970

It is old fashioned, even reactionary to remind people that free enterprise has done more to reduce poverty than all the government programs dreamed up by Democrats.

As Governor of California, 1972

Government does not solve problems. It subsidises them.

11 December 1972

Heaven help us if government ever gets into the business of protecting us from ourselves.

12 April 1973

The United States has much to offer the Third World War.

1975

Recession is when your neighbour loses his job. Depression is when you lose your job. And recovery is when Jimmy Carter loses his.

Speech in New Jersey, 1980

I've noticed that everybody who is for abortion has already been born.

21 September 1980

No arsenal or no weapon in the arsenals of the world is so formidable as the will and moral courage of free men and women.

Inauguration speech, 20 January 1981

This Administration's objective will be a healthy, vigorous, growing economy.

Ibid.

It is not my intention to do away with government. It is rather to make it work – work with us, not over us; stand by our side, not ride on our back. Government can and must provide opportunity, not smother it; foster productivity, not stifle it.

Ibid.

I hope you're all Republicans.
   To surgeons as he entered the operating room, 30 March 1981

The years ahead will be great ones for our country, for the cause
of freedom and the spread of civilisation. The West will not
contain Communism, it will transcend Communism. We will
not bother to denounce it, we'll dismiss it as a sad, bizarre chapter
in human history whose last pages are even now being written.
   Notre Dame University, 17 May 1981

We who live in free market societies believe that growth,
prosperity and ultimately human fulfilment, are created
from the bottom up, not the government down. Only when
the human spirit is allowed to invent and create, only when
individuals are given a personal stake in deciding economic
policies and benefiting from their success – only then can
societies remain economically alive, dynamic, progressive,
and free. Trust the people. This is the one irrefutable lesson of
the entire post-war period contradicting the notion that rigid
government controls are essential to economic development.
   29 September 1981

The size of the Federal Budget is not an appropriate barometer
of social conscience or charitable concern.
   5 October 1981

Cures were developed for which there were no known diseases.
   Commenting on Congress and the federal Budget, 1981

Government has an important role in helping develop a
country's economic foundation. But the critical test is whether
government is genuinely working to liberate individuals by
creating incentives to work, save, invest, and succeed.
   30 October 1981

She's the best man in England.
   On Margaret Thatcher

Government is the people's business and every man, woman and child becomes a shareholder with the first penny of tax paid.

Address to the New York City Partnership Association, 14 January 1982

We don't have a trillion-dollar debt because we haven't taxed enough; we have a trillion-dollar debt because we spend too much.

Address to National Association of Realtors, 28 March 1982

Eighty per cent of pollution is caused by plants and trees.

Ibid.

In an ironic sense, Karl Marx was right. We are witnessing today a great revolutionary crisis – a crisis where the demands of the economic order are colliding directly with those of the political order. But the crisis is happening not in the free, non-Marxist West, but in the home of Marxism-Leninism, the Soviet Union ... [Communism will be] left on the ash heap of history.

June 1982

It is the Soviet Union that runs against the tide of history ... It is the march of freedom and democracy which will leave Marxism-Leninism on the ash heap of history as it has left other tyrannies which stifle the freedom and muzzle the self-expression of the people.

Speech to both Houses of Parliament, 1982

Balancing the Budget is like protecting your virtue – you have to learn when to say no.

September 1982

The Constitution was never meant to prevent people from praying; its declared purpose was to protect their freedom to pray.

Radio address to the nation on prayer, September 1982

Let us beware that while they [Soviet rulers] preach the supremacy of the state, declare its omnipotence over individual man, and predict its eventual domination over all the peoples of the earth, they are the focus of evil in the modern world ... I urge you to beware the temptation ... to ignore the facts of history and the aggressive impulses of any evil empire, to simply call the arms race a giant misunderstanding and thereby remove yourself from the struggle between right and wrong, good and evil.

Speech to the National Association of Evangelicals, 8 March 1983

I call upon the scientific community in our country, those who gave us nuclear weapons, to turn their great talents now to the cause of mankind and world peace, to give us the means of rendering those nuclear weapons impotent and obsolete.

Address to the nation, 23 March 1983

There are no such things as limits to growth, because there are no limits on the human capacity for intelligence, imagination and wonder.

Address to the University of South Carolina, Columbia,
20 September 1983

History teaches that wars begin when governments believe the price of aggression is cheap.

Address to the nation, 16 January 1984

We will always remember. We will always be proud. We will always be prepared, so we may always be free.

Normandy, 6 June 1984

The men of Normandy had faith that what they were doing was right, faith that they fought for all humanity, faith that a just God would grant them mercy on this beachhead or the next. It was the deep knowledge – and pray God we have not lost it – that there is a profound moral difference between the use of force for liberation and the use of force for conquest.

Ibid.

The poet called Miss Liberty's torch, the lamp beside the golden door. Well, that was the entrance to America, and it still is. And now you really know why we're here tonight. ... the glistening hope of that lamp is still ours. Every promise every opportunity is still golden in this land. And through that golden door our children can walk into tomorrow with the knowledge that no one can be denied the promise that is America.

... her heart is full; her torch is still golden, her future bright. She has arms big enough to comfort and strong enough to support, for the strength in her arms is the strength of her people. She will carry on in the eighties unafraid, unashamed, and unsurpassed.

... in this springtime of hope, some lights seem eternal; America's is.

Republican National Convention, 23 August 1984

Abraham Lincoln recognised that we could not survive as a free land when some men could decide that others were not fit to be free and should therefore be slaves. Likewise, we cannot survive as a free nation when some men decide that others are not fit to live and should be abandoned to abortion or infanticide ... there is no cause more important for preserving that freedom than affirming the transcendent right to life of all human beings, the right without which no other rights have any meaning.

Abortion and the Conscience of the Nation (1984)

Die-hard Conservatives thought that if I couldn't get everything I asked for, I would jump off the cliff with the flag flying – go down in flames. No, if I can get 70 or 80 per cent of what it is I'm trying to get ... I'll take that and then continue to try to get the rest in the future.

New York Times, 6 October 1985

We will never forget them, nor the last time we saw them – this morning, as they prepared for their journey, and waved good-bye, and slipped the surly bonds of earth to touch the face of God.

Speech about the *Challenger* disaster, 28 January 1986

Government growing beyond our consent had become a lumbering giant, slamming shut the gates of opportunity, threatening to crush the very roots of our freedom. What brought America back? The American people brought us back – with quiet courage and common sense; with undying faith that in this nation under God the future will be ours, for the future belongs to the free.

State of the Union address, 4 February 1986

The nine most terrifying words in the English language are, 'I'm from the government and I'm here to help'.

2 August 1986

Government's view of the economy could be summed up in a few short phrases: If it moves, tax it. If it keeps moving, regulate it. And if it stops moving, subsidise it.

Remarks to the White House Conference on Small Business, 15 August 1986

Surround yourself with the best people you can find, delegate authority, and don't interfere.

Fortune, 15 September 1986

The other day, someone told me the difference between a democracy and a people's democracy. It's the same difference between a jacket and a straitjacket.

Remarks at Human Rights Day event, 10 December 1986

How do you tell a Communist? Well, it's someone who reads Marx and Lenin. And how do you tell an anti-Communist? It's someone who understands Marx and Lenin.

Remarks in Arlington, Virginia, 25 September 1987

Mr Gorbachev, open this gate! Mr Gorbachev, tear down this wall!

Speech near the Berlin Wall, 1987

A friend of mine was asked to a costume ball a short time ago. He slapped some egg on his face and went as a liberal economist.

11 February 1988

Freedom is the right to question and change the established way of doing things. It is the continuous revolution of the marketplace. It is the understanding that allows us to recognise shortcomings and seek solutions.

Address to students at Moscow State University, 31 May 1988

The best minds are not in government. If any were, business would hire them away.

Attributed

In America, our origins matter less than our destination, and that is what democracy is all about.

1992

When you see all that rhetorical smoke billowing up from the Democrats, well ladies and gentleman, I'd follow the example of their nominee; don't inhale.

Republican National Convention, 1992

For you see, my fellow Republicans, we are the change!

Ibid.

This fellow they've nominated claims he's the new Thomas Jefferson. Well let me tell you something; I knew Thomas Jefferson. He was a friend of mine and Governor ... You're no Thomas Jefferson!

Ibid.

After watching the State of the Union address the other night, I'm reminded of the old adage that imitation is the sincerest form of flattery. Only in this case, it's not flattery, but grand larceny: the intellectual theft of ideas that you and I recognise as our own. Speech delivery counts for little on the world stage unless you have convictions, and, yes, the vision to see beyond the front row seats.

RNC Annual Gala, 3 February 1994

Although the political landscape has changed, the bold ideas of the 1980's are alive and well. Republican candidates swept every major election across the country last year ... and as a result, it seems that our opponents have finally realised how unpopular liberalism really is. So now they're trying to dress their liberal agenda in a Conservative overcoat.

Ibid.

However, our task is far from over. Our friends in the other party will never forgive us for our success, and are doing everything in their power to rewrite history. Listening to the liberals, you'd think that the 1980s were the worst period since the Great Depression, filled with suffering and despair. I don't know about you, but I'm getting awfully tired of the whining voices from the White House these days. They're claiming there was a decade of greed and neglect, but you and I know better than that. We were there.

Ibid.

It was leadership here at home that gave us strong American influence abroad, and the collapse of imperial Communism. Great nations have responsibilities to lead, and we should always be cautious of those who would lower our profile, because they might just wind up lowering our flag.

Ibid.

Now, as most of you know, I'm not one for looking back. I figure there will be plenty of time for that when I get old.

But rather, what I take from the past is inspiration for the future, and what we accomplished during our years at the White House must never be lost amid the rhetoric of political revisionists.
Ibid.

The Democrats may remember their lines, but how quickly they forget the lessons of the past. I have witnessed five major wars in my lifetime, and I know how swiftly storm clouds can gather on a peaceful horizon. The next time a Saddam Hussein takes over Kuwait, or North Korea brandishes a nuclear weapon, will we be ready to respond? In the end, it all comes down to leadership, and that is what this country is looking for now.
Ibid.

The Great Society is only great in power, in size, and in cost.
Attributed

Government does not generate revenue, it merely consumes it.
Attributed

I've been accused of being pro-business. Well, I just have to say: Guilty as charged.
Attributed

We have long since discovered that nothing lasts longer than a temporary government program.
Attributed

A broader reading of history shows that appeasement, no matter how it is labelled, never fulfils the hopes of its appeasers.
Attributed

Republicans believe every day is the 4th of July, but Democrats believe every day is April 15th.
Attributed

John Redwood
b. 1951; Conservative MP 1987–, Cabinet minister 1993–95

' ... ... '
As Welsh Secretary singing the Welsh national anthem

No Change, No Chance.
Leadership campaign slogan

I have always said that we need a steady nerve under fire, that we need to return to common-sense policies in health, education and Europe that brings us closer to the views of the nation. This is not lurching right but getting it right.
Action not Words (1996)

We should forget all this business about right or left. The old labels have much less meaning today.
Ibid.

Labour's constitutional blueprint is nothing less than a plan for the destruction of UK democracy.
1999

The EU project is to create a country called Europe.
2001

There is no point in saving the currency if we lose the country that goes with it.
May 2003

I have more government than I want, more government than I need, more government than I can afford.
June 2003

Ralph Reed
b. 1961; US Christian Coalition

We need laws that reflect the moral law and the law of God
again, what is right and what is wrong, what is just and what is
unjust.

Attributed

Jacob Rees-Mogg
b. 1969; Conservative MP 2010–

I'm a man of the people. Vox populi, vox Dei.

BBC interview with Andrew Neil, 26 January 2011

Stiffen your sinews, summon up the blood, imitate the action
of a tiger. For that is how you should behave to our European
partners, not like Bagpuss.

House of Commons, 24 October 2011

It is amazing how united the Conservative Party has been so
far today. We had a Eurosceptic statement from the Prime
Minister and then a Eurosceptic speech from the Foreign
Secretary, so it can only be the Liberal Democrats who are
inveigling us down the path of unrighteousness.

Ibid.

I am glad to say, Mr Deputy Speaker, that the requirement not
to be rude about judges applies only to judges in this country.
It does not apply to judges in the EU, so let me be rude about
them. Let me indulge in the floccinaucinihilipilification of EU
judges and quote from the book of Amos about them: 'For I
know your manifold transgressions and your mighty sins: they
afflict the just, they take a bribe, and they turn aside the poor
in the gate from their right.'

House of Commons, 21 February 2012

'Aspiration' is one of those ghastly political jargon words, but it's hard to find a better word.

Total Politics, 9 July 2012

It was easier to get cannabis in Hinton Blewett than a copy of *The Spectator*.

The Independent, 6 January 2013

Ernest Renan

1823–92; French philosopher and writer

He is very unwise who tries to shut a door against the future.

Attributed

Rod Richards

b. 1947; Conservative MP 1992–97

They are all the same. They're short, they're fat and they are fundamentally corrupt.

Junior Welsh Office Minister on Welsh Labour Councillors, 1995

Cardinal Richelieu

1585–1642; French Chief Minister of the Crown

Not the least of the qualities that go into the making of a great ruler is the ability of letting others serve him.

Political Testament (1687)

If the poor are too well off they will be disorderly.

Attributed

Nicholas Ridley

1929–93; Conservative MP 1959–92, Cabinet minister 1983–90

Trees have to be cut down and replanted.

As Environment Secretary, 1989

The [European Monetary Union] is a German racket designed to take over the whole of Europe. It has to be thwarted. This rushed takeover by the Germans on the worst possible basis, with the French behaving like poodles to the Germans, is absolutely intolerable.

The Spectator, 14 July 1990

Seventeen unelected reject politicians with no accountability to anybody, who are not responsible for raising taxes, just spending money, who are pandered to by a supine parliament which is also not responsible for raising taxes.

Ibid., on the European Commission

Malcolm Rifkind

b. 1946; Conservative MP 1975–97, Cabinet minister 1986–97

The future is not what it used to be.

On *Talking Politics*, BBC Radio, 1989

Old politicians never die, they just simply wade away.

On John Stonehouse

Scotland needs the Labour Party as much as Sicily needs the Mafia.

1992

Conservatives are not reactionary defenders of the status quo. Sometimes if you want things to stay the same, things have to change.

Speech to Conservative Mainstream, 7 June 2005

That is the sad problem with the Liberal Democrats: they always wish to be all things to all people – to go for the middle way. I am reminded of a remark I once heard, which I thought was rather good: if Christopher Columbus had been a Liberal Democrat, he probably would have been content with discovering the mid-Atlantic.

Lords reform debate, 9 July 2012

Blessed are the young, for they shall inherit the national debt.

Misquoting Herbert Hoover

He has as much claim to the mantle of Margaret Thatcher as Silvio Berlusconi had to that of Julius Caesar.

On Ed Miliband's likeness to Thatcher, 19 November 2012

Pat Robertson
b. 1930; US televangelist

You don't go out and kick a mad dog. If you have a mad dog with rabies, you take a gun and shoot him.

On Libyan leader Colonel Gaddafi

A dark land teeming with homosexuals.

On Scotland (paraphrased), 1999

John Rodgers
1906–93; Conservative MP 1950–79

With the coming of television [the average youth] now stays indoors three or four nights a week. Those who are worried about the problem of growing juvenile delinquency should take some comfort from the fact that here is a medium which can attract the young.

1953

Theodore Roosevelt

1858–1919; US President 1901–09

There is a homely adage which runs 'Speak softly and carry a big stick, you will go far.'
  1901

It is hard to fail, but it is worse never to have tried to succeed. Do what you can, with what you have, where you are.
  Attributed

Sir Hugh Rossi

b. 1927; Conservative MP 1966–87

Home ownership stabilises society, engenders pride in possessions and self-respect, and gives the individual and the family personal independence and freedom. We know that it fulfils the great desire of the vast majority of people in this country ... Their (Socialist) vision of a society amounts to a form of serfdom where people are municipal tenants with nothing to call their own, subjected to the patronage and paternalism of local political barons ... we do not have to wait for Fritz Lang's *Metropolis* or even George Orwell's *1984*. It is here and now. It is to be seen in districts of Glasgow, Sheffield, Liverpool...
  1977

Our nuclear power stations are as safe as they can possibly be, and are getting safer all the time.
  As Environment Minister, 1986

Jean Jacques Rousseau

1712–78; French philosopher

It should be remembered that the foundation of the social contract is property; and its first condition, that everyone should be maintained in the peaceful possession of what belongs to him.

A Discourse in Political Economy (1758)

Salman Rushdie

b. 1947; novelist

The true Conservatives of Britain are now in the Labour Party, while the radicals are all in blue.

Quoted by Brian Walden, *Sunday Times*, 1989

S

Michael Hicks Beach, Viscount St Aldwyn
1837–1916; British Conservative politician

In my opinion, pensions ... are worse than a waste of public
money: they are the greatest possible incentive to the absence
of self-reliance and thrift.
    1907

Norman St John Stevas
1929–2012; Conservative MP,1964–87, Cabinet minister 1979–81

The twentieth century may not be a very good thing but it is
the only century we've got.
    1970

It wasn't an election. It was an assumption.
    On Margaret Thatcher's election as Leader of the Conservative
    Party, 1975

The tragedy is that the present government are much more
concerned with the use of comprehensive schools as a means of
social engineering to further the egalitarian society which they
favour, than they are with the educational wants or otherwise
of comprehensive schools.
    1976

There is another threat which is more subtle and more
deadly and that is the collapse into a society which is neither
Communist nor Conservative, but is simply valueless –
an amoral rootless society, indifferent to the spiritual,
contemptuous of the arts, in which pornography not religion,

would be the opium of the people, and the horrors of the 'Clockwork Orange' society would be translated from fantasy to reality. There is only one answer to that: we have to revivify and renew moral and religious education in our schools.

1977

But I mustn't go on singling out names. One must not be a name-dropper, as Her Majesty remarked to me yesterday...

Daily Telegraph, 1979

I have nothing against Hampstead. I used to live there myself when I was an intellectual. I gave that up when I became Leader of the House.

1980

I used to be in favour of women priests but two years in the Cabinet cured me of them.

As an ex-member of Margaret Thatcher's Cabinet, 1981

Lord Salisbury

1830–1903; Prime Minister 1885–86, 1886–92, 1895–1902

No lesson seems to be so deeply inculcated by the experience of life as that you never should trust experts.

1877

English policy is to float lazily downstream, occasionally putting out a diplomatic boathook to avoid collisions.

Ibid.

Old King Tarquin knew what he was about when he symbolised the surest way of enslaving a community by striking off the heads of the tallest poppies.

1883

It has always been our intention that the people in their
localities should govern themselves – and that the attempt
to imitate continental plans by drawing all authority
from the central power, though it might produce a more
scientific, a more exact, and for the moment a more effective
administration, yet was destitute of the two essentials of all
good government that was suited to the facts and idiosyncrasies
of the particular community for whom it was designed, and did
not teach the people to take that active interest in their own
government which is the only training that makes a man a true
and worthy citizen.

Newport, 1885

I have four departments – the Prime Minister's, the Foreign
Office, the Queen and Randolph Churchill; the burden of them
increases in that order.

1886

We are part of the community of Europe and we must do our
duty as such.

10 April 1888

The perils of change are so great, the promise of the most
hopeful theories is so often deceptive, that it is frequently the
wiser part to uphold the existing state of things, if it can be
done, even though, in point of argument, it should be utterly
indefensible.

1890

The federated action of Europe is our sole hope of escaping
from the constant terror and calamity of war.

1897

The Chamberlain family govern the country as if they were
following hounds – where according to hunting conventions it
is mean-spirited to look before you leap.

Letter to A. J. Balfour, 1904

A violent, isolated, artificial improvement in the institutions of
a community, undertaken without regard to the condition
of the other portions of the machinery in concert with which
it is to work, is a danger so great that no improvement at all is
almost to be preferred.

Attributed

The Cabinet is the creature of the House of Commons. It
springs from the House of Commons and dwells in the House
of Commons. It is checked and corrected by the House of
Commons and by the shrug of the shoulders of the private
members of the House the Cabinet can be shattered.

Attributed

The bestowal on any class of a voting power disproportionate
to their stake in the country, must infallibly give to that class a
power potential of using taxation as an instrument of plunder
and legislation as a fountain of gain ... and when universal
suffrage was reached, it would be simple despotism.

Attributed

Roger Scruton

1944; political philosopher and musicologist

The basic premise of conservatism is that worthwhile
institutions are hard to build, and easy to destroy, and that a
life without institutions is seriously impoverished.

The Times, 1983

The idea of social justice on which the welfare state is founded
– where social justice is supposed to be something other than
charity, a right of the recipient rather than a virtue of the one
who gives – seems to sponsor and condone a corruption of the
moral sense.

Conservative Texts (1991)

The welfare state that is built upon this conception seems to move precisely away from the Conservative conception of authoritative and personal government, towards a labyrinthine, privilege sodden structure of anonymous power, nurturing a citizenship that is increasingly reluctant to answer for itself, increasingly void of personal responsibility, and increasingly parasitic on the dispensations of a bureaucracy towards which it can feel no gratitude.

Ibid.

The welfare state promises more than it can provide, grows like a cancer in the economic order, and finally threatens the process of wealth-creation itself. If the lot of the poor is changed by the welfare state, it is because something else changes also – namely, the productive capacity upon which the welfare state depends, and which it also threatens to extinguish.

Ibid.

John Seeley

1834–95; English historian and essayist

I believe that the [War Ministry] are entirely wrong in thinking that they can substitute tanks for cavalry ... That seems to me a most extraordinary misreading of the lessons of the war ... It would be the most extraordinary misconception of the truth to imagine that in applying science to war the first thing to get rid of is the horse. On the contrary, every advance in science has made the horse a more and more indispensable weapon of war. Heavy artillery fire, heavy machine-gun fire, gas, aeroplane observation – all these make rapid movement more essential.

Former Secretary of State for War, 1921

Seneca

1st century; Greek philosopher, dramatist and statesman

The foremost art of the kings is the power to endure hatred.
Thyestes

If you judge, investigate; if you reign, command.
Attributed

William Shakespeare

1564–1616; dramatist

O thoughts of men accurst!
Past, and to come seem best, things present worst!
King Henry IV, Part II

Let them obey that know not how to rule.
Ibid.

The first thing we do, let's kill all the lawyers.
Ibid.

Not all the water in the rough rude sea
Can wash the balm off an appointed king.
King Richard II

Give every man your ear, but very few your voice,
Take each man's censure but reserve your judgement.
Hamlet

There's hope a great man's memory may outlive his life by half
a year.
Ibid.

Men's evil manners live in brass, their virtues we write in water.

Ibid.

We must not make a scarecrow of the law,
Setting it up to fear the birds of prey,
And let it keep one shape, till custom make it
Their perch and not their terror.

Measure for Measure

Some are born great, some achieve greatness, and some have greatness thrust upon 'em.

Twelfth Night

When our actions do not, or fears do make us traitors.

Macbeth

George Bernard Shaw

1856–1950; Dramatist and intellectual

Charity deals with symptoms instead of causes.

Man and Superman (1903)

Money … enables us to get what we want instead of what other people think we want.

The Intelligent Woman's Guide to Socialism (1928)

Michael Shersby

1933–97; Conservative MP 1972–97

The police force in Britain is a reactionary force. It has to respond…

1990

Edward Shils

1910–95; American sociologist

Human beings need the help of their ancestors; and they need the help which is provided by their own biological ancestors and they need the help of the ancestors of their communities and institutions, of the ancestors and they need the help of the ancestors of their communities and institutions ... The destruction or the discrediting of these cognitive, moral, metaphysical, and technical charts is a step into chaos.

Tradition (1981)

Samuel Smiles

1812–1904; Victorian moralist

The spirit of self-help is the root of all genuine growth in the individual, and, exhibited in the lives of the many; it constitutes the true source of national vigour and strength.
Help from without is often enfeebling in its effects, but help from within invariably invigorates.

Self Help (1859)

Adam Smith

1723–90; moral philosopher and political economist

Every individual is constantly exerting from himself to find out the most advantageous employment for whatever capital he can command. It is his own advantage, indeed, and not that of society, which he has in view. But the study of his own advantage naturally, or rather necessarily leads him to prefer that employment which is most advantageous to society.

Wealth of Nations (1776)

The property which every man has in his own labour, as it
is the original foundation of all other property, so it is the most
sacred and the most inviolable.
Ibid.

There is no art which one government sooner learns of another
than that of draining money from the pockets of the people.
Ibid.

Nobody but a beggar chooses to depend chiefly upon the
benevolence of his fellow citizens.
Ibid.

The uniform constant and uninterrupted effort of every man
to better his condition, the principle from which public and
national, as well as private opulence is originally derived is
frequently powerful enough to maintain the natural progress of
things towards improvement, in spite of both the extravagance
of government and of greater errors of administration.
Ibid.

Great nations are never impoverished by private, though they
sometimes are by public prodigality and misconduct. The
whole, or almost the whole public revenue, is in most countries
employed in maintaining unproductive hands.
Ibid.

Without any intervention of law ... the private interests and
passions of men naturally lead them to divide and distribute
the stock of every society, among all the different employments
carried on in it, as nearly as possible in the proportion which is
most agreeable to the interests of the whole society.
Ibid.

Edward Smith-Stanley
1799–1869; Prime Minister 1852, 1858–59, 1866–68

When I first came into Parliament, Mr Tierney, a great Whig authority, used always to say that the duty of an opposition was very simple – it was to oppose everything and propose nothing.
Attributed

Alexander Solzhenitsyn
1918–2008; Russian novelist

I have spent my whole life under a Communist regime, and I will tell you that a society without any objective legal scale is a terrible one indeed. But a society with no other scale than the legal one is not quite worthy of man either.
Commencement address, Harvard University, 1978

[I]t is time to remember that the first thing we belong to is humanity. And humanity is separated from the animal kingdom by thought and speech and they should naturally be free. If they are fettered we go back to being animals.
Letter to the Writer's Union, Moscow, quoted in the *New York Times*, 15 November 1969

Anna Soubry
b. 1956; Conservative MP 2010–

What we now need to do is stop people in the party engaging in quite a lot of twattery. I came into politics to fight lefties.
On backbench squabbling, *Total Politics*, 24 April 2012

Thomas Sowell

b. 1930; American economist, philosopher and author

Compassion is the use of tax money to buy votes. Insensitivity is the objection to the use of tax money to buy votes.

Attributed

Herbert Spencer

1820–1903; sociologist

Conservatism defends those coercive arrangements which a still lingering savageness makes requisite. Radicalism endeavours to realise a state more in harmony with the character of the ideal man.

1850

An argument fatal to the Communist theory, is suggested by the fact ... that a desire for property is one of the elements of our nature.

Social Statistics (1851)

Liberty of each, limited by the like liberties of all, is the rule in conformity with which society must be organised.

Ibid.

Feudalism, Serfdom, slavery, all tyrannical institutions, are merely the most vigorous kind to rule, springing out of, and necessary to, a bad state of man. The progress from these is the same in all cases – less government.

Ibid.

All Socialism involves slavery.

The Man versus the State (1884)

The Republican form of government is the highest form of government: but because of this it requires the highest type of human nature – a type nowhere at present existing.

Essays (1891)

Society exists for the benefit of its members; not the members for the benefit of society.

Principles on Ethics (1892–93)

A Frenchman who having been three weeks here, proposed to write a book on England, after three months found that he was not quite ready, and after three years concluded that he knew nothing about it.

Study of Sociology (1873)

Ivor Stanbrook

1924–2004; Conservative MP 1970–92

It is the normal British practice for the wife to go where her husband desires.

1982

Adlai Stevenson

1900–65; American statesman

Patriotism is not a short and frenzied outburst of emotion but the tranquil and steady dedication of a lifetime.

Speech to American Legion, 1952

A wise man does not try to hurry up history.

Ibid.

Leo Strauss

1899–1973; American political philosopher

The difficulty of defining the difference between liberalism
and conservatism with the necessary universality is particularly
great in the United States, since this country came into being
through a revolution, a violent change or break with the past.
One of the most Conservative groups here calls itself the
Daughters of the American Revolution.

Liberalism: Ancient and Modern (1968)

Jonathan Swift

1667–1745; satirist and writer

Confine the expression of popular feeling within rigid limits,
surround it with iron bands, and a spark may cause a terrific
explosion. Leave it free and like gunpowder scattered in the
open air, even if set alight it will do no damage.

Attributed

T

Sir Peter Tapsell

b. 1930; Conservative MP 1959–64, 1966–; Father of the House 2010–

A single European currency was first proposed by the Nazi Reichsbank to Hitler at the time of Dunkirk. Now it is EU policy.

   2001

Michael Taylor

b. 1942; political scientist

I suggest that the more the state intervenes in such situations, the more 'necessary' (on this view) it becomes, because positive altruism and voluntary cooperative behaviour atrophy in the presence of the state and grow in its absence. Thus, again, the state exacerbates the conditions which are supposed to make it necessary. We might say that the state is like an addictive drug: the more of it we have, the more we 'need' it and the more we come to 'depend' on it.

   The Possibility of Cooperation (1987)

Norman Tebbit

b. 1931; Conservative MP 1970–92, Cabinet minister 1981–87

I grew up in the thirties, with an unemployed father. He didn't riot. He got on his bike and looked for work.

   Conservative Party Conference, October 1981

The Labour Party is not dead, just brain dead.

   Attributed

The trigger of today's outburst of crime and violence ... lies in the era and attitudes of post-war funk which gave birth to the permissive society.

The Guardian, 4 November 1985

I hope Mrs Thatcher will go until the turn of the century looking like Queen Victoria.

1987

The word 'conservative' is used by the BBC as a portmanteau word of abuse for anyone whose views differ from the insufferable, smug, sanctimonious, naïve, guilt-ridden, wet, pink orthodoxy of that sunset home of the third-rate minds of that third-rate decade, the 1960s.

The Independent, 24 February 1990

Liberals are Enid Blyton Socialists – a dustbin for undecided votes.

Attributed

Those who stand outside the town hall and scream and throw rotten eggs are not the real unemployed. If they were really hard up they would be eating the eggs.

Attributed

Why don't you go and have another heart attack?

To Labour MP Tom Litterick

Take a sedative.

To Denis Healey

I'm older than you are sonny, and you can take me on when you grow up.

Attributed

The cricket test – which side do you cheer for? Are you still looking back to where you came from or where you are?

On the loyalties of British immigrants

Maastricht is like that famous dead parrot. They may try to nail it on the perch again but nobody will believe it is still alive.
>   1992

I am not impressed by being called anti-European by those who were in short trousers when I began campaigning for Britain to enter the Common Market.
>   1993

That foul abomination, that running sore of Britain's politics, John Major's political tar baby, John Smith's self-imposed political ball and chain, the crumbling altar of the xenophobic paranoiac world of Monsieur Delors.
>   On the Maastricht Treaty

Perhaps election fever is developing into something more like sleeping sickness, as the utter boredom of a contest in which almost all the attention seems to be on personalities and polls wears us all down. I just wish they would get on with it.
>   On the upcoming general election, *Daily Telegraph*, March 2010

Why shouldn't a mother marry her daughter? Why shouldn't two elderly sisters living together marry each other? I quite fancy my brother!
>   On equal marriage, 21 May 2013

Alfred, Lord Tennyson
1809–92; Poet Laureate

For I dipt into the future, far as human eye could see;
Saw the vision of the world, and all the wonder that
would be...
Yet I doubt not through the ages one enduring purpose runs,
And the thoughts of men are widened with the process of
the suns.
>   *Locksley Hall* (1838)

A doubtful throne is ice on summer seas.
  Idylls of the Kings (1869)

'Forward' rang the voices then, and of the many mine was one.
Let us hush this cry of 'Forward' till ten thousand years have
gone.
  Locksley Hall Sixty Years After (1887)

When was age so cramm'd with menace? Madness? written,
spoken lies?
  Ibid.

Tertullian

c.150–225; Christian theologian

Prevention of birth is a precipitation of murder.
  Attributed

Carol Thatcher

b. 1953; daughter of Margaret Thatcher

After all she's done, I think this is an act of gutless treachery.
As far as I'm concerned Tory is now a four-letter word.
  To a journalist outside her home, 22 November 1990

Oh Mum, it's me. I think you're a heroine. [Bursts into tears] I
don't know how you made that speech. It's just so awful what
they've done – your party are complete shits.
  Speaking to her mother on the evening of 22 November 1990

Being the only girl in the world who can say that her mother was
Britain's first woman Prime Minister is honour enough for me.
  13 June 1992

I now have to spell Thatcher when I make table reservations at restaurants – but I can cope with that.

The Independent, 28 December 1993

Denis Thatcher

1915–2003; husband of Margaret Thatcher

For forty years I have been married to one of the greatest women the world has ever produced. All I could produce – small as it may be – was love and loyalty.

On Margaret Thatcher

Bit worried. Bloody bad business with those polls. They just won't budge.

On the 2001 general election

Margaret Thatcher

1925–2013; Member of Parliament 1959–93, Cabinet minister 1970–74, Prime Minister 1979–90

I wasn't lucky, I deserved it.

On winning a school prize, aged nine

This woman is headstrong, obstinate and dangerously self-opinionated.

Report on Margaret Roberts by the ICI Personnel Department, rejecting her job application, 1948

Every Conservative desires peace. The threat to peace comes from Communism which has powerful forces ready to attack anywhere. Communism waits for weakness, it leaves strength alone. Britain must therefore be strong, strong in her arms, strong in her faith, strong in her own way of life.

Margaret Roberts election leaflet, 1950

It is expensive to be in politics. One has to be mobile, one has to be well groomed, and one has to entertain.

The Guardian, March 1962

The legal system we have and the rule of law are far more responsible for our traditional liberties than any system of one man one vote. Any country or government which wants to proceed towards tyranny starts to undermine legal rights and undermine the law.

Conservative Party Conference, October 1966

Civil servants have not got the expertise at their disposal which a merchant bank has. If they had such expertise, they would probably be working very successfully for a merchant bank.

1967

We must recognise certain groups of people who need help, but the rest of us must take responsibility for ourselves, and we must stop being such a subsidised-minded society.

At the Scottish Conservative Party Conference, May 1969

No woman in my time will be Prime Minister or Foreign Secretary – not the top jobs. Anyway I wouldn't want to be Prime Minister. You have to give yourself one hundred per cent to the job.

1969

This business of the working class is on its way out I think. After all, aren't I working class? I work jolly hard, I can tell you.

London Evening News, October 1969

We are not in politics to ignore people's worries; we are in politics to deal with them.

Attributed

Many of our troubles are due to the fact that our people turn to politicians for everything.

Attributed

It costs just as much to train a bad teacher as it does to train a good teacher.

1973

Please don't use the word tough. People might get the impression that I don't care. And I do care very deeply. Resilient, I think.

August 1973

I don't want to be leader of the party – I'm happy to be in the top dozen.

1974

We failed the people.

On the Heath government, *Daily Telegraph*, February 1974

We should back the workers, not the shirkers.

February 1974

It was then that the iron entered my soul.

On her time in the Heath Cabinet

The charm of Britain has always been the ease with which one can move into the middle class.

London Evening Standard, October 1974

Some Chancellors are micro-economic. Some Chancellors are fiscal. This one is just plain cheap … If this Chancellor can be Chancellor, anyone in the House could be Chancellor.

On Denis Healey, January 1975

Look Keith, if you're not going to stand, I will.

To Sir Keith Joseph after he decided not to stand against Edward Heath for the party leadership

Forget that I'm a woman. Forget the accusations that I am
a Right Winger demanding privilege – I had precious little
privilege in my early years.

> February 1975

We must build a society in which each citizen can develop his
full potential, both for his own benefit and for the community
as a whole.

> 1975

I've got my teeth into him, and I'm not going to let go.

> On Edward Heath during the leadership contest, February 1975

To me it is like a dream that the next name in the list after
Harold Macmillan, Sir Alec Douglas-Home and Edward Heath
is Margaret Thatcher.

> February 1975

The better I do, the more is expected of me. I am ready for
that. I think I have the strength to do anything that I feel has to
be done.

> *Daily Telegraph*, September 1975

You cannot bring about prosperity by discouraging thrift.
You cannot strengthen the weak by weakening the strong.
You cannot help strong men by tearing.
You cannot help the wage earner by pulling down the wage payer.
You cannot further the brotherhood by encouraging class
hatred.
You cannot help the poor by destroying the rich.
You cannot establish sound security on borrowed money.
You cannot keep out of trouble by spending more than you earn.
You cannot build character and courage by taking away man's
initiative and independence.
You cannot help men permanently by doing for them what they
could and should do for themselves.

> Abraham Lincoln, kept by Mrs Thatcher in her handbag

We must have an ideology. The other side have got an ideology they can test their policies against. We must have one as well.
1975

I sometimes think the Labour Party is like a pub where the mild is running out. If someone does not do something soon, all that is left will be bitter and all that is bitter will be left.
Ibid.

In a Socialist society, parents should be seen and not heard.
Conservative Party Conference, 10 October 1975

They have the usual Socialist disease; they have run out of other people's money.
Ibid.

The first duty of a government is to uphold the law, and if it tries to bob, weave and duck round that duty when it is inconvenient the governed will do exactly the same thing, and then nothing will be safe, not home, not liberty, not life itself.
1975

Let our children grow tall, and some grow taller than others.
Speech in the United States, 1975

The Budget gives away the money the Chancellor has not even borrowed yet.
On Denis Healey's 1976 Budget

We look to our alliance with NATO as the precise guarantee of our own security and, in the world beyond Europe, the United States is still the prime champion of freedom ... We believe in the Conservative Party that our foreign policy should continue to be based on a close understanding with our traditional ally, America.
1976

If your only opportunity is to be equal then it is not opportunity.

28 November 1976

For the Conservative Party politics has always been about something more than gaining power. It has been about serving the nation. We are above all a patriotic party ... nothing that's bad for Britain can ever be good for Conservatives.

1976

Ladies & Gentlemen, I stand before you tonight in my green chiffon evening gown, my face softly made up, my hair softly waved ... The Iron Lady of the western world? Me? A cold warrior? Well, yes – if that is how they wish to interpret my defence of the values and freedom fundamental to our way of life.

Referring to the Soviet Magazine *Red Star*, which was the first to call her the Iron Lady, 1976

Sometimes I've heard it said that Conservatives have been associated with unemployment. That's absolutely wrong. We'd have been drummed out of office if we'd had this level of unemployment.

On the Labour government's employment record, 1977

We want a society in which we are free to make choices, to make mistakes, to be generous and compassionate. That is what we mean by a moral society – not a society in which the state is responsible for everything, and no one is responsible for the state.

At Zurich University, 14 March 1977

My great fear is that when the time comes, I might fail.

April 1977

Let me tell you a little about my extremism. I am extremely careful never to be extreme. I am extremely aware of the dangerous duplicity of Socialism, and extremely determined to turn back the tide before it destroys everything we hold dear. I am extremely disinclined to be deceived by the mask of moderation that Labour adopts whenever an election is in the offing, a mask now being worn by all those who would 'keep the red flag flying here'.

Conservative Party Conference, 14 October 1977

We do not believe that if you cut back what government does you diminish its authority. On the contrary, a government that did less, and therefore did better, would strengthen its authority.

Ibid.

Choice is the essence of ethics. If there were no choice there would be no ethics, no good, no evil. Good and evil only have meaning in so far as man is free to choose.

1977

We must learn again to be one nation or one day we shall be no nation.

1978

There are still people in my party who believe in consensus politics. I regard them as Quislings, as traitors ... I mean it.

Ibid.

Marxists get up early to further their cause. We must get up even earlier to defend our freedom.

Daily Mail, May 1978

If you wash your hands of Northern Ireland you wash them in blood.

Conservative Party Conference, 13 October 1978

There are two ways of making a Cabinet. One way is to have in it people representing the different points of view within the party, within the broad philosophy. The other way is to have

in it only the people who want to go in the direction which
every instinct tells me we have to go: clearly, steadily, firmly,
with resolution. As Prime Minister, I could not waste my time
having internal arguments.

    1979

I am not a consensus politician – I'm a conviction politician.

    Ibid.

Let us make this country safe to work in. Let us make this
country safe to walk in. Let us make it a country safe to grow
up in. Let us make it a country safe to grow old in.

    Party political broadcast, 30 April 1979

Where there is discord may we bring harmony. Where there is
error, may we bring truth. Where there is doubt, may we bring
faith. Where there is despair, may we bring hope.

    Quoting St Francis of Assisi on the steps of 10 Downing Street,
    May 1979

In the age of materialism we stand for value. In an age of
selfishness we believe in service. In an age of sectional interests
we still uphold the flag of patriotism, honour, family, courage,
integrity and self-sacrifice. We do not equate permissiveness
with civilised behaviour. We will neither permit ourselves,
nor encourage others to overstep the bounds of conscience,
morality and the law. It is because we are the party of freedom
that we are also the party of the law.

    Attributed

Unless we change our ways and our direction, our greatness as
a nation will soon be a footnote in the history books, a distant
memory of an offshore island, lost in the mist of time like
Camelot, remembered kindly for its noble past.

    2 May 1979

We should not underestimate the enormity of the task which lies ahead. But little can be achieved without sound money. It is the bedrock of sound government.

May 1979

The mission of this government is much more than the promotion of economic progress. It is to renew the spirit and solidarity of the nation.

6 June 1979

When I look at him [Edward Heath] and he looks at me, I don't feel that it is a man looking at a woman. More like a woman being looked at by another woman.

To Sir John Junor, 1979

If someone is confronting our essential liberties, if someone is inflicting injuries and harm, by God I'll confront them!

1979

Any woman who understands the problems of running a home will be nearer to understanding the problems of running a country.

Ibid.

Pennies don't fall from heaven, they have to be earned on earth.

Sunday Telegraph, November 1979

Nobody would remember the Good Samaritan if he had only good intentions, he had money as well.

1980

Iron entered my soul. You need a touch of steel. Otherwise you become like India rubber.

BBC Radio, March 1980

To those waiting with baited breath for that favourite media catchphrase, the U Turn, I have only one thing to say. You turn if you want to. The Lady's not for turning.

Conservative Party Conference, 10 October 1980

I want my money back!

Dublin EC Summit, November 1980

If a woman like Eva Peron with no ideals can get that far, think how far I can go with all the ideals I have.

Sunday Times, 1980

I don't mind how much my Ministers talk, as long as they do what I say.

1980

You belong to the North East, why don't you boost it? Not always standing there as moaning minnies. Now stop it!

Description of journalists on Tyneside

If you have conviction people are much more likely to come out and support you. Most of the great faiths upon which our own moral values are founded would never have got started if their prophets had gone out to the people and said: 'Brothers, I believe in consensus.'

News of the World, September 1981

Our judgement is that the presence of the Royal Marines garrison ... is sufficient deterrent against any possible aggression.

Attributed

Oh, those poor shopkeepers.

Visiting Toxteth after the 1981 riots

Competition works. It is thanks to Freddie Laker that you can cross the Atlantic for so much less than it would have cost in the early 1970s.

Speech to Conference, 1981

The people of the Falkland Islands, like the people of the United Kingdom, are an island race. They are few in number but they have the right to live in peace, to choose their own way of life and to determine their own allegiance. Their way of life is British; their allegiance is to the Crown. It is the wish of the British people and the duty of Her Majesty's government to do everything that we can to uphold that right. That will be our hope and our endeavour, and, I believe, the resolve, of every Member of this House.

House of Commons, 3 April 1982

When you stop a dictator there are always risks, but there are great risks in not stopping a dictator. My generation learned that long ago.

1982

Gentlemen, I have spent the night thinking about this Peruvian (peace) initiative and I have to tell you that if it is your decision to accept then you will have to find another Prime Minister.

To the War Cabinet, May 1982

It is exciting to have a real crisis on your hands when you have spent half your life dealing with humdrum issues like the environment.

May 1982

Just rejoice at the news and congratulate our armed forces and the Marines. Rejoice!

To journalists, following the retaking of South Georgia, 1982

We have ceased to be a nation in retreat. We have instead a new found confidence – born in the economic battles at home and tested and found true 8,000 miles away ... And so today, we can rejoice at our success in the Falklands and take pride in the achievement of the men and women of our task force. But we do so, not as some flickering of a flame which must soon be dead. No, we rejoice that Britain has rekindled that spirit which has fired her for generations past and which today has begun to burn as brightly as before. Britain found herself again in the South Atlantic and will not look back from the victory she has won.

3 July 1982

There are forces more powerful and pervasive than the apparatus of war. You may chain a man, but you cannot chain his mind. You may enslave him, but you will not conquer his spirit. In every decade since the war Soviet leaders have been reminded that their pitiless ideology only survives because it is maintained by force. But the day will come when the anger and frustration of the people is so great that force cannot contain it. Then the edifice cracks; the mortar crumbles ... one day, liberty will dawn on the other side of the wall.

In Berlin, 29 October 1982

Most of us have stopped using silver every day.

Attributed

Successful businessmen do not take jobs in nationalised industries.

1982

Oh, Lord, teach me to learn that occasionally I make mistakes.

Quoting her favourite poem, BBC Radio, 1982

If you want anything said, ask a man; if you want anything done, ask a woman.

The Changing Anatomy of Britain (1982)

Oh, I have got lots of human weaknesses, who hasn't?

The Times, 1983

State socialism is totally alien to the British character.
>1983

You can strike your way down, but you have to work your way up.
>Ibid.

Will this thing jerk me off?
>Firing a field gun on the Falkland Islands, January 1983

If you are pronouncing a new law that wherever Communism reigns against the will of the people, even though it's happened internally, there the United States shall enter, then we are going to have really terrible wars in the world.
>Condemning the US invasion of Grenada, 1983

I was brought up by a Victorian Grandmother. We were taught to work jolly hard. We were taught to prove yourself; we were taught self-reliance; we were taught to live within our income. You were taught that cleanliness is next to Godliness. You were taught self-respect. You were taught always to give a hand to your neighbour. You were taught tremendous pride in your country. All of these things are Victorian values. They are also perennial values. You don't hear so much about these things these days, but they were good values and they led to tremendous improvements in the standard of living.
>LBC Radio, April 1983

I was asked whether I was trying to restore Victorian values. I said straight out I was. And I am.
>1983

It's a pity about Ronnie (Reagan), he just doesn't understand economics at all.
>Ibid.

And what a prize we have to fight for: no less than the chance to banish from our land the dark, divisive clouds of Marxist socialism.

Scottish Conservative Party Conference, May 1983

It's a result that will reverberate through our history. Its consequences will outlive most of us here tonight.

On the 1983 election result, 7 June 1983

Socialism and Britain go ill together. It is not the British character.

Director Magazine, September 1983

We got a really good consensus during the last election. Consensus behind my convictions.

1984

I love being at the centre of things.

Ibid.

I would feel desperate if I had been without a good regular income for twenty weeks.

Ibid.

I came to office with one deliberate intent – to change Britain from a dependent to a self-reliant society, from a give-it-to-me to a do-it-yourself nation, to a get-up-and-go instead of a sit-back-and-wait Britain.

The Times, 8 February 1984

What do you think of those two then?

To male advisers, while holding up page 3 of *The Sun* in front of them

I am always on the job.

Interview on *Aspel & Co*, LWT, 1984

In the Conservative Party we have no truck with outmoded Marxist doctrine about class warfare. For us it is not who you are, who your family is or where you come from that matters, but what you are and what you can do for your country that counts.

1984

What we've got is an attempt to substitute the rule of the mob for the rule of the law. It must not succeed.

On the Miners' Strike, 1984

Scabs? They are lions!

On working miners, Conservative Party Conference, 13 October 1984

Beer and sandwiches at No.10? No, never.

Rejecting idea of negotiations to end the Miners' Strike

I am an ally of the United States. We believe the same things, we believe passionately in the same battle of ideas, we will defend them to the hilt. Never try to separate me from them.

To Mikhail Gorbachev at their first meeting in 1984

The bomb attack on the Grand Hotel early this morning was first and foremost an inhuman, undiscriminating attempt to massacre innocent, unsuspecting men and women staying in Brighton for our Conservative Conference. Our first thoughts must at once be for those who died and for those who are now in hospital recovering from their injuries. But the bomb attack clearly signified more than this. It was an attempt not only to disrupt and terminate our conference; it was an attempt to cripple Her Majesty's democratically elected government. That is the scale of the outrage we have all shared, and the fact that we are gathered here now, shocked but composed and determined, is a sign not only that this attack has failed but that all attempts to destroy democracy by terrorism will fail.

Conservative Party Conference, 12 October 1984

In church on Sunday morning – it was lovely and we haven't had many lovely days – the sun was coming through the stained glass window and falling on some flowers. It just occurred to me that this was the day I was not meant to see. Then all of a sudden I thought 'there are some of my dearest friends who are not seeing this day'.

> Following the IRA bomb attack on the Cabinet in Brighton, October 1984

I like Mr Gorbachev. We can do business together.

> On Mikhail Gorbachev, December 1984

We had to fight the enemy without in the Falklands. We always have to be aware of the enemy within, which is more difficult to fight and more dangerous to liberty.

> On the Miners' Strike, 1984–85

If they do not wish to confer the honour, I am the last person who would wish to receive it.

> On Oxford University's decision not to give her an honorary degree, 1985

Yes, unemployment breeds frustration, but it's an insult to the unemployed to suggest that a man who doesn't have a job is likely to break the law.

> Conservative Party Conference, 11 October 1985

I took a pair of old scissors. I cut the card into pieces and sent it back to them in their prepaid envelope with a letter protesting against a gross invasion of privacy.

> On receiving a credit card

I may not be Prime Minister at six o'clock.

> To colleagues just before the No Confidence Debate over Westland, 26 January 1986

I know nothing about diplomacy, but I know I want certain things for Britain.

   1986

Has he resigned or has he gone for a pee?

   To Cabinet colleagues on Michael Heseltine's resignation,
   January 1986

If you want to cut your own throat, don't come to me for a bandage.

   To Robert Mugabe on South African sanctions, July 1986

There is just one thing I would like to make clear. The rose I am wearing is the rose of England.

   A dig at Labour's red rose logo, Conservative Party Conference,
   1986

Dr Johnson could have said: when you know you are going to be privatised, it concentrates the mind wonderfully.

   1986

What did it ever do for me?

   On feminism

The Labour Party believes in turning workers against owners; we believe in turning workers into owners.

   Sunday election rally speech, 1987

Popular capitalism is on the march ... Of course, there will always be people who, in the name of morality, sneer at this and call it 'materialism'. But isn't it moral that people should want to improve the material standard of living of their families, by their own effort? Isn't it moral that families should work for the means to look after their old folk? Isn't it moral that people should save, so as to be responsible for themselves? ... And it is for government to work with that grain in human nature to strengthen the strand of responsibility and independence: it benefits the family; it benefits the children; it is the essence of freedom.

Scottish Conservative Party Conference, May 1987

I feel more genuine affection this time. I think I have become a bit of an institution and, you know, the sort of thing people expect to see around the place.

At the start of the general election campaign, May 1987

This is only the third time of asking. I hope to go on and on and on.

During the general election campaign, May 1987

I exercise my right as a free citizen to spend my own money in my own way, so that I can go on the day, the time, to the doctor I choose and get out fast.

On why she chooses to use private healthcare, causing a political storm during the general election campaign, June 1987

We've got a big job to do in some of those inner cities, a really big job.

To party workers at Conservative Central Office, 12 June 1987

There is no such thing as Society. There are individual men and women, and there are families.

1987

It would be fatal for us to stand just where we are now. What would be our slogan for the 1990s if we did that? Would 'consolidate' be the word that we stitch on our banners? Whose blood would run faster at the prospect of five years of consolidation?

Conservative Party Conference, 9 October 1987

We are in the fortunate position, in Britain, of being, as it were, the senior person in power.

To a reporter en route to Moscow, 1987

I've seen and heard so many things on the BBC that infuriate me almost every day of the week – tendentious reporting, unfair comment, unbearable violence and vulgarity – that I hesitate to say yes when any part of the BBC asks me to do anything.

To George Urban, 29 June 1988

I totally disagree about sanctions as did the previous Labour government and unlike him [Neil Kinnock] I am not prepared to stand there comfortably in this house and impose starvation and poverty on millions and millions of black South Africans and black children.

Defending her opposition to sanctions against South Africa, 1988

We have not successfully rolled back the frontiers of the state in Britain only to see them reimposed at a European level, with a European super-state exercising a new dominance from Brussels.

1988

Make all you can, save all you can, give all you can.

Quoting John Wesley, 1988

We have become a grandmother.

To reporters outside 10 Downing Street, 1989

He is another one of us.

On John Major

Human rights did not begin with the French Revolution ... [they] really stem from a mixture of Judaism and Christianity ... [we English] had 1688, our quiet revolution, where Parliament exerted its will over the King ... it was not the sort of revolution that France's was ... 'Liberty, equality, fraternity' – they forgot obligations and duties, I think. And then, of course the fraternity went missing for a long time.

Interview with *Le Monde*, 1989

363

It took us a long time to get rid of the effects of the French
Revolution 200 years ago. We don't want another one.
  30 June 1989

You can't buck the market.
  On Chancellor Nigel Lawson's attempts to shadow the Deutsche
  Mark, 1989

I went to Oxford University, but I've never let that hold me back.
  Conservative Party Conference, 13 October 1989

I am staying my own sweet, reasonable self.
  Following the resignation of Nigel Lawson, October 1989

Advisers advise, Ministers decide.
  On her relationship with Sir Alan Walters, 26 October 1989

Unassailable, unassailable.
  Description of Nigel Lawson in an interview with Brian Walden,
  29 October 1989

If we let it succeed no small country will feel safe again.
  On Iraq's invasion of Kuwait, 2 August 1990

All right, George, all right. But this is no time to go wobbly.
  To George Bush, August 1990

Beneath its contrived self-confidence lies a growing certainty
that the world and history has passed it by and that if Britain
rejects it as I believe it will, Socialism must return forever to its
proper place – the reading room of the British Library where
Karl Marx found it – Section: history of ideas. Subsection:
nineteenth century. Status: archaic.
  Conservative Party Conference, 1 October 1990

Ours is a creed which travels and endures. Its truths are
written in the human heart. It is the faith which once more has

given life to Britain and offers hope to the world. We pledge in this Party to uphold these principles of freedom and to fight for them. We pledge it to our allies overseas, and we pledge it to this country we are proud to serve.

The conclusion of Margaret Thatcher's final speech to a Conservative Party Conference, 12 October 1990

Others bring me problems, David brings me solutions.

On David (later Lord) Young, 1990

As leader of the Progressive Conservatives I thought he put too much stress on the adjective and not enough on the noun.

On Canadian Premier Brian Mulroney

Yes, the Commission wants to increase its powers, yes, it is a non-elected body and I do not want the Commission to increase its powers at the expense of the House, so of course we differ. The President of the Commission, Mr Delors, said at a press conference the other day that he wanted the European Parliament to be the democratic body of the Community. He wanted the Commission to be the Executive and he wanted the Council of Ministers to be the Senate. No! No! No!

30 October 1990

I'm still at the crease, though the bowling's been pretty hostile of late. And, in case anyone doubted it, can I assure you that there will be no ducking the bouncers, no stonewalling, no playing for time? The bowling's going to get hit all round the ground. That's my style.

Lord Mayor's Banquet, 12 November, 1990

I'm naturally very pleased that I got more than half the parliamentary party and disappointed that it's not enough to win on the first ballot so I confirm it is my intention to let my name go forward for the second ballot.

Outside the Paris embassy, November 1990

I fight on, I fight to win.
> Upon leaving Downing Street for the Commons, 21 November 1990

Having consulted widely among colleagues, I have concluded that the unity of the Party and the prospects of victory in a general election would be better served if I stood down to enable Cabinet Colleagues to enter the ballot for the leadership.
> 1990

Margaret Thatcher: Europe is strongest when it grows through willing cooperation and practical measures, not compulsion or bureaucratic dreams.
Alan Beith: Will the Prime Minister tell us whether she intends to continue her personal fight against a single currency and an independent central bank when she leaves office?
Dennis Skinner: No, she's going to be the governor (laughter)
Margaret Thatcher: What a good idea! I hadn't thought of that. But if I were, there'd be no European Central bank, accountable to no one, not least of all to national Parliaments. Because the point of that kind of Europe with a central bank is no democracy, taking powers away from every single Parliament, and having a single currency, monetary policy and interest rates, which takes all political power away from us. As my Right Honourable Friend [Nigel Lawson] said in his first speech after the proposal for a single currency, a single currency is about the politics of Europe. It is about a federal Europe by the back door. So I'll consider the Honourable Gentleman's [Mr Skinner's] proposal. Now, where were we? I'm enjoying this, I'm enjoying this!
Michael Carttiss: Cancel it. You can wipe the floor with these people!
> No Confidence Debate, 22 November 1990

It's a funny old world.
> At a Cabinet meeting following her resignation, 27 November 1990

I shan't be pulling the levers, but I shall be a very good back-seat driver.

On her role following her departure from No. 10, 1990

Carol Thatcher: Can you manage the supermarket shopping?
Margaret Thatcher: Good heavens, yes, dear, I've opened enough of them.

December 1990

Every Prime Minister needs a Willie.

On William Whitelaw, 1991

One is an ordinary person, and don't you forget it!

To Eve Pollard, 1991

In my view dictators do not surrender. They have to be well and truly defeated.

Independent on Sunday, 20 January 1991

I have never been defeated by the people. It is my great pride.

Interview with Barbara Walters, February 1991

If you have a good Thatcher, you keep your home water- and wind-proof.

Ibid.

Home is where you come to when you've nothing better to do.

11 May 1991

A hung parliament would hang the future of our country. Just look at some countries that have had coalition governments. You may have read about Belgium in the papers in the last few weeks. It took them 100 days to form a new government. What would have happened if anything vital had come up during that time? Did it help their main decisions? Did it help their deficit to come down? Not a bit of it. They've got one of the worst deficits in Europe. Not surprising with a coalition government. No one has got the guts to stand up and say no to public expenditure. So they get a big deficit. Does continuous coalition government help them to stand up against the tyrant? No. When we wanted to buy munitions they wouldn't sell them to us. So, do not go for coalitions – ever.

22 March 1992

I do not accept the idea that all of a sudden Major is now his own man. There isn't any such thing as Majorism.

25 April 1992

People who start things don't often see the end of them – take Moses and the Promised Land.

On her premiership, 1992

True gentlemen deal with others for what they are, not for who their fathers were.

1993

Given time, it would have been seen as one of the most far-reaching and beneficial reforms ever made in the working of local government.

On the Community Charge (Poll Tax), 1993

It would be the equivalent of having the Prime Minister of England invite the Oklahoma City bombers to 10 Downing Street, to congratulate them on a job well done.

On President Clinton's welcome of Gerry Adams

What is this thing called consensus? Consensus is something you reach when you cannot agree.

Attributed

When the time is right.

The mantra for joining the European Exchange Rate Mechanism

They have a new colour. They call it gold; it looks like yellow to me.
    On the Liberal Democrats

The sheer professionalism of the British civil service, which
allows governments to come and go with a minimum of
dislocation and a maximum of efficiency, is something other
countries with different systems have every cause to envy.
    1993

It is the people's turn to speak. It is their powers of which we
are the custodians.
    Calling for a referendum on Maastricht, 1993

We have been a little like an accomplice in a massacre. We
cannot carry on like that.
    On the West's role in Bosnia, 17 April 1993

It was treachery with a smile on his face. Perhaps that was the
worst thing of all.
    Describing her betrayal by the Cabinet, BBC TV, 1993

The lesson of this century is that Europe will only be peaceful
if the Americans are on this continent.
    18 April 1993

In my day that would have required the occasional use of the
handbag. Now it will be a cricket bat. But that's a good thing
because it will be harder.
    On John Major's negotiations on the Maastricht Treaty, 1993

I personally could never have signed this Treaty.
    On the Maastricht Treaty, 12 June 1993

... He is probably the most formidable leader we have seen
since Gaitskell ... I see a lot of Socialism behind their front
bench but not in Mr Blair – I think he genuinely has moved.
    On Tony Blair, BBC TV, 1994

Your President, President Clinton, is a great communicator.
The trouble is, he has absolutely nothing to communicate.

To American political observer, Daniel Forrester, March 1994

They have hit at everything I believed in.

On John Major's government, 1995

It is lovely to be back at this address – which I still think of as
home ... Though, come to think of it, Gladstone did form his
fourth administration when he was over eighty. So you have
much to look forward to.

At a No. 10 dinner marking her seventieth birthday, 1995

I haven't changed. Well, you wouldn't expect me to, would you?

26 September 1995

They tell me I have become an 'ism' in my own lifetime. I
didn't know quite how to take that to start with. But they
assure me it's a compliment – one of the better 'isms'. They say
all sorts of things about you when you've left office. They don't
always wait for that. Do they, John?

Ibid.

So to those who say it's time to ease up, to relax and to give the
other side a chance, I say (if I may coin a phrase):
'NO!' 'NO!' 'NO!'

Ibid.

I would say of the [Tony Blair] Labour leader, as I once said of his
[Neil Kinnock] predecessor: if it's that easy for him to give up
the principles in which he DID believe, won't it be even easier
for him to give up the principles in which he does NOT believe?

On Tony Blair, 8 October 1996

We introduced the Community Charge. I still call it that. I like
the Poles – I never had any intention of taxing them.

On the Poll Tax, Nicholas Ridley Memorial Lecture, 22 November 1996

The whole of Mr Blair's strategy in creating the boneless
wonder that calls itself New Labour is to reassure the electorate
in its illusion.

On New Labour, 1 April 1997

US journalist: Back in the States people are thinking about
Tony Blair as the new Margaret Thatcher. What do you think
about that?
Margaret Thatcher: Well I think they have got the sex wrong for
a start. And I think they have got the willpower wrong. I think
they have got the reasoning wrong. I think they have got the
strength wrong.

9 April 1997

The fight-back begins now!

In a telephone conversation with Michael Portillo the day after the
1997 general election

The true way to give the Scots more control over their future
is, by contrast, to cut back what government spends and
controls, leaving more freedom of choice for the people. That,
though, is the last thing which so many still Socialist-minded
Scottish politicians want.

Ibid.

I do not believe that most Scots want to end the Union.
But separation is the destination towards which the present
devolution proposals lead. They represent a negation of our
shared history and an abdication of our joint future. Scottish
voters can do no greater service to their country than to
reject them.

On the devolution referendum. *Scotsman*, 9 September 1997

Democracies, like human beings, have a tendency to relax
when the worst is over.

10 December 1997

America's duty is to lead: the other Western countries' duty is to support its leadership.

Ibid.

Britain's reputation should be of vital importance to the government of the day. Our reputation sustains our interests. The Pinochet case has sullied that reputation ... This is a Pandora's box which has been opened – and unless Senator Pinochet returns safely to Chile, there will be no hope of closing it.

On the arrest of General Pinochet, 6 July 1999

President Pinochet was this country's staunch, true friend in our time of need when Argentina seized the Falkland Islands. I know – I was Prime Minister at the time. On President Pinochet's express instructions, and at great risk, Chile provided enormously valuable assistance.

6 October 1999

Much of the evil which still stalks the world was planted and cultivated first by Communism.

5 November 1999

The idea that men must govern themselves not by the arbitrary commands of a ruler but by their own considered judgement is the means whereby chaos is replaced by order, violence by the peaceful resolution of differences, and tyranny by freedom.

7 December 1999

A new political alliance of the English-speaking peoples would allow us to foster those values that have been so important in our peace and prosperity and thus encourage that same peace and prosperity around the world.

Speech to the English Speaking Union, 7 December 1999

Liberty is a plant of slow growth and one that demands constant and careful attention. Yet there seems to be an inevitability about it, for liberty is man's natural and desired condition.

Ibid.

Creating the practical circumstances in which freedom can flourish requires more than the mere parroting of empty phrases like 'human rights'.

Ibid.

My friends, we are quite the best country in Europe. I've been told I have to be careful about what I say and I don't like it. In my lifetime all our problems have come from mainland Europe and all the solutions have come from the English-speaking nations across the world.

Speech to Scottish Tories in 1999

Your detention in Britain was a great injustice which should never have taken place.

Letter to General Pinochet, 2000

The claim that contrary to what appeared the case at the time, the Cold War wasn't really won, or if it was, it wasn't won by the Cold Warriors but in spite of them. Perhaps I should say 'in spite of us'. But the revisionists are wrong, and the Right was right.

Speech to the Hoover Institution, 19 July 2000

In this twenty-first century the dominant power is America; the global language is English; the pervasive economic model is Anglo-Saxon capitalism – so why imprison ourselves in a bureaucratic Europe?

19 July 2000

We know what works – the Anglo-Saxon model of liberty, property, law and capitalism. And we know where it works – everywhere it's actually applied. We must not be paralysed by false modesty or even good manners. Promoting the values that find their expression in America isn't imperialism, it's liberation.

Ibid.

In Britain, we have been enduring one of the worst summers on record. And I'm talking about the government, as well as the weather.

Ibid.

I was told beforehand my arrival was unscheduled, but on the way here I passed a local cinema and it turns out you were expecting me after all. The billboard read The Mummy Returns.

Conservative Party Conference, 22 May 2001

Today's Labour Party has no discernible principles at all. It is rootless, empty and artificial. And when anything real or human surfaces despite the spin – it's the bitter, brawling, bully that we hoped we'd seen the last of twenty years ago.

Ibid.

To surrender the pound, to surrender our power of self-government, would betray all that past generations down the ages lived and died to defend.

Ibid.

Obviously this is a very disappointing result. But let me say this. William Hague campaigned tirelessly from first to last. He was a bonny fighter. But make no mistake, the Conservative Party will be back.

On the resignation of William Hague, 8 June 2001

Ken Clarke has many qualities. But I have no doubt that Iain Duncan Smith would make infinitely the better leader. I am confident that, if elected leader, Iain will restore the Conservative Party's faith and fortunes. He deserves support.

Endorsing Iain Duncan Smith for Leader of the Conservative Party, 2001

In many respects the challenge of Islamic terror is unique, hence the difficulty Western intelligence services encountered trying to predict and prevent its onslaughts. The enemy is not, of course, a religion – most Muslims deplore what has occurred. Nor is it a single state, though this form of terrorism needs the support of states to give it succour. Perhaps the best parallel is with early Communism. Islamic extremism today, like Bolshevism in the past, is an armed doctrine. It is an aggressive ideology promoted by fanatical, well-armed devotees. And, like Communism, it requires an all-embracing long-term strategy to defeat it.

On Islamic terrorism, 11 February 2002

America will never be the same again.

After the Twin Towers attacks, 11 February 2002

The events of September 11 are a terrible reminder that freedom demands eternal vigilance. And for too long we have not been vigilant. We have harboured those who hated us, tolerated those who threatened us and indulged those who weakened us.

11 February 2002

The fundamental role of government in a free society is to create a framework where the talents and abilities of the people can flourish. I remember once comparing this framework with another frame – the one which surrounds a picture. You need that frame, certainly: but it mustn't over-shadow the painting itself – for that's where the true worth really lies.

Message to Chapman University Conference, 4 May 2002

Evil, it is true, has always been with us. But evil was never so technically sophisticated, never so elusive, never so devoid of scruple, and never so anxious to inflict civilian casualties. The West must prevail – or else concede a reign of global lawlessness and violence unparalleled in modern times.

9 December 2002

'Europe' in anything other than the geographical sense is a
wholly artificial construct. It makes no sense at all to lump
together Beethoven and Debussy, Voltaire and Burke, Vermeer
and Picasso, Notre Dame and St Paul's, boiled beef and
bouillabaisse, and portray them as elements of a 'European'
musical, philosophical, artistic, architectural or gastronomic
reality. If Europe charms us, as it has so often charmed me, it
is precisely because of its contrasts and contradictions, not its
coherence and continuity.

   Statecraft (2003)

Constitutions have to be written on hearts, not just paper.

   Ibid.

What we should grasp, however, from the lessons of European
history is that, first, there is nothing necessarily benevolent
about programmes of European integration; second, the desire
to achieve grand utopian plans often poses a grave threat to
freedom; and third, European unity has been tried before, and
the outcome was far from happy.

   Ibid.

The new dogma about climate change has swept through the
left-of-centre governing classes ... and provides a marvellous
excuse for worldwide, supra-national Socialism.

   Ibid.

It is always exhilarating to visit New York. But nowadays it
is also ennobling. This was the city which terrorists hated so
much that they sought to tear out its very heart. But that heart
still beats – proudly, strongly, passionately. Out of the ashes,
from amid the tears, New Yorkers are once again rebuilding
their City and their lives. Truly they are an inspiration to the
world.

   On the 9/11 attacks, 14 May 2003

I am proud that Britain stood by America in this conflict. Our own Prime Minister was staunch; and our forces were superb. But, above all, it is President Bush who deserves the credit for victory. First in Afghanistan, and now in Iraq, the forces of tyranny and darkness have been routed. These victories have made our nations and our allies more secure. They have shown all who are tempted to do us harm that they will have to pay the price of their actions. Yes: the world remains dangerous. But it is yesterday's weakness, not today's resolve, which is to blame for the risks we face.

Speech to The Atlantic Bridge, 14 May 2003

For years, many governments played down the threats of Islamic revolution, turned a blind eye to international terrorism, and accepted the development of weaponry of mass destruction by dictators. Indeed, some politicians were happy to go further, collaborating with the self-proclaimed enemies of the West for their own short-term gain – but enough about the French!

14 May 2003

Socialism is like one of those horrible viruses. You no sooner discover a remedy for one version, than it spontaneously evolves into another. In the past, there was nationalisation, penal taxation and the command economy. Nowadays Socialism is more often dressed up as environmentalism, feminism, or international concern for human rights. All sound good in the abstract. But scratch the surface and you'll as likely as not discover anti-capitalism, patronising and distorting quotas, and intrusions upon the sovereignty and democracy of nations. New slogans: old errors.

Ibid.

This heinous attack upon America was an attack upon us all. With America, Britain stands in the front line against Islamist fanatics who hate our beliefs, our liberties and our citizens. We must not falter. We must not fail.

On the fifth anniversary of the 9/11 attacks, 2006

I might have preferred iron, but bronze will do. It won't rust. And, this time I hope, the head will stay on.

> Unveiling her statue in Parliament, after a previous marble one was decapitated, 22 February 2007

I wholeheartedly support *The Sun*'s campaign for a referendum on the new EU treaty.

Yet again the British people are being told that the changes in the Treaty are not important, that they are technical, and that in any case we have either blocked or gained opt-outs in all the worst cases.

Well, we've heard it all before only to see more and more powers grabbed by Brussels.

So yet again *Sun* readers are standing up for Britain and calling our government to account.

This Treaty is a blueprint for a European Constitution in all but name – a Constitution which has already been rejected.

But that's one little 'technicality' the Brussels bureaucrats want us to forget.

So may I say to the Prime Minister, don't believe the assurances from Brussels, they gave similar ones to me!

It's not too late to listen and it's not too late to act.

This Treaty matters Prime Minister, so be bold and let the British people have the final say!

> *The Sun*, 29 September 2007

Today, some find it all too easy to forget the sufferings of those years. Just as Communism had many apologists who sought to blind us to its horrors and failures, so there are people who now talk almost nostalgically about the past and deride all that has been achieved over the last two decades. Our duty is to remember and remind. To forget the past would dishonour all those who fought heroically to resist Communism's evil – it would also place us in danger of repeating its mistakes.

> Message to the Prague Conference on European Conscience and Communism, 30 May 2008

I never hugged him. I bombed him.
> On Colonel Gaddafi of Libya, 2011

Clarence Thomas
b. 1948; US Supreme Court Justice

Conservatives should be no more timid about asserting the responsibilities of the individual than they should be about protecting individual rights.
> July 1991

James Thompson
1700–48; Scottish poet

When Britain first, at Heaven's command
Arose from out of the azure main,
This was the charter of the land,
And guardian angels sang this strain,
Rule Britannia, rule the waves,
Britons never will be slaves.
> 1740

Henry David Thoreau
1817–62; American author and philosopher

There will never be a really free and enlightened state until the state comes to recognise the individual as a higher and independent power, from which all its own power and authority are derived, and treats him accordingly.
> *Walden* (1854)

Anyone in a free society where the laws are unjust has an obligation to break the law.
> On liberty

Alexis de Tocqueville
1805–59; French writer and statesman

When the religion of a people is destroyed, doubt gets hold of
the higher powers of the intellect, and half paralyses all the
others. Every man accustoms himself to have only confused and
changing notions on the subjects most interesting to his fellow
creatures and himself.

Democracy in America (1840)

I know of no country, indeed, where the love of money has
taken stronger hold on the affections of men and where
a profounder contempt is expressed for the theory of the
permanent equality of property.

Ibid.

In democracies, nothing is more great or brilliant than
commerce: it attracts the attention of the public, and fills
the imagination of the multitudes; all energetic passions are
directed towards it.

Ibid.

Leo Tolstoy
1828–1910; Russian novelist

Government is an association of men who do violence to the
rest of us.

On government

Harry Truman
1884–1972; US President 1944–52

It is a recession when your neighbour loses his job. It's a
depression when you lose your own.

13 April 1958

The buck stops here.

Popularised by the paperweight that sat on Truman's desk in the
White House

I have found the best way to give advice to your children is to
find out what they want and then advise them to do it.

Attributed

The Republican Party either corrupts its liberals or expels them.

Attributed

Men make history and not the other way round. In periods
where there is no leadership, society stands still. Progress
occurs when courageous skilful leaders seize the opportunity
to change things for the better.

Attributed

Desmond Tutu

b. 1931; South African bishop, Archbishop Emeritus of Cape Town

Freedom and liberty lose out by default because good people
are not vigilant.

Sermon

Mark Twain

1835–1910; American novelist

It is by the goodness of God that in our country we have those
three unspeakable precious things; freedom of speech, freedom
of conscience, and the prudence never to practice either of them.

Following the Equator (1897)

V

Peter Viereck
1916–2006; American philosopher

Conservatism, which is for politics what classicism is for literature, is in turn the political secularisation of the doctrine of original sin. In contrast, radicalism is Rousseau's 'natural goodness of man, collectivised into a touching political faith in the 'masses'. Nazi radicalism equates Rousseau's Noble Savage with the radical mass (the Volk); Marxist radicalism equates him with the economic mass (the proletariat). But he is not worshipped like this by the churches. The churches, Protestant, Catholic, or ... Jewish, draw the fangs on the noble savage and clip his ignoble claws.

Conservatism Revisited (1946)

Virgil
70–19 BC; Roman poet

Others, I suppose will more subtly mould the breathing bronze, draw forth the living features from the marble, plead causes better, mark with the rod the wanderings of the sky and foretell the rising stars; Thou, Roman, be mindful to rule the peoples with imperial sway (these shall be thy arts) to impose the way of peace, to spare the conquered and put down the proud.

The Aeneid

Voltaire
1694–1778; philosopher

I detest your views, but I am prepared to die for your right to
express them.
Attributed

Liberty was born in England from the quarrels of tyrants.
Lettres philosophiques (1733)

W

David Waddington

b. 1929; Conservative MP,1968–74, 1979–91, Cabinet minister 1987–90

Sentences served should be much closer to sentences passed.
> As Home Secretary, 1990

The vast majority of offences are committed not by determined young professionals but by dishonest youngsters left to their own devices.
> Ibid.

William Waldegrave

b. 1946; Conservative MP 1979–97, Cabinet minister 1989–97

We said zero, and I think any statistician will tell you that when you're dealing with very big numbers, zero must mean plus or minus a few.
> On hospital waiting lists, 1992

In exceptional cases it is necessary to say something that is untrue to the House of Commons. The House of Commons understands that and has always accepted that.
> As Minister for Open Government, 1994

Peter Walker

1932–2010; Conservative MP

Rivers and lakes are polluted past praying for. Seas are overfished. Forests are vanishing. Pollution of the air and the water are threatening the two previously most predictable and essential elements in man's very existence … As our cities become more congested, our lives more merchandised, and our leisure more pre-packaged, there must be growing awareness that nature is now our most precious possession.

1970

Dame Irene Ward

1895–1980; Conservative MP

Is my right honourable friend saying that Wrens' skirts must be held up until all sailors have been satisfied?

> Responding to Navy Minister's statement that new women's uniforms would be dealt with as soon as male officers had theirs. House of Commons, 1940

George Washington

1732–99; US President 1789–97

Government is not reason. Government is not eloquence. It is force. And, like fire, it is a dangerous servant and a fearful master.

> Attributed

Associate yourself with men of good quality if you esteem your own reputations; for 'tis better to be alone than in bad company.

> *Rules of Civility* (c.1748)

To be prepared for war is one of the most effectual means of preserving peace.

> First annual address to Congress, 1790

The very idea of the power and the right of the people to establish government, presupposes the duty of every individual to obey the established government.

> Farewell Address, 1796

J. C. Watts

b. 1957; US Congressman

The American dream does not happen by asking Americans to accept what's immoral and wrong in the name of tolerance.

GOP Radio Response, 4 February 1997

If liberals can't beat you, if they're losing on the issues, they do one of two things. They either call you a bigot or a racist. Or they sue you.

Attributed

My father taught that the only helping hand you're ever going to be able to rely on is the one at the end of your sleeve.

Attributed

Auberon Waugh

1939–2001; British journalist

... the small troupe of exhibitionists, failed vaudeville artists, juicy young Boy Scouts and degenerate old voluptuaries which is the Liberal Party.

Attributed

Contradictions between the individualistic, free-market stance and traditional Conservative appeals to authority, patriotism, law and order are two a penny, and have often been remarked on. The electoral calculation has always been that the two opposed camps – the 'individualists' who are trying to make money, and the 'Conservatives' who already have it – will make common cause at the end of the day.

The Spectator, 1989

It is an alarming thought that if we are ever invaded by monsters from outer space, the man who will be appointed to save us as Minister for Monsters will be this joke yobbo who could easily be mistaken for the traditional plumber with a cleft palate who has lost his dentures down the lavatory.

On Denis Howell MP

Evelyn Waugh

1903–66; British novelist and social commentator

The trouble with the Conservative Party is that it has never turned the clock back a single second.

Attributed

I believe that man is, by nature, an exile and will never be self-sufficient or complete on this earth; that his chances of happiness and virtue, here, remain more or less constant through the centuries and, generally speaking, are not much affected by the political and economic conditions in which he lives

Attributed

I believe that inequalities of wealth and position are inevitable and that it is therefore meaningless to discuss the advantages of their elimination; that men naturally arrange themselves into a system of classes; that such a system is necessary for any form of cooperative work, more particularly the work of keeping a nation together.

Mexico: An Object Lesson (1939)

He is not a man for whom I ever had esteem. Always in the wrong, always surrounded by crooks, a most unsuccessful father – simply 'Radio personality' who outlived his prime.

Ibid., on Winston Churchill, 1965

Daniel Webster
1782–1852; American statesman

Let our object be our country, our whole country and nothing but our country.
   1825

Duke of Wellington
1769–1852; Prime Minister 1828–30, 1834–39

I don't know what effect these men will have upon the enemy, but, by God, they terrify me.
   On a new draft of soldiers sent out during the Peninsular War

Nothing except a battle lost can be half so melancholy as a battle won.
   Comment after the Battle of Waterloo

Nobody cares a damn about the House of Lords. The House of Commons is everything in England and the House of Lords nothing.
   To Thomas Creevy in Brussels

An extraordinary affair, I gave them their orders and they wanted to stay and discuss them.
   As Prime Minister, on his first Cabinet, 1828

I never saw so many shocking bad hats in my life.
   On seeing the first reformed House of Commons, 1832

Don't quote Latin. Say what you have to say and then sit down.
   Advice to a new MP

I have no small talk and Peel has no manners.
   Attributed

Hugo Charteris, 11th Earl of Wemyss
1857–1937; Scottish Conservative politician

We grow corn, oats, hay and straw. Motors do not eat oats, they do not eat hay and they do not lie on the straw and when horses are done away with, it will not be worthwhile our growing these agricultural articles of consumption having lost our best customer.

    1903

Paul M. Weyrick
1942–2008; American religious political activist and commentator

… the Old Right tends to be intellectual and upper class. It is an accurate generalisation that the New Right tends to be middle class, blue-collar and ethnic in its origins.

    Blue Collar or Blue Bird? The New Right Compared with the Old Right
    (1982)

Though the upper classes had more intellectual expertise, they tended to become deficient in something that was strong in the working middle classes: values.

    Ibid.

Well-bred, well-heeled youth allowed right and wrong to become blurred, and tradition to become a romantic decoration. Respect among working people was a consciously instilled value.

    Ibid.

Reginald James White
British scholar

Conservatism is less a political doctrine than a habit of mind, a mode of feeling, a way of living. And the human content of the

Party is no less amorphous than the so called 'creed'. The Party is, in fact, the perfect secular analogy of its great historical ally, the Church of England. It contains not only the convinced and the converted who think they know what they believe. It contains also the vast residue of politics which would be hard put to describe itself as anything else at all.

The Conservative Tradition (1970)

William Whitelaw

1918–99; Conservative MP 1955–83, Cabinet minister 1970–74, Deputy Prime Minister 1983–87

I have always said it is a great mistake ever to pre-judge the past.

As Northern Ireland Secretary, 1972

They are going about the country stirring up complacency.

On Labour ministers, 1974

I have the thermometer in my mouth and I am listening to it all the time.

On party morale, 1974

Those who say that I am not in agreement with the policy are, rightly or wrongly, quite wrong.

On the party's immigration policy

It is never wise to appear to be more clever than you are. It is sometimes wise to appear slightly less so.

1975

It is both possible and moral, to love one's country and hate its government ... In the long run those who shout 'racialist' loudest will do real damage to race relations and the true interests of the ethnic minority groups in our society by their obstinate refusal to face facts and to recognise the genuine worries and fears of so many of our fellow citizens ... I do not believe we have any hope of promoting the sort of society which we want unless we are prepared to follow a policy which is clearly designed to work towards the end of immigration.

1976

From 6.45 a.m. to lights out at 9.30 p.m. life will be conducted at a brisk tempo. Much greater emphasis will be put on hard and constructive activities, on discipline and tidiness, on self-respect and respect for those in authority.

As Home Secretary, announcing 'short, sharp, shock' treatment for juvenile offenders, 1979

I can assure you that I definitely might take action.

As Home Secretary, 1981

Ann Widdecombe

b. 1947; Conservative MP 1987–2010

I think the rest of the world will think we're mad, and indeed we are. We've turned out the greatest Prime Minister in the post-war years simply because of short-term nerves.

BBC TV news, 22 November 1990

He has something of the night about him.

On Michael Howard, former Home Secretary, 20 May 1997

Hunting is not a pesticide, so we must ask what it is. It is cruelty. I am not against killing foxes or culling deer. I am against the chase, the cruelty involved in prolonging the terror of a living, sentient being that is running for its life.

On fox hunting, House of Commons, 28 November 1997

I believe the death penalty is a deterrent, I think the statistics clearly show that, I think you have a moral responsibility to the innocent to have it available to the courts.

BBC News, 16 February 1999

In *The Wizard of Oz*, the Man of Straw had no brain. I can show you one with no heart and no courage as well. He and his friend Tony promised to be 'tough on crime and tough on the causes of crime'. All they've been tough on is the dwindling number of people trying to fight crime.

Conservative Party Conference, 2000

The real bigots are those who believe that those who dissent have no right to do so, and that the state itself should silence them.

On those who call equal marriage opponents bigots, Conservative Party Conference, 2012

He could have been a political giant had he only learned to distinguish between toughness and bullying and decisiveness and autocracy, if he had known when to stop delivering punishment, if his smile did not remind me of the face of the proverbial tiger, and if he had some humanity.

On Michael Howard, *Strictly Ann* (2013)

Oscar Wilde

1854–1900; writer

The state in the end depends on the vigour of the character of the individuals which make it up; and that character is strengthened by the effort to find a way out of difficulties and hardships, and is weakened by the habit of looking to state help. If individual gifts and attainments were infallible signs of wisdom and goodness ... and the knowing, clever and talented (vile word!) were always rational; if the mere facts of science confined or suppressed the softening humanising influences of the moral world ... then indeed, political power might not unwisely be conferred as the honorarium or privilege of having passed through all the forms of the National School.

The Soul of Man under Socialism (1895)

Spencer Compton, Earl of Wilmington

1673–1743; British Conservative politician, Prime Minister 1742–43

No Sir, you have a right to speak, but the House will have a right to judge whether they will hear you.

As Speaker, on whether Members had a right to be heard,
Hatsell's Precedents (1818)

Woodrow Wilson

1856–1924; US President 1913–21

A Conservative is a man who sits and thinks – mostly sits.

Attributed

Nicholas Winterton

b. 1938; Conservative MP 1971–2010

Certain elements of the British Medical Association leadership have gone over the top and taken fully entrenched positions,

On health reforms, 1989

Sir Kingsley Wood

1881–1943; British Conservative politician

Are you aware it is private property? Why, you'll be asking me to bomb Essen next.

As Secretary of State for the Air, on plans to bomb the Black Forest,
1939

Y

Lord Young of Graffham

b. 1932; businessman and Conservative politician, Cabinet minister 1984–89

The idea of a pilot scheme is to see whether it will fly.
As Employment Secretary, 1989

Oh look – with hindsight you can always look back.
As former Trade and Industry Secretary, responding to government criticism of the 1985 Harrods/House of Fraser takeover, 1990

Index